More Praise for *Pursuit of Passionate Purpose*

"A great process for living a life of passion while achieving your heart's desire. Full of real-life examples that will inspire you to look deep at your life, your business and your dreams, then move forward with clarity and purpose."

> —Larry Winget
> Author of *Shut Up, Stop Whining and Get a Life!*

"In the many years I have known Theresa Szczurek, she proved to be the epitome of passionate purpose herself, with unflagging energy and generosity to the many people she affects. Her book is another expression of passionate purpose written with style. It will help all it touches. It's a great business book."

> —Margaret Hansson
> Inventor of the baby carrier, founder of Gerry Baby
> Products Company, and Chair, Purecycle Corporation
> and ERTH Technologies, Inc.

"As usual, Dr. Szczurek has written an excellent book with lots of practical guidance for those who are searching for their own passionate pursuit in their career. The structured program, detailed in the book, will be a great help to those who are intent on finding the career that will get rid of the 'Do I have to go to work today?' syndrome."

> —Don Vanlandingham
> Retired Chairman and CEO, Ball Aerospace &
> Technologies Corp.

"Buy this book and discover that even with all of life's uncertainties and surprises, there is a process that can lead you to success. Discover the power of ideas like the Allowing Strategy and how they can lead you to follow your natural path to fulfillment in your work and your life."

> —Joe Calloway
> Author of *Becoming a Category of One*

"By sharing true stories of wisdom from 80 people, Theresa Szczurek inspires us all to create the life we want to live, on purpose, with passion. Her exciting book teaches the premise, path, and outcome to actualize this success, both personally and professionally."

>—LeAnn Thieman
>Coauthor of *Chicken Soup for the Nurse's Soul, Chicken Soup for the Christian Woman's Soul,* and *Chicken Soup for the Caregiver's Soul*

"In the process of living life, certain questions start to percolate: What is my purpose? What do I *care* about? What should I *do* about it? In business as in life, the answers come from personal discovery. Theresa Szczurek's book offers extremely practical advice, and stories from her research provide companionship along the way."

>—Cynthia Kneen
>Management consultant, author of the award-winning book, *Awake Mind, Open Heart,* and *Shambhala Warrior Training*

"When achievers make decisions to change their direction, they frequently are alone in their process. Theresa provides excellent insights into how successful people pass through their circle of change to revitalize themselves and discover their next passionate pursuit."

>—Carolyn M. Romero, CPA
>Treasurer, Business & Professional Women/USA

"A simply marvelous book! Theresa Szczurek has synthesized many concepts into a coherent and practical process. *Pursuit of Passionate Purpose* will change your life."

>—Gregory J. P. Godek
>Author of *1001 Ways to Be Romantic*

"*Pursuit of Passionate Purpose* distills the compelling experiences of real people into a practical framework for creating passion and meaning in your work—and in your *life*. It speaks to the passion and power that come from aligning your head and your heart with a purpose that fits your unique gifts and values. Without oversimplifying the complexities, it describes the steps required to find a passionate purpose that will work for you. It also provides useful strategies for overcoming the barriers that keep people from following their passion. This book rings with the practical wisdom that Theresa Szczurek has derived from her research and consulting. She succeeds at balancing intellectual with emotional wisdom, and spirituality with worldly practicality. This book will be valuable to people who are fine-tuning their careers and will be *invaluable* to people who are considering major changes."

> —Kenneth W. Thomas
> Author of *Intrinsic Motivation at Work* and coauthor of
> the Thomas-Kilmann Conflict Mode Instrument

"*Pursuit of Passionate Purpose* is a sure recipe for business success. Step by step we learn about energizing our passion, moving forward on our determined path and making our career count. Szczurek tells individual's stories of pursuing passion and cleverly juxtaposes her own tale into play to give the reader lively examples of the passionate journey. Here is a treasure for corporate, government, and nonprofit leaders."

> —Marilyn E. Blair
> Editor, *ODPractitioner Journal,* Organization Development
> Network

"In pursuing life's purpose, everyone deserves a little guidance. In her book, Theresa Szczurek offers a complete road map to anyone committed to a passionate pursuit of life's journey."

> —André Pettigrew
> Assistant Superintendent, Denver Public Schools

"Finally, here is the book that people of all ages need. *Pursuit of Passionate Purpose* provides a practical approach on how to live a meaningful life. It helps you determine why you are here and how to pursue it."

> —Eric Chester, CSP, CPAE
> Author of *Employing Generation Why*

"Through her own life and interviews with many others, Theresa Szczurek helps us appreciate the power of polarities and shows us how to tap this power to benefit both ourselves and the organizations and communities in which we live and work."

> —Barry Johnson, PhD
> Author of *Polarity Management*™ *Identifying and Managing Unsolvable Problems*

"*Pursuit of Passionate Purpose* brings focus and meaning to one's life, both personal and professional. It applies to a broad audience and wide variety of business areas and provides a good framework for those pursuing entrepreneurial or new business creative endeavors."

> —Alexander E. Bracken
> Executive Director, Bard Center for Entrepreneurship
> Development, University of Colorado at Denver

"The core of any successful and confident person is passion—passion for work, passion for life, and passion for self. Theresa Szczurek has created a realistic and terrific formula to ignite or rekindle this critical factor for everyone who wants to create their 'work' versus having a 'job.' This book is a Keeper!"

> —Dr. Judith Briles
> Author of *The Confidence Factor*

Pursuit of
Passionate
Purpose

Pursuit of
Passionate
Purpose

Success Strategies for a
Rewarding Personal and
Business Life

Theresa M. Szczurek, PhD

WILEY

John Wiley & Sons, Inc.

Published by John Wiley & Sons, Inc., Hoboken, New Jersey.
Published simultaneously in Canada.

Theresa M. Szczurek encourages readers to send her feedback. E-mail her at
tms@TMSworld.com and visit www.TMSworld.com or www.pursuitofpassionatepurpose.com

Trademarks and registered trademarks belong to their respective owners.

Limit of Liability/Disclaimer of Warranty: While the publisher and author have used their best
efforts in preparing this book, they make no representations or warranties with respect to the
accuracy or completeness of the contents of this book and specifically disclaim any implied
warranties of merchantability or fitness for a particular purpose. No warranty may be created
or extended by sales representatives or written sales materials. The advice and strategies
contained herein may not be suitable for your situation. The publisher is not engaged in
rendering professional services, and you should consult a professional where appropriate.
Neither the publisher nor author shall be liable for any loss of profit or any other commercial
damages, including but not limited to special, incidental, consequential, or other damages.

For general information on our other products and services please contact our Customer
Care Department within the United States at (800) 762-2974, outside the United States at
(317) 572-3993 or fax (317) 572-4002.

Wiley also publishes its books in a variety of electronic formats. Some content that appears in
print may not be available in electronic books. For more information about Wiley products,
visit our web site at www.wiley.com.

Library of Congress Cataloging-in-Publication Data:

Szczurek, Theresa M., 1955–
  Pursuit of passionate purpose : success strategies for a rewarding
personal and business life / Theresa M. Szczurek.
    p. cm.
  Includes bibliographical references and index.
  ISBN 0-471-70324-9 (cloth)
1. Success in business.   2. Success—Psychological aspects.   3.
Self-actualization (Psychology)   I. Title.
  HF5386.S97   2005
  650.1—dc22
2004016893

Printed in the United States of America.

10 9 8 7 6 5 4 3 2 1

To all people everywhere who,
by pursuing passionate purpose,
are on the path toward the real rewards of life.
You are the spirit of life.

And, especially, to those who have supported me in my pursuits.

Contents

People Whose Stories Are Prominently Shared

Karen Bernardi, realtor

Fred Ramirez Briggs, foundation director

Tom Chappell, personal care products entrepreneur

Jim Collins, author of *Good to Great* and coauthor of *Built to Last*

Richard Connolly, blacksmith

Ann Cooper, realtor

Leslie Durgin, social services administrator

Katie Ewig, administrative assistant

Morris Frank and Buddy, helpers of the blind

Carol Grever, author of *My Husband Is Gay*

Johnny Halberstadt, running champion, footwear inventor, and retail business owner

Margaret Hansson, inventor and entrepreneur

Josephine Heath, stateswoman and nonprofit executive

Wendy James, secret service agent

Lauren Ward Larson, national blood donation advocate

André Pettigrew, public administrator

Mark Plaatjes, running champion, physical therapist, and retail business owner

Joseph Rush, physicist

Jonathan Sawyer, engineer and entrepreneur

Ellie Sciarra, tap dancer

Howard "Binx" Selby III, community leader

Linda Shoemaker, attorney and societal change agent

Lynda Simmons, real estate developer, architect, and community builder

Kevin Streicher, advertising salesperson

Nathan Thompson, data storage entrepreneur

Oakleigh Thorne II, environmental educator

Liz Valles, controller and musician

Don Vanlandingham, retired corporate executive

Shinzen Young, mindfulness meditation teacher

Margot Zaher, life coach

Acknowledgments

If I have seen further, it is by standing upon the shoulders of giants.

Sir Isaac Newton[1]

This research project and book, in being both a pursuit of passionate purpose and the means for relationships along the way, has provided deep meaning to my life. The intention is to help others in finding a practical formula for a fulfilling life, and in the process I have personally received real rewards. You and time will determine the book's usefulness and whether it represents further insights. This pursuit has gripped me, and many other people, for over five years. In the process, I have stood on the "shoulders of many giants" and have benefited from connections with many people and spiritual forces along the way. Heartfelt thanks go to each and every being in this web of life who contributed to this journey.

I am grateful to all my teachers—my parents and relatives, the nuns at St. Mary School, and my other educators over the years especially Wayne Boss, Larry Cornwall, Natalie Goldberg, John Hess, Paul Humke, Barry Johnson, Shinzen Young, and these educators' lineage of teachers.

Thanks to members of the Radish team including the employees, investors, customers, partners, and consultants who supported the entrepreneurial pursuit of passionate purpose. Thanks for the dedication, hard work, creativity, good times, and the challenges that, now looking back, were gifts in themselves and the impetus for starting this endeavor. Thanks also to my previous employers and my coworkers there. Special thanks to my associates and clients of Technology and Management Solutions.

Participants in this research project generously shared their wisdom. Everyone has a story and every tale is worthwhile. Those stories, encompassing the deepest sorrows and greatest joys of the world, show how to create a life worth living. Only a fraction of these accounts can be shared in this book. For their willingness to offer insights to help others, I thank: Carlos Aguirre, Ben Alexandra, Martha Arnett, Karen Ashworth, Karen Bernardi, Gigi Boratgis, Marlena Boratgis, Lisako Bridgewater, Fred Ramirez Briggs, Tom Chappell, Jim Collins, Richard Connolly, Ann Cooper, Virginia Corsi, Eleanor Crow, James E. Davis, Glen Deiner, Leslie Durgin, Alan Ehrlich, Katie Ewig, Jacqueline Frischknecht, Emerson W. Fullmer, Gordon Gamm, Jean Gore, Carol Grever, Theresa Grills, Leslie Gura, Ida Halasz, Johnny Halberstadt, Margaret Hansson, Paul W. Harris, David Hawkins, Frances Hawkins, Josephine Heath, David Hofmockel, Wendy James (Desmond), Bridget Jeffrey, Eileen Joseph, Cynthia Kemper, Lauren Ward Larson, Anny Lee, Mariella Mathia, Adrian Miller, Ron Moitzfield, Diane Moshman, Alyson Mulvany, Deborah Myers, Harry Nachman, Stephanie Nestlerode, Larry O'Hara, A. R. "Pete" Palmer, Mark Palmer, Kathey Pear, André Pettigrew, Mark Plaatjes, Phyllis Postlewait, Brooks Preston, Sean Redmond, Joseph Rush, Jonathan Sawyer, Ellie Sciarra, Howard "Binx" Selby III, Marsha Semmel, Diana Sherry, Linda Shoemaker, Scott Shor, Lynda Simmons, Sara E. Smith, Scott Snider, Eli Spanier, Kevin Streicher, Jeanne Teleia, Caroline Thompson, George Thompson, Nathan Thompson, Oakleigh Thorne, William Tieman, Deben Tobias, Liz Valles, Robin Van Norman, Don Vanlandingham, Mark Walker, Lola Wilcox, Shinzen Young, Margot Zaher, and a number of people who chose to remain anonymous.

Critical book reviewers, research methodology inquisitors, and/or data collection instrument and inventory pretesters provided insightful perspectives and probing questions that made the study and book stronger. I am indebted to Jim Collins, Reg Gupton, Paul Harris, Sina Simantob, Mike Winseck, Shinzen Young, and the Associated Consultants International writers group members Marilyn Blair, Leilani Henry, Cynthia Kneen, Mary Miura, Gene Morton, Lola Wilcox, Chuck Wilcox, and Al Persons.

My thanks go to dedicated research and administrative assistants: Tracey Bloser, Lisako Bridgewater, Jo Moeller, Meridee Silbaugh, Lindsey May Smith, Sara E. Smith, and especially to Wendy James Desmond.

Thanks, also, to those who helped with the audio/visual communications including graphics artist, Mikell Yamada; web site designers Jeff McEwan and Ben Alexandra; Channel 54 Community Access TV of Boulder, especially Pat Halsey, for video production training and equipment used to interview participants; Ken Fong, my friend and workshop video editor; as well as Mark Camacho at 81 Media International for promotional video production. I also send thanks to Stephanie Nestlerode and Tara Hu for an inspiring calligraphy of "balancing head and heart."

I am grateful to my clients, employers, sponsors, and workshop/ presentation attendees for providing an audience as well as applications, feedback, suggestions, and questions.

A large team of people provided various kinds of professional support and encouragement along the way. I send thanks to publicist Meryl Moss and staff; members of ACI—Lee Hogan, Gaynelle Winograd, and the writers group; Cynthia Kneen for her methodology for writing a book; colleagues and mentors at the Colorado Independent Publisher's Association, Maui Writer's Conference, and National Speakers Association especially Dorie McCubbrey, Kay Baker, Judith Briles, Don Cooper, and Sam Horn; Emissaries of Divine Light, Sunrise Credit Union, Diana de Winton, and Bill Becker who provided me space for a writing retreat; naming focus group participants Carol Grever, Linda Jacobson, Francois Pellissier, Jennifer Pollman, Wolf Reitz, Lynn Sherretz, Scott Snider, and Robert Taylor; Linda Fong and Binx Selby who inspired my writing practice; and colleagues who were sounding boards and provided insights: Cheryl Bell, Alexander Bracken, Rick Brearton, Anthony Brittain, Richard Felstein, Jim Ferenc, Catharine Harris, Lois Hart, Akira Hasegawa, Jeremy Hunter, Christina Kauffman, Carl Lawrence, Bill Mooney, Harvey Moshman, Audrey Nelson, Denis Nock, Sean Redmond, Marcia Schirmer, Kathy Simon, Susan Skjei, Linda Tharp, Kenneth Thomas, Alan Weiss, Carol Ann Wilson; and a wide range of friends and colleagues too numerous to list who have provided ideas, comments, contacts, or encouragement.

I express my gratitude to all of those who lovingly volunteered to care for my daughter Annie when I was consumed with this project including Rosa Chapiro, Betty Forster, Dick Forster, Denise McCorvie, the other Girl Scout troop leaders, Unitarian Universalist Fellowship Religious Education program leaders, many other friends, and especially Ann Drumm.

To my personal support network, I send loving thanks to my women's group members Martha Arnett, Robin Carrington, Julia Hoilien, Dianne Ladd, Doris Schneider, and Lynn Sawyer; and special friends Laura Ferenc, Janice Stachyra, Anita Targan, and Annette Taylor.

I would like to make special note and deeply thank my trusted agent and strategic advisor John Willig of Literary Services, Inc. and the professional team at John Wiley & Sons, especially my talented editor Matt Holt and Tamara Hummel, Michelle Patterson, and Deborah Schindlar.

Three people provided tremendous support over years to this pursuit of passionate purpose. I am deeply indebted for having them involved in so many parts of the project and for being the wind under my wings: Nancy Balch, who also provided me a haven so I could write "in monk mode" for over seven months; Dr. Jackie Frischknecht, who offered invaluable suggestions on word and book structure, and Dr. Ida Halasz, my coach since the early days of this project who relentlessly asked difficult questions, provided astute research advice, and unwavering encouragement.

Special thanks to my daughter Annie for her love, patience, and enthusiasm and for helping me maintain balance between my head and heart. Finally, I am deeply grateful to my spouse and partner in business and life, Richard A. Davis, who, in addition to running his own business and being a fabulous father, has helped the entire journey in every possible way.

PART ONE

INTRODUCTION: GET ON YOUR PATH

Premise: You can live a more rewarding life and produce remarkable results.

Path: Use the "Pursuit of Passionate Purpose" formula.

Outcome: Knowledge of how to turn a good life into a great life and reap real rewards.

1

1 Pursuit Brings Real Rewards

Premise: There is a formula, a model, for success.

Path: Discover why and how to implement the formula.

Outcome: Knowledge of how to effectively use this book.

The summit at 19,340 feet was in sight now. After another hour of persistent climbing, I breathlessly whispered, "*Yes!* Here is the summit of Kilimanjaro, the highest point in Africa." Indeed, the Pursuit of Passionate Purpose formula helped me succeed on that five-day, arduous trek just as it had in other parts of my life. With my business card from Radish Communications Systems to represent the young venture I had cofounded and painstakingly nurtured, the moment was captured in a photo—my baby, Radish, and me on top of the world!

Fierce winds blew on Kili. Similarly, but unknown to me, the winds of change were furiously blowing in my professional life at home.

It had started nearly four decades earlier. I grew up in a large, blue-collar, Polish family in the suburbs of Chicago, with a solid education at St. Mary of Czestochowa Catholic School. As my personal foundation of core values took form, my determination also gained strength. My motto became: "If it is to be, it is up to me."

Twenty years after that beginning, I was living my dream—or so I thought—climbing the career ladder in a Fortune 100 company. But I didn't realize the price I would have to pay for my position as one of the highest ranked women in my division. The lack of a personal life and 60-hour workweeks were taking their toll. Behind my back, colleagues resented my promotions. My boss instructed me to act without integrity:

3

On top of Mount Kilimanjaro at 19,340 feet, with my Radish business card, I began to feel the winds of change.

"Kill Larry or Larry is going to kill you." Then the company sent that boss, instead of me, to announce the new product I had worked on for three years. My head, the rational thinker, had dominated decisions to this point. Now my heart, the creative feeler, cried out, "What you really want is balance in life—deep connection with people and meaningful work in an environment where people can contribute and be rewarded to the fullest. Make changes. Follow your heart, in harmony with your head. Pursue passionate purpose."

I was like many people today who hear the wake-up call and are searching for meaning. Hungry for practical solutions, these people are asking, **"What is the formula for getting what I want in work and in life? How can I live a rewarding life?"**

Similarly, the employers of these workers seek to improve productivity and generate superior results.

TURN THE WORST OF TIMES INTO THE BEST OF TIMES

Especially in the worst of times, as Dickens[1] would say, when terrorism, war, economic downturn, drought, layoffs, bankruptcies, ethical tests, or other challenges surface, you need to ignite your passion.

Just as exercise strengthens your muscles, adversity strengthens who you are and stimulates stronger flow of spirit. And that is why the worst of times—when adversity strikes—can become the best of times.

Your challenge, and the challenge of all organizations, is to keep that human life force flowing. But how?

The pursuit of meaningful intention ignites passion. The primary purpose of this book is to help you live a great life with the rewards you desire.

> **The *pursuit* of passionate purpose, *as well***
> ***as its attainment,* and relationships along the**
> **way bring the real rewards in life.**

RESEARCH OVERVIEW

This project began because people kept asking me how I had accomplished certain remarkable things. Combining these inquiries with an unshakable calling to help others, I examined what had delivered results and brought real rewards in both my business and personal life. I also wanted to know if others had produced positive outcomes using similar methods. This led to the key question: What distinguishes those who find and fulfill a passionate purpose from those who don't?

After reviewing others' work and not finding the answer, I designed and undertook a rigorous, multiyear, research study to answer the question. The project goal was to distill a systematic and practical approach that others could use to get all they want in life. To ensure substantive conclusions, I collected data from a representative sample of adult Americans using one-on-one interviews and written surveys. The participants represented both genders from various occupations, ethnic and age groups, and geographic locations, with a range of personal and professional purposes. As I incorporated the wisdom of more than 80 research participants—those who had found and pursued passionate purpose and those who had not—success strategies and a step-by-step process emerged.

I derived conclusions from extensive analysis of all the data. Not every participant stated every point summarized here, and a few provided inputs counter to these conclusions. The findings of this study, however, are consistent with the majority of the data. All personal stories and quotes in this book, unless otherwise noted, are from my research participants.

ABOUT PASSIONATE PURPOSE

Passionate purpose is an intention or goal pursued with passion—intense enthusiasm, zeal, fervor, and interest.[2] As a purpose connected to the Pursuer's values and gifts, it is significant. The more meaningful the purpose, the more intense is the passion and the more noteworthy is the impact.

What It Is

There is a human need for purpose. In *Man's Search for Meaning,*[3] Viktor Frankl reports, "Man actually needs the striving and struggling for some goal worthy of him." Joseph Campbell in *The Hero with a Thousand Faces*[4] writes that nearly all cultures carry a common myth about the hero's journey. The hero leaves home in service of a worthwhile purpose, encounters obstacles and hindrances, eventually succeeds, and returns home to be of further service. Kenneth Thomas[5] explains, "We seem to need to see ourselves as going somewhere—as being on a journey in pursuit of a significant purpose."

Passionate purposes and pursuit toward them are as varied as snowflakes—some are grandiose and others are quite modest. Some are professional; others are personal. Only you can choose a meaningful purpose. Although the examples in this book focus more on business-oriented endeavors, the concepts apply to all areas of life.

The word *purpose* in this book encompasses a range of aspirations, from a grand reason for living to narrow objectives. Purpose is used interchangeably with the terms *aim, target, goal,* and *intention.* You can make an impact and reap real rewards whether you align your passion with a core purpose, broad intention, or smaller goals. Some people recognize an enduring purpose that is the overall "why" of life, and others do not. Still, most people agree that having purpose is important and that purpose brings meaning to life.[6]

Almost everyone needs and wants a reason to get out of bed in the morning.[7] Some people, called *Passionate Pursuers,* find and commit to a worthwhile purpose, keep the fire burning during the pursuit, and continue until they produce results. *Seekers* may strive for a long time to discover it. Still others, *In-between'ers,* are taking a break.

Passionate purpose optimally engages your whole self, or *spirit,* in the pursuit. Spirit, your source for intuition and insights, is built from three energy centers of the self:

1. *Head* (intellect, mind, or cognition) stems from mental effort, logical thinking, talking, and imagination.
2. *Heart* (passion) emanates from desire, emotions, and feelings.
3. *Hands* (body) can spring from physical exertion, body sensations, touch, taking action, and doing.

Why It Is Important

A passionate purpose is one of the best gifts you can give yourself and others. You experience joy and build self-confidence in your ability to make a meaningful difference while living a rewarding life.

> *There is one quality which one must possess to win, and that is definiteness of purpose, the knowledge of what one wants, and a burning desire to possess it.*
>
> NAPOLEON HILL, *Think and Grow Rich*[8]

Having a clear purpose about which you are passionate is essential for getting what you want in work and life. With the pursuit of purpose comes fulfillment, and from that experience comes meaning and a feeling of success. Not only the individual benefits—businesses, families, churches, and organizations gain positive results when people align personal passion with organizational purpose.

In reading *Good to Great,*[9] I asked myself, "How do you turn a good life into a great life?" Jim Collins writes, "It is impossible to have a great life unless it is a meaningful life. And it is very difficult to have a meaningful life without meaningful work." Then I realized this study, which had absorbed me for over five years, really was exploring that critical question. The pursuit of passionate purpose is the quest to make a meaningful difference as your life's work. This book shows you *how* to transform a good life into a great life.

How do you measure success in the pursuit of passionate purpose? You have to define it by what you believe is meaningful. Likewise, you define greatness individually—but at the broadest level, it means a life that delivers what you want and find meaningful. These are your real rewards.

How Pursuing Passionate Purpose Feels

It feels great. Pursuit of passionate purpose is the quest of a meaningful goal that you care about deeply. It is the course of action or path you take on the journey to a desired destination. In the optimal pursuit, you reap what Kenneth Thomas[10] calls intrinsic rewards of meaningfulness, choice, competence, and progress that create more motivation for the pursuit. These are also real rewards from the pursuit. You may also experience what Mihaly Czikszentmihalyi[11] calls *flow*—a state of focused concentration where you become so involved in the activity that nothing else seems to matter. There is a sense of delight and deep satisfaction.

THE SUCCESS FORMULA

In interviewing people from all walks of life, I asked, "What brings meaning to your life?" There were many responses, but the majority essentially said:

- Love (deep, caring relationships with the interconnected web of life including people, animals, nature, and spirit)
- Meaningful work (a worthwhile way to contribute, grow, and make a difference)

My research affirms what others have said through the ages: The pursuit of passionate purpose and relationships along the way bring meaning to life.

A "two-four-six rule" is the basis for successfully pursuing passionate purpose and reaping real rewards. The *two-step* formula is:

1. Follow the proven *four-stage* process.
2. Apply *six* success strategies.

Consider this metaphor. Think of the pursuit of passionate purpose as a journey to a desired destination:

- The process is the step-by-step path you take to get from point A to point B. Your whole self—head, heart, and hands—becomes a unified vehicle to get you where you want to go. Your hands (body) serve as the engine. Your heart (passion) is the fuel. Your head (intellect, mind, or cognition) is the navigator guiding you along.
- The strategies are the principles of operation and lubrication that keep the vehicle working efficiently and moving forward on the journey. They can also act as catalysts to convert your vehicle from a bicycle into a sports car or rocket ship. Bring the proper people and

the rest of the interconnected web of life along as your travel companions and support crew who provide encouragement, stimulation, and all kinds of help.

Follow the Proven Process

First, discover what you value and your unique gifts—what you are passionate about. Next, find a worthwhile purpose that aligns with your passion. The purpose gives focus and passion fuels your pursuit. In pursuing the purpose, you may need to change, grow, and accept as your journey unfolds. Eventually, you assess progress. If you have achieved your goal or done everything possible to reach it, you continue the cycle of your life by reaffirming what you value and determining what is next. If not, you continue the pursuit, perhaps with some adjustments.

This iterative, ongoing process, shown in Figure 1.1, has four stages of development:

1. *Know and Nurture the Person* (exploring who I am and what I value).
2. *Find Passionate Purpose* (determining what I want and do not want).

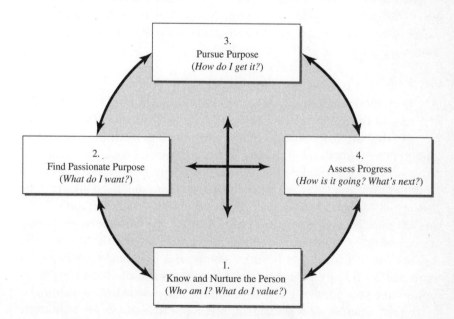

Figure 1.1   Four phases in the Pursuit of Passionate Purpose.

3. *Pursue Purpose* (establishing how I get it).
4. *Assess Progress* (evaluating how things are going and what is next).

The circular graphic is intentional in representing the process. The hoop[12] or *mandala,*[13] which means "magic, sacred circle" in Sanskrit, can be found in all cultures and periods of time as a symbol of wholeness. As one of the essential shapes of creation, it corresponds to the cycle of life.

In following this process, you are on the hero's journey,[14] universally found in myths and reality. You initially build a core foundation at home (know the person), then go off to engage in a worthwhile cause (find and pursue passionate purpose), overcome obstacles, eventually succeed, and then come back home to be of service to the greater community (assess progress and begin the cycle again).

Although movement is typically clockwise, movement between stages can be multidirectional. It is possible to jump on the pursuit at any stage and even move between stages while skipping one. You may start helping a worthy cause (pursuing someone else's purpose) without determining that it is your own aim or that you are passionate about it. Later, it becomes your own purpose, and as an unexpected consequence you get to know yourself better. The late David Hawkins, professor emeritus of philosophy, said, "We need to explore the relationship between means and ends. Purposes grow out of situations. One may find the pursuit first and then this brings the purpose."

My Path

My story illustrates this four-stage process. Although I did not realize it at the time, I started the *Assess Progress* stage as challenge after challenge arose in the corporate setting. Finally, when my boss made the product announcement without me, I decided to make changes. I took an educational leave of absence to explore through an eye-opening adventure trip to the South Pacific who I was and what was important to me. I embarked on the *Know and Nurture the Person* stage. Seeing children, families, and wildlife in Australia, New Zealand, and Fiji, I realized that I had been neglecting an important part of myself—my need for deep connections to people, being close to nature, and having a family. But how could I balance my heart and head? During the *Find Passionate Purpose* stage, I found what appeared to be the answer. I quit the company and moved to Colorado to be close to the outdoors, good friends, and a possible spouse. In addition, I started my consulting firm and enrolled in a PhD program. Immersed in the *Pursue Purpose* stage, I was now following my heart, in harmony with my head, while pursuing passionate purpose.

Had I arrived? My journey brought me back full circle to the *Assess Progress* stage with the next set of challenges. Could I consult, be a serious student, and nurture a relationship? This tale continues throughout the book.

Pursuits over Time

Over time, this circular process can be viewed as a continuous, upward spiral as shown in Figure 1.2. The ascending movement depicts the passage through eras of life.[15]

While some people have a passionate purpose that consumes their entire existence, others pursue simultaneous passionate purposes part-time, as shown in Figure 1.3. Professor Hawkins continues, "The idea of *a* purpose seems unduly restrictive. Life can have many purposes—commitments, involvements, and interests. Sometimes one is dominant, sometimes another."

Figure 1.2 Evolution of the pursuit over time.

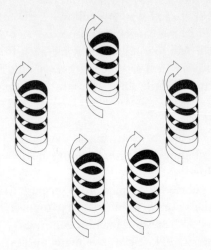

Figure 1.3   Simultaneous pursuits of passionate purpose.

Apply Success Strategies

There is more to the successful pursuit than following the four-stage process. Success requires using six vital strategies throughout the journey.

1. Polarity Strategy

Polarities, or opposites, exist in all of life—including in ourselves. My participants mentioned tension between their head and heart, between making a difference and making a living, between family and work. In pursuing passionate purpose, there is a polarity between the purpose (or intent) and the results (or impact). The Polarity Strategy is about integrating all parts of a person, organization, or system. Instead of seeing a polarity as a problem to solve, effective Passionate Pursuers honor opposites in life and allow dynamic movement between interdependent poles. The synergy of two or more poles working together in harmony is stronger and more stable than the efforts of just one side.

2. Attraction Strategy

Effective Passionate Pursuers attract what they want by maintaining a broad intention, while thinking, feeling, and taking action to get it. They direct the energy of their head, heart, and hands and encourage other people and resources in the web of life to help attain the purpose. In seeking a desired outcome, you need to be clear about what you want, visualize getting it, believe you will get it, talk as if you have it, feel passionately about getting it, and take action to attain that purpose while being flexible and open to the possibilities. Heart energy or passion about the outcome is the most vital. The Attraction Strategy means holding a broad intention and opening to opportunities that are everywhere, while thinking, feeling passionately, and taking action to get what you want.

3. Persistence Strategy

Persistence is the act of steadily pursuing purpose despite hindrances or obstacles. Effective Passionate Pursuers mindfully persevere with focused determination toward their goal using a divide-and-conquer approach. Once committed to a clear purpose or destination, they divide the journey into parts and conquer the whole, piece by piece. Working with unremitting will toward a portion until they make some progress, they establish a positive feedback loop. The outcome is real rewards—tangible results, positive feedback, and a stronger self with more confidence and passion, which fuels the next pursuit stage.

4. Allowing Strategy

Allowing is also called surrender, nonresistance, letting go, or equanimity. Effective Passionate Pursuers maintain clarity about *what* they want, while they allow *how* they get it to unfold. They are receptive to options and without attachment to a certain outcome, yet they remain persistent. The Allowing Strategy is about surrendering, without interference, to the natural flow, instead of struggling and resisting.

5. Connections Strategy

The most effective Passionate Pursuers are connected to the web of life. This support network includes the self and the right people, animals, plants, spiritual forces, and environment. Participants in my study agree that proper people are the greatest energizer for their pursuits and improper people are the biggest hindrance. It is vital to build relationships with and bring along on life's journey the *proper* people and support web, which serve as positive forces. Bring the proper people along and lessen the impact of the improper ones.

6. Pack Strategy

When you go on a trip, you typically pack a bag. Effective Passionate Pursuers use this success strategy to appropriately pack for the journey. They bring along essential energizers, such as their whole self and supportive people, while ridding themselves of draining forces, such as discouraging people and limiting attitudes.

My Path

My painful corporate experiences helped me realize that I was out of balance. By moving into the right environment and deciding to honor all of me, the *Polarity Strategy* brought me a sense of wholeness. While holding a broad intention to find the real formula for getting all that I wanted in life, I opened to the possibilities. In applying the *Attraction Strategy,* I thought passionately about my envisioned outcome and took action to pull what I wanted toward me. Before long, the opportunities for a relationship, degree program, and consulting practice found me. With the *Persistence Strategy,* I "divided and conquered" by focusing and persevering on one piece at a time. This required me to practice the *Allowing Strategy.* I let go of attachment to my corporate management identity and learned to allow life's journey to unfold. The *Connections Strategy* was at work— many people and spiritual forces helped me on this path. Through this part of my life's journey, I learned about building trust with the proper people. In bringing my values and gifts along, and striving to remove the obstacles of my own impatience, fears, and polarity imbalance, I learned how to use the *Pack Strategy.*

The Most Important Lessons Learned

My minister asked our congregation, "If you could put a note in the cookie jar to be read by your children's children, what would you share as the most important lessons you have learned about life?"

This book is for the child within each of us that yearns to make everything possible out of life. And so, for our children and our children's children, this is the note for the cookie jar:

Every person can live a more meaningful, satisfying life and produce extraordinary results. The pursuit of passionate purpose, not only its attainment, and relationships along the way bring the real rewards to life. Recognize success as maintaining integrity of effort as well as making your goal.

On your life's journey, follow this proven four-stage process:

1. Get to know who you are—what you value and what are your gifts; then nurture all parts of you—head, heart, and hands—into the whole person you want to be.

2. Foster your passion, align it to meaningful purpose, and commit to it fully.
3. Pursue your purpose by developing and implementing a focused plan.
4. Appreciate your progress and make adjustments along the way.

Throughout the journey, apply these six strategies:

1. Honor opposites in life and encourage dynamic movement between them.
2. Envision broadly what you want and, while being open to all possibilities, direct your thinking, feeling, and doing energy to attract it toward you.
3. Persist with enjoyment in the process by dividing and conquering piece by piece until you reach your goal.
4. Surrender to and allow the natural flow of life without attachment to a certain outcome.
5. Make deep connections to the proper people and web of life and lessen the impact of the improper ones.
6. Find out what energizes you and what discourages you. Bring the energizers along and leave discouragers behind. Enjoy!

ORGANIZATION OF THE BOOK

Pursuit of Passionate Purpose weaves my story with those of other individuals to illustrate the process and success strategies. The three concepts at the beginning of each part and chapter define its logical structure. This threefold logic is often used in Buddhism[16] to deepen understanding:

- *Premise:* The basic assumption supporting the contents.
- *Path:* The method of attainment.
- *Outcome:* The result or fruition.

Part One of this book lays the foundation and distinguishes those with passionate purpose from those without it. *Passionate Pursuers,* who have a different profile than *Seekers* and *In-between'ers,* effectively achieve their purposes.

The *two-step* formula for a rewarding business and personal life is then discussed in Parts Two and Three:

1. *Follow the Proven Process* explores how people move through four stages in pursuing passionate purpose.
2. *Apply Success Strategies* provides six principles of operation and lubrication that facilitate forward movement on the journey.

Part Four offers ways to use the approach to help others as well as yourself in various personal and professional pursuits. Look for boxes throughout the book with practical pointers to help you use the *Pursuit of Passionate Purpose* concepts.

This book offers a tested approach and practical suggestions to support your pursuits, whether personal or professional. My hope is that it will inspire and assist you in living your dreams.

2 Profiles of People on Their Path

Premise: People have different characteristics in pursuing passionate purpose.

Path: Determine what profile fits you.

Outcome: Knowledge of how to pursue a passionate purpose.

Ordinary people become *extraordinary* and produce extraordinary results when they align their passion with a meaningful purpose. People fall into profiles in their pursuit of passionate purpose:

- *Passionate Pursuers* have found and are actively pursuing their purpose.
- *Seekers* are striving to find and align their interests with a worthwhile purpose.
- *In-between'ers* are taking a break between pursuits.

A very few people in the study, *Existers,* don't seek or pursue passionate purpose. One such person describes himself as "passionate presence—I just am." This is fine, too, although this book does not focus on these people.

People change over time. A person who was a Passionate Pursuer may have transitioned to an In-between'er, become a Seeker, and now is again a Passionate Pursuer.

17

WHAT YOU CAN GET FROM THIS CHAPTER

This chapter profiles those with passionate purpose, those seeking it, and those resting between pursuits. Use the *Pursuit Inventory* to help assess how proficient you are in pursuing a passionate purpose. The Inventory also provides direction on where to focus your energy. Next, consider the following three profiles and assess where you fit. Use the tools provided, such as the *Passionate Purpose Indicator,* to determine your typical profile based on two dimensions: intensity of passion and clarity of purpose. With your profile, you are better equipped to benefit from this book.

MY PATH—THE JOURNEY TO A REWARDING LIFE

After breaking up with the wrong man and putting consulting on the back burner, I focused on the Degree Plan—finishing my doctorate—as my passionate purpose. I call each of the many pursuits of passionate purpose within my life's path a *plan,* with its own name. When I had achieved that goal, I went back to my core and pursued an entrepreneurial dream, the Business Plan, in harmony with a family life.

As I tell the story, once upon a time there were two former Bell Laboratories engineers, Richard A. Davis, who was known as the RAD, and Theresa Szczurek, who became known as the ISH for "Including Szczurek Happily." We had a vision for a better way to communicate and a desire to build a strong business based on our values. As Passionate Pursuers, we founded Radish Communications Systems.

It was the start of a thrilling roller-coaster ride as a Passionate Pursuer that brought some of the greatest highs in my life. This pursuit of passionate purpose encompassed the conception, gestation, labor, birth, and early years of my baby's (Radish's) growth, and the joy of sharing in her life. This is the story of then encountering and resolving the challenges that are typical in the journeys of most heroes. This is the account of eventually succeeding and living happily ever after as, at first, an In-between'er, then a Seeker and, in due course, a renewed Passionate Pursuer focused on my grand purpose in life. This is the report of lessons learned along the way that stimulated new thinking and novel approaches to living a rewarding life.

USE THE PURSUIT INVENTORY

How proficient are you at following the four-stage process while pursuing passionate purpose? Are there certain strategies that could use polishing? The Pursuit Inventory (see Table 2.1 on pages 20 and 21) can help you answer these questions and get a better sense of yourself.

It may help you determine whether the Passionate Pursuer profile fits you. It is also valuable for Seekers and In-between'ers who want to evaluate their use of the success formula. Although they are not likely to be actively going for a meaningful intention now, they may from previous experience be skillful at many or most of these tactics. And, they may soon be back in the pursuit.

After obtaining your score, only you can determine what level is appropriate for you. The higher the score, the closer you are to matching the optimal Passionate Pursuer profile and to using the formula effectively for the pursuit of passionate purpose: Follow the process and apply the success strategies.

PASSIONATE PURSUERS

Are you a Passionate Pursuer—have you aligned your passion with a worthwhile purpose?

A Passionate Pursuer—Richard Connolly's Story

Richard Connolly, blacksmith, could have spent his life employed in the automotive industry to have more financial security and to do what his family wanted. But instead, this 50-year-old Taoist is living his passion as a blacksmith in a small town in Arizona. "Relationships with other people and work bring meaning to my life. My intention is to create beautiful things. When I get up I can't wait to get to work. I am living every boy's dream."

It wasn't always this way for Connolly, the fifth child in a large Irish family, but life circumstances helped him open to the opportunity and find his passionate purpose. "I had jobs that I didn't like. I pursued things that my family was into and that were expected of me. Then I got laid off from the automotive industry in the '70s and was hired to restore carriages. I loved it so much that I went to school and learned blacksmithing

Table 2.1 Pursuit Inventory

Identify a purpose you are (or were) pursuing: _____

Based on your perceptions, indicate how OFTEN each statement describes who you are while pursuing this purpose. Using a 1–5 scale where 1 is rarely and 5 is most of the time, write the appropriate number of points in the corresponding column. Sum all the numbers to get your total points.

Don't over analyze; mark your initial reaction to the statement.

Purpose I am pursuing: _____	Rarely or Never	Seldom	Sometimes	Frequently	Most or All of Time
Number of points per response in this column	1	2	3	4	5
1. On an ongoing basis, I take action to learn more about who I am.					
2. I recognize my values and gifts.					
3. I work to nurture my self-confidence and self-esteem, curiosity, energy, integrity of effort, optimism, passion, regeneration, values, and wholeness.					
4. I have passion that is aligned with a worthwhile purpose.					
5. I have what it takes to keep my passion burning.					
6. I am committed to a meaningful purpose.					
7. I develop and implement an appropriate plan, build partnerships, and promote along the way.					
8. I enjoy the process of getting where I am going.					
9. I define success as maintaining integrity of effort in the pursuit of the purpose, regardless of whether the desired results are attained.					
10. I evaluate and appreciate progress.					
11. I make midcourse adjustments and am flexible when necessary.					
12. I honor opposites in life and allow a dynamic flow between interdependent poles, thereby creating a more balanced whole.					

Purpose I am pursuing: _____ _____	Rarely or Never	Seldom	Sometimes	Frequently	Most or All of Time
13. I have a clear, yet broad, vision of a successful outcome.					
14. I attract opportunities in line with a broad intention by opening to the possibilities and focusing my personal energy, as well as energy from others in the web of life, to get what I want.					
15. I break the purpose into parts and persistently work piece-by-piece with unremitting will until progress is made.					
16. I can surrender to the natural flow and let go of attachment to the outcome.					
17. My inner self supports the pursuit of this purpose.					
18. I involve the proper people, animals, plants, spiritual forces, and environment from the web of life and leave improper ones behind.					
19. I bring energizers or encouraging forces along on my journey.					
20. I remove hindrances or obstacles that block me.					
Total points = _____					

Scoring

Only you can determine what level is appropriate for you. Follow the process and apply the success strategies. The higher the score, the closer you are to the optimal Passionate Pursuer profile.

100–81   You are an effective Passionate Pursuer. Most likely you flow with ease while working toward your dream.

80–61   You have many useful skills in pursuing what you want. Some minor modifications will help you more smoothly attain what you want in life.

60–41   Your practice for finding and pursuing purpose, intentions, and goals needs work. Now is the time to assess and take action for improvement.

Below 41   Immediate attention is needed. You have lots of room for improvement. If you are a Seeker or In-between'er, focus, as your passionate purpose for now, on knowing and nurturing yourself.

Your answer to individual questions tells you where to focus more energy. If you scored 1 or 2 on any one, focus on these elements as you continue through this book.

by apprenticing. There was a time when I needed more money, like when my kids had certain demands, and I tried going back to a more traditional job. An injury would take me away from that job and throw me back into this. Blacksmithing just feels right. Rather than fighting in the auto industry, I am relaxed about it. My family thought I was silly. They said, 'Find something with a retirement.' Later, my dad was very proud of me."

Connolly gets into a "creative flow" and watches his work emerge. "I get a snapshot in my brain of the finished piece—a complete flash. My job is to figure out how to make that. I take the hot iron out of the fire. If I push with the hammer, it gets confusing. If I just hold the piece in my hand and in my heart, I don't have to decide. It is so natural. Without thinking, I watch it take shape. I am not shaping it. It is 'doing by not doing.' I am watching it happen. This is a place that is so peaceful. I don't have to think or plan. I am part of it. I am its instrument. I am the tool. I think two hours have passed and six hours have gone by.

"The feeling I get when I work encourages me. I am also supported by seeing my day's effort and seeing the finished product. While I make things for others, I also make them beautiful for me. The money and lack of a steady income occasionally discourage me. Pressure from customers disturbs the flow. Also this work requires hard, physical labor—sometimes too hard. I overcome these negative forces by exercising and lifting weights. If I am strong, my job is easy. I gave up the horseshoeing part because it was too hard on my body. And, I am charging more for my work."

Connolly now has two passionate purposes that require flexibility and some adjustments. "A friend set me up on a date for my birthday. We were instantly attracted. Since I was alone for so long and Kate is so precious to me, I go to great lengths now to be with my wife. I changed my schedule, starting work earlier and ending earlier. I set limits and at 6 P.M. go home."

Connolly has advice for those who cannot find their passionate purpose. "There is something in everyone's life that you are drawn to or look forward to. Life keeps putting this in your path. You have a choice to walk around it or to take it. It may be scary to take it, but fear can be a great motivator. Perhaps it comes so often it might be annoying. It is so easy to deny. It may be so obvious. You may daydream about it, or it may be the favorite thing you do. If it weren't your work, it would be your hobby. Realize that a fire needs a little air to stoke it. . . . Follow your heart instead of your wallet.

"If you love what you're doing, you'll be good at it, and you will make money. When you have free time, what do you do to feel good? Find a job that gives you this feeling. If you are in a horrible situation, you can walk away. Just be willing to accept the consequences of your decisions. Believe that you can do whatever you want."

Profile of Passionate Pursuers

While each person is different and may even change over time from pursuit to pursuit, the most effective Pursuers use the *two-step* formula for successfully pursuing passionate purpose: (1) Follow the process and (2) employ success strategies.

Follow the Proven Four-Stage *Process*

1. *Know and Nurture the Person.* Get to know who you are and nurture your whole self.
2. *Find Passionate Purpose.* Foster passion, align it with a worthwhile purpose, and commit fully to the purpose.
3. *Pursue Purpose.* Develop and focus on implementing a plan by persistently involving people in partnership, resources, and communication.
4. *Assess Progress.* Evaluate progress, recognize success, appreciate, and determine what's next.

Apply Six *Success Strategies*

1. *Use the Polarity Strategy.* Instead of seeing a polarity as a problem to solve, honor opposites in life and allow dynamic movement between interdependent poles.
2. *Use the Attraction Strategy.* Hold a broad intention and remain open to opportunities that are everywhere, while thinking, feeling passionately, and taking action to get what you want.
3. *Use the Persistence Strategy.* Mindfully persevere with focused determination using a divide-and-conquer approach.
4. *Use the Allowing Strategy.* Be clear on *what* you want and allow *how* you get it to unfold.
5. *Use the Connections Strategy.* Bring the proper people and web of life along and lessen the impact of improper ones.
6. *Use the Pack Strategy.* Pack energizers and remove hindrances for the journey.

Effective Passionate Pursuers exercise techniques to help them productively use the formula. Techniques that have proven to be especially valuable, such as Mindfulness Meditation,[1] are mentioned throughout the book.

Challenges of Passionate Pursuers

Finding a passionate purpose does not automatically mean you will easily pursue and achieve it. Not everyone with a passionate purpose has mastered the process and strategies of effective Passionate Pursuers.

People typically must resolve blockages, friction, obstacles, or negative behaviors. Have you met any of these—doubter, critic or judge, dabbler, procrastinator, coward or victim, obsessive thinker, grudge carrier, perfectionist, controller, sloth, or fighter? (Rising above hindrances is explored in Chapter 12.)

What Do Passionate Pursuers Get from This Book?

Why should someone who is actively working on a passionate purpose read this book? Even if you have found passion and aligned it with an important purpose, you may still encounter challenges during your quest. Pursuers may find in this book:

- Practical pointers and tested techniques, especially during a particular stage of the process, to help you more easily succeed in your pursuit. These suggestions can remove obstacles, adjust your attitude, keep you focused on goal completion, offer alternative approaches, and move you to the next level or outcome.
- An understanding of how best to use the four-stage process and the guiding strategies.
- Encouragement and a recharge to keep your passion burning.
- Tools to assess when to continue, change, or move on.
- Validation or explanation of what you may have been doing already, thereby encouraging you to continue, as well as suggestions to strengthen your use of the formula.

At one time, I was president of a foundation that helped low-income women attain economic self-sufficiency through education. These women were often struggling to work, raise a family, and complete their college degree. One recipient of a foundation scholarship shared that more than the actual dollars, the gift told her, "Keep going. You can do it." Likewise, this book can provide encouragement for Passionate Pursuers.

SEEKERS

Are you a Seeker—someone striving to find your passion and align it with a meaningful purpose?

A Seeker—Katie Ewig's Story

Katie Ewig, administrative assistant, is 25 years old and has not yet been able to find or commit to a passionate purpose. Treading water as she works as a temporary administrative assistant at a museum, she continues to search. While she has a lot going for her, including a bachelor's degree in environmental studies and a supportive family who wants her to find something she likes doing, Ewig has some internal constraints. She admits, "I'm too frozen and paralyzed to leap into something. In the back on my mind, I am fearful."

Perhaps an internal imbalance, which allows one part of her to dominate decision making, contributes to her dissatisfaction. "My head gets priority over my heart when making decisions because I am terrified of financial instability.

"Last summer, I had a job working with kids in nature. It felt great and time went by quickly. I couldn't believe I was getting paid for doing what I enjoy. There was a coming together of my two parts, a balancing of my head and heart. There was peace. However, I viewed it as my last chance to do environmental work."

Ewig concluded that environmental work would not provide the income she desired so that she could travel and socialize with her friends. In the values conflict between money and pursuing what she knew she loved, her financial fears won and she left the passionate purpose behind. Unwilling to commit to this purpose or unable to creatively explore how to mold it into something that would balance her values conflict, she remains a frustrated yet active Seeker.

However, recently Ewig has brought more heart into her search. "I am taking the advice of a counselor: 'Be patient, take the pressure off of yourself, give yourself a few years, there is no time limit.' I now have faith that I will in time figure it out."

Postlude: After being laid off and taking time during unemployment to explore what to do next, Ewig concluded that she felt best working with kids. So she worked part-time in retail while completing the requirements for an elementary education teaching license. Today, she is a summer camp counselor and is seeking a permanent teaching position.

Profile of Seekers

Seekers are those striving for passionate purpose and the knowledge to appropriately pursue it. There are many different kinds of Seekers. Some people may be confused about their purpose; others may not find intense interest, energy, devotion, or liking for what they are doing. Still others have not found a way to link their passion with a viable purpose. As circumstances change, even Passionate Pursuers encounter times when they need to reaffirm their passion or purpose; thus they become temporary Seekers again.

Constraints typically hamper seekers, especially those who cannot find a passionate purpose over the long term:

- *Internal constraints:* "We have met the enemy and he is us."[2] Research shows that internal, often self-imposed, limitations are the biggest hindrance for people.[3] Seekers may have low self-esteem or a weak sense of self that breeds fears, lack of courage, self-doubt, and weak confidence. Or, they may be "out-of-balance," allowing one part of themselves to dominate and overpower messages from another part. They may, in some way, be hindering their own creativity or energy flow.
- *External constraints:* Often restrictions come externally from family, other people, societal influences, lack of resources, or challenges of life. Some external factors may ultimately stem from internal restrictions. If you have low self-esteem and do not value your inner voice, other people may more easily influence you.

A Long-Term Seeker with Internal and External Constraints—Dawn's Story

Dawn[4] retired a few years ago after 32 years as a primary school teacher in the public schools. "I envy those people with passions that consume their lives. I don't value myself enough to give myself credit for passion. I enjoy birding, walking outdoors in nature, and doing these with people. But I haven't been able to identify this as passion."

Dawn worked to know herself better and to discover what was holding her back from finding a passionate purpose. "Poor self esteem, depression, lack of time, fear of failure, and fear of disapproval held me back. My energy was going to keep things together. I felt I wasn't capable. I only had one child because I didn't feel confident that I could handle more."

People and circumstances influenced Dawn's self-esteem. Growing up in a chaotic, physically abusive family, Dawn shares, "I was fearful of my dad and his punitive actions. From third grade through junior high, I played the trumpet. I got satisfaction from playing; it was fun and I wanted to do it.

"In junior high school, I became fearful about my ability to do things. Someone compared me to my siblings and gave me feedback saying, 'You shouldn't go to college. You're not smart enough.' That was a turning point. I quit the trumpet because of fear of failure. It was a relief in some way. Later as a teacher, I was always careful to not demean anyone. I value the child and realize that this is one thing I can do well."

Dawn also recognized opposition between various parts of herself.

I haven't resolved the tension between my heart and head. They are in conflict. My heart says one thing and the head says another.

DAWN, retired teacher and Seeker

Over the years, Dawn made some progress in overcoming restraining forces. "I had personal therapy and started taking antidepression medication. This made a big difference. I recognized that I have wonderful things in life with my family, income, and a good job."

Dawn has advice for those who cannot find passionate purpose. "Beating yourself up doesn't help. Relax more. Don't think that it must be so big. Honor yourself and what you are doing. Don't think you have to put a label on it."

Her life can give us hope. "One of my purposes now is being happy. I am committed and really working on it." (Getting beyond internal constraints is discussed further in Chapters 3 and 12.)

A Seeker Affected by External Influences—Bob's Story

Bob,[5] a hard-working, gentle soul, was a good math and science student in high school and loved anything mechanical, especially cars. With encouragement from relatives, who as successful engineers had stressed the high salaries in this profession, this Eagle Scout started working toward a mechanical engineering degree. It just did not connect with him. The harder he worked the worse his grades grew until his Junior year he came close to flunking out. This wake-up call encouraged him to rediscover himself. He had always enjoyed leading the younger scouts and coaching a youth baseball team. Finally he gravitated to teaching.

Bob knew he loved kids, but why did it take him so long to decide to become a teacher? It is not that Bob and some other Seekers do not know deep down what they want to do. It may look like they are wandering around aimlessly without a purpose, but it may be that outside influences are confusing them. Societal factors, including parental guidance, sway them toward something in conflict with their true purpose. His heart says teach, but everyone else says engineering, make money, or whatever. So now there is a conflict between the messages from the inner voice and the outside world. It takes resolution of the conflict of these polarities before one can find and commit to a passionate purpose.

What Do Seekers Get from This Book?

Seekers are trying to understand and recognize what is holding them back from finding and committing to passionate purpose. With self-awareness, Seekers can nurture themselves to lessen negative effects, resolve conflicts, or break free of constraints. It sounds simple, and indeed for some people, it can be. For many others, however, it's a huge lifelong challenge.

As a Seeker, you are offered tactics in this book to "Know and Nurture the Person." Once you develop awareness, you can choose whether to make changes. Research indicates what actions would help. Then it is up to you to passionately pursue the action plan that is right for you. Seekers may need, and can get from this book, suggestions to:

- Discern your values, so you can define what is meaningful and use that to spark your passion.
- Evaluate your gifts and traits, determine how together with your values they define your passion, and then align your passion with a worthwhile purpose.
- Determine how to nurture yourself into the person you want to be and take steps to:
  —Foster passion.
  —Strengthen self-esteem, develop more confidence, diminish self-doubt, or build other traits.
  —Strive to open to the possibilities, overcome fears, leave frustration and exhaustion from your search behind, and find the courage to commit.

—Acquire additional skills or knowledge.

—Find repressed energy, conquer laziness, maintain effort, or break through other blocks.

* Balance the whole self—head, heart, and hands.
* Identify external factors influencing the situation and determine how to reduce their impact.

If you are a Seeker, be kind to yourself and patient, but be open and persistent in your search. Realize that this book may be one of many steps in your search. Beyond this book, some Seekers may need to get help from other professionals to address depression, emotional disorders, or other mental health issues. This approach worked for Dawn, it may work for you.

Once you begin to know and nurture yourself, you can use other approaches in this book to find and embrace passionate purpose, pursue it, and assess progress on your journey.

IN-BETWEEN'ERS

Are you an In-between'er—resting between pursuits?

An In-Between'er—Lynda Simmons's Story

When Lynda Simmons, real estate developer, architect, and community leader, finally decided to move on from being president and CEO of Phipps Houses, her retirement was announced on the front page of the *New York Times* real estate section. Simmons is an architect who delivered on her passionate purpose of "creating better lives through enduring and beautiful communities." Over 23 years, she worked to transform a small, old organization into the largest, not-for-profit, housing developer in the United States. With a staff of 500, this establishment owned and managed 3,600 apartments (of which she built 3,000) for homeless, low- and moderate-income tenants. Additionally, the business managed 5,800 units for other owners, including two of New York City's largest hospitals. Simmons was responsible for nearly $1 billion worth of real estate and an annual cash through-put of around $90 million. "I wasn't building apartments, I was creating community. This was my conscious ministry. Beauty is biologically important; 'housing' is not enough to develop people. We incorporated trees, play spaces, and beauty.

"We organized human development programs for education, job training, recreation, social, and other services for residents and their surrounding neighborhoods. We can't create humane communities anywhere unless
we create one out of our own organization. . . . Meaningful work is the
most powerful tool in the development of a person. Love and work bring
meaning to life."

Simmons worked in a difficult environment. "Developing in the rough
and tumble of New York City was stressful, as was managing the operations
and finances of 16 companies. I loved it. For eight of my ten-year presi-
dency, I had severe chronic fatigue syndrome. I couldn't work a full day.
Initially seeing the buildings going up would keep my fire burning. Then,
I worked to create a strong organization, which took all the artistry I had.
My meditation practice also was key. My spirituality sustained me through
most of the years, because I never doubted that I was doing what we were
meant to do—help others and develop my own talents."

The time came when Simmons finally let go. "I was completely identified with my creations. Eventually, I decided to retire at 58 years old and
focus on my personal, inner life—spiritual, emotional, and physical. I was
exhausted, the organization had become an institution with a strong creative culture, and I knew I had achieved what I wanted."

So she transitioned into what she calls her "reconstruction/reorientation"
phase. For nine years, she has used physical therapies and the study and
practice of Buddhist meditation, sculpture, and nature to get healthy. In
one sense, "healing" is her passionate purpose. In another perspective,
she is "in-between" and working on knowing and nurturing herself.
Now seeking her next passionate purpose, she says, "I am ready for
something."

Simmons has this advice to those taking on a passionate purpose. "Stick
with it. Strive to live a major life. And use your heart in decision making.
In the end it feels better."

Profile of In-Between'ers

An In-between'er has known and pursued passionate purpose. Yet, the time
came to let go and take a break. Being on the sideline, instead of in active
play, presents opportunities to reorient and rejuvenate. This is the time to
get to know and nurture yourself. After the right amount of space in this
neutral zone,[6] which only you can define, you will once again be ready to
move on to the next stage of your life's overall purpose. And you don't have

to be in-between purposes; you can just be resting in-between significant pieces of the same purpose.

An in-between time represents an important part of the cycle of life. Each day is a metaphor for life with a comparable cycle of dawn, day, sunset, and night. In every 24-hour sequence, you need to find time to rest and nourish. And so it is with passionate purposes. There is a time in-between to replenish and feed the soul.

Too often, we do not honor this downtime. We might even beat ourselves up for not having a clear purpose and energy. Have you ever asked, "What's wrong with me?" Perhaps nothing is wrong. It may just be the natural cycle of life seeking the necessary downtime for rejuvenation.

Difficulty in Resting—Brian's Story

Every day Brian,[7] an avid hiker, retreats to nature for aggressive physical exercise, emotional solace, and spiritual replenishment. This is his monastery. In one sense, he is addicted to it. But every few months, he asked, "What is wrong with me? I have no energy. I am feeling tired rather than revitalized during my hikes." Eventually through the help of his friends, he realized, "When did I last take a day off from this routine? The best athletes know they cannot exercise every day. I must give myself a rest day to rebuild; in resting I become stronger."

The attitude against taking a break is pervasive through our society for much more than physical fitness. Some people will not give themselves permission to rest. They harbor fears of not being able to get started again, losing control, or facing other unforeseen consequences. (Overcoming fear is addressed in Chapter 12.)

Other parts of Brian's life have the same familiar pattern. A creative entrepreneur who took his company from an idea to a thriving operation, Brian refused to give himself a break even after successfully selling the company. He immediately went on to start another venture and did not allow himself to be an In-between'er. While he is now working hard in pursuing this new purpose, it somehow feels empty and shallow. He feels as if he has not found his true passionate purpose. Because he did not allow himself to go into the neutral zone and renew, he constrained the next pursuit. Instead of being in a state of effortless flow, Brian uses tremendous effort, which drains him even further.

For Brian, being in-between is just too difficult. He harbors a fear that he might never get back on track. His work is the source for too much of his sense of worth and identity. He also feels pressure from his father not to depart from prescribed societal norms of what a man "should" do as the breadwinner. In reality, if Brian allowed some time to know and nurture himself, he could reconnect with meaning and reignite his passion.

What Do In-Between'ers Get from This Book?

In-between'ers can use this book to:

- Receive validation of resting periods or neutral zones as valuable and honorable and give themselves and others permission to be in the neutral zone.
- Learn how to have the most constructive in-between time.
- Reaffirm and strengthen use of the process and strategies of Passionate Pursuers.
- Assess if and when the time is right to begin again and embrace the next passionate purpose.
- Revisit, when the time is right, the questions "Who am I?" and "What do I value?" in the *Know and Nurture the Person* stage.

UNDERSTAND YOUR PROFILE

What about you? Are you a Passionate Pursuer, Seeker, or In-between'er? Understanding your profile and its underlying nature will allow you to use the tools in this book to help you pursue passionate purpose and reap the real rewards of life.

Use the Passionate Purpose Indicator

The Passionate Purpose Indicator (PPI), shown in Figure 2.1, provides a simple, visual representation based on two dimensions: intensity of passion and clarity of purpose.

Level of passion varies from indifferent to intense. Are you extremely passionate, indifferent, or somewhere in the middle? Do you have a purpose now that is aligned with this passion? Clarity of purpose can range from clear to confused. Are you perfectly clear about your purpose, perplexed, or somewhere in the middle?

Use the indicator to assess your current situation. Answer these questions:

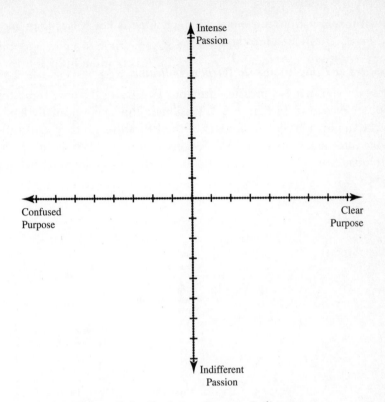

Figure 2.1 Passionate Purpose Indicator.

- How intense is my passion (intense, indifferent, or somewhere in the middle)?
- Is my passion aligned with a purpose? How clear is this purpose (perfectly clear, confused, or somewhere in the middle)?

Consider where you fall on the PPI. If you have multiple interests and intentions, you will find it helpful to complete this inquiry several times. Your clarity and intensity may vary from day to day; this is natural and human.

What you feel, not what others see, is most important. The indicator should be based on your own perception since visible level of passion varies. One person's passion may be brightly burning like a bonfire while another's may appear as a subtle glow like the embers of a fire. Both are hot, but the visual manifestations are quite different. One is not better than another; they are just unique unto themselves.

Profiles and the Passionate Purpose Indicator

How do you match a profile with your Passionate Purpose Indicator response? As shown in Figure 2.2, Passionate Pursuers optimally hang out in the upper right quadrant (III) of the PPI although they can shift and move into quadrants II and IV. Seekers will more likely be in the lower left quadrant (I). They may also be in the upper left (II) and lower right (IV).

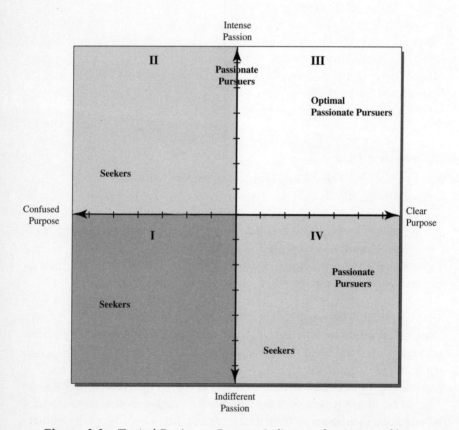

Figure 2.2   Typical Passionate Purpose Indicator of various profiles.

In-between'ers, who honor where they are, may identify their in-between time as a passionate purpose in itself and may be more in the upper right (III). Or, perhaps they will be on the left side with lack of clarity of purpose. They are left off this figure because their situations can vary so much.

One thing is certain: Change is constant, and it is natural to move to different places on the PPI as your passion and clarity of purpose fluctuate. A Passionate Pursuer in the upper right (III) may encounter some doubt. She will then move more to the left. Or if she becomes discouraged, her passion level may drop, and she may move down. This movement is why we all need support and recharges to keep us on course.

The movement can be quick, or it can be slow. Sue[8] started the "Pursuit of Passionate Purpose" workshop with confusion about her purpose and with a level of passion right in the middle. Being on the left side of the "purpose" axis and in the middle of the "passion" axis, she was a Seeker. When asked two months later, she had moved to the upper right quadrant (III). Having completed some important work in the session and afterward, Sue opened up to the possibilities. During a spontaneous visit to another city, she became clear on moving there and designing a community for aging baby boomers.

Pleasure over Pain

When your passion is intense and your purpose is clear (upper right quadrant of the Passionate Purpose Indicator), you generally feel good. When there is indifference and a confused purpose, you don't feel as good. Preferring to feel good, people like having passionate purpose and seek it. Following the Pursuit of Passionate Purpose process moves you to more intense passion and a clear purpose. This begins with knowing yourself—your values and gifts (see Chapter 3).

Lack of Alignment

Sometimes people have strong passion, but no clear purpose related to it. So on Figure 2.2, they would be in the upper left quadrant. Alternatively, people may spend their time pursuing a well-defined purpose, but it is not in harmony with their passion. They would be in the lower right quadrant of Figure 2.2. They have not determined how to align their passions with a worthwhile purpose, or they may not know how to build passion for their purpose. (Aligning passion with purpose is covered in Chapter 4.)

Profiles and Stages

The stages of the process, shown in Figure 2.3, are linked with the profiles. Passionate Pursuers move throughout the process but may often find themselves in the *Pursue Purpose* and *Assess Progress* stages asking, "How do I get it?" and "How's it going?" Consistent with the PPI in Figure 2.2, they tend to be in the upper right quadrant. Those with the most effective use of strategies may move more easily among the stages.

Seekers may spend more time in the *Know and Nurture the Person* and *Find Passionate Purpose* stages answering the questions: "Who am I" and "What do I want?" Or, they may be pursuing a purpose without much passion for it, since they may not have determined who they really are and what really excites them. Perhaps being disenchanted, they have stopped any pursuit at all and are really In-between'ers, hanging out and going through the motions of life. On the PPI in Figure 2.2, seekers tend to be in the lower left quadrant.

In-between'ers may be resting somewhere between the *Assess Progress* and *Know and Nurture the Person* stages. They may be in that stage to determine who they are, or more likely, they have temporarily moved off the path altogether.

A person may have had a passionate purpose sometime in life, but at another time may be in-between or searching for a purpose. It is natural to move from one profile to another as you live life.

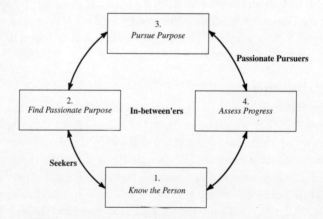

Figure 2.3 Profiles with four-stage process.

SUMMARY

- Most people fall into one of the following three profiles in the pursuit of passionate purpose:
  1. *Passionate Pursuers* have found and are actively pursuing their purpose.
  2. *Seekers* are striving to find and align their interests with a worthwhile purpose.
  3. *In-between'ers* are taking a break between pursuits.
- The Pursuit Inventory helps assess proficiency in using the process and applying the strategies. It helps identify areas that need attention.
- Passionate Pursuers find passionate purpose, keep the fire burning during the pursuit, and produce positive results. They have a profile with certain characteristics.
- Seekers are looking for passionate purpose. They may be constrained in some way, internally or externally from people, society, or situations.
- In-between'ers have known and pursued passionate purpose. Yet, the time has come to let go and take a break. Being in the neutral zone, rather than in active play, presents opportunities to reorient and rejuvenate. The in-between phase represents an important part of the cycle of life.
- While each person is different and may even change over time from pursuit to pursuit, the most effective Pursuers follow the *two-step* formula:
  1. Follow the proven process.
  2. Apply success strategies.
- Effective Passionate Pursuers follow the *four stages* of the process:
  1. Know and nurture the self.
  2. Foster and align passion with a worthwhile purpose, and then commit fully.
  3. Develop and implement a plan for "How do I get it?"
  4. Evaluate progress, recognize success, appreciate, and determine what is next.

(continued)

- Passionate Pursuers skillfully apply the *six* success strategies:
    1. Use the Polarity Strategy.
    2. Use the Attraction Strategy.
    3. Use the Persistence Strategy.
    4. Use the Allowing Strategy.
    5. Use the Connections Strategy.
    6. Use the Pack Strategy.
- The Passionate Purpose Indicator provides a simple, visual representation based on two dimensions: intensity of passion and clarity of purpose.
- It is natural to move from one profile to another.
- Passionate Pursuers move through all four stages of the process, but expend more time in the *Pursue Purpose* and *Assess Progress* stages. Seekers may spend more time in the *Know and Nurture the Person* and *Find Passionate Purpose* stages. In-between'ers may temporarily be off the path, or hanging out in the *Assess Progress* and *Know and Nurture the Person* part of the process.

PART TWO

FOLLOW THE
PROVEN PROCESS

Premise: There is a way to get where you want to go.
Path: Begin and follow the four-stage process.
Outcome: Movement on the journey of life.

3 Know and Nurture the Person

Premise: Start with who you are now.

Path: Get to know the self and nurture it into a whole person.

Outcome: Become who you want to be.

You cannot pursue purpose until you find it, and you cannot find passionate purpose until you know what you are seeking. During this stage, you determine or reconfirm "Who am I?" by looking at your values, gifts, and traits. Answers to the question help you define what you are passionate about. By nurturing yourself, you strengthen your sense of self and become the whole person you want to be. Thus, the first stage in the pursuit of purpose is: Know and nurture yourself, the person.

WHAT YOU CAN GET FROM THIS CHAPTER

Passionate Pursuers, Seekers, and In-between'ers all benefit from the knowledge of self. For some, especially Seekers and In-between'ers, this is the most vital part of the process.

KNOW YOURSELF

The sages[1] since antiquity have said, "Know Thyself." It is not surprising that Passionate Pursuers have learned how to know themselves. But how can you become familiar with and understand yourself better?

Understanding has two critical elements:

1. *Values:* Core beliefs, ideology, ethics, morals, attitude, and ideals—define who you are and what is meaningful to you.
2. *Gifts:* Talents, experience, abilities, aptitude, education, and traits—mold how you can uniquely contribute.

Your values define what is meaningful to you. The intersection of your values and your gifts, as shown in Figure 3.1, describes *what you are passionate about.* What you are passionate about makes your heart sing and brings more passion.

Traits are personal characteristics that allow you to effectively use your values and gifts. Eight essential traits are found in effective Passionate Pursuers.

People in my study strongly agree that having meaning is important to them. Furthermore, they strongly agree that purpose brings meaning to their lives.[2]

People are more satisfied while pursuing a purpose than they were before having a purpose, and they are even more satisfied after achieving it. But that satisfaction fades over time. For most therefore, the *pursuit* of passionate purpose, *not merely its attainment,* brings meaning and satisfaction to life.

The sources of meaning mentioned in my study are consistent with human needs, which move from basic survival needs, to love, and on to growth.[3] People report that pursuit of passionate purpose brings growth.[4]

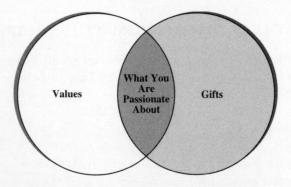

Figure 3.1   Intersection of values and gifts.

Generally, people in my study had met their basic survival needs and found their meaning in fulfilling love and growth needs. It is easy, however, for survival needs to resurface. Just miss a few meals and the physiological need for food returns. If you get sick or lose your job, satisfying basic needs quickly becomes the top priority.

People with a healthy sense of self or trust that the Universe will provide for them, still seek, even in trying times, to fulfill their higher needs and purposes. Consider Paul Harris, whose New York boss secretly blocked his transfer to Colorado. Infuriated and committed to living true to his convictions, he moved anyway. "With hardly any financial cushion to fall on, I put the family in the car and we headed west. Although I didn't have a job lined up, I trusted in my abilities and knew that something would work out."

Aligning Values with Gifts

- Values define meaning. Aligning values with gifts sparks passion.
- Meaning is important to people.
- Purpose is a source of meaning.
- Meaningful purpose unleashes more passion.
- Passion fuels the pursuit.
- Passion, along with other personal traits, determines how effectively you pursue your purpose.
- Pursuit of passionate purpose, not only its attainment, brings satisfaction.

My Path—Discovering My Values

My values, on which we built Radish, were formed years earlier. "What is wrong with me?" I asked myself in confusion. "I don't want to get out of bed in the morning and go to work. I used to love being an engineer. This is not like me." Eventually, I heard my inner voice reply, "You need a change. You want to work with people and use your heart along with your head. Why not initiate a transfer to the marketing side of the firm?"

I responded to the message from deep inside me, and the company supported my career change. I became a product line manager in the international division, guiding a team to bring telecommunications solutions to world markets. This was the right move. My tremendous energy, motivation, and passion, told me that I value meaningful work interacting with many people. My Career Plan was to climb the corporate ladder.

After I had worked long and hard, the next promotion came. That is when I overheard my coworkers whispering behind my back. "She doesn't deserve it. Why did she get promoted?" It was as if someone had shot an arrow through my heart. Finally, I heard my heart cry through my inner voice, "You have no one with whom to share this hard-earned prize. You need deeper connections with loving people and balance in life. You value family and friends, along with a way to contribute professionally. Make some changes, Theresa!"

I joined a church and made some friends outside work, decorated my house, began entertaining, and started hiking again with new friends. It helped ease some of the pain.

Yet, the challenges continued. My boss warned me: "Theresa, you need to kill Larry, or he is going to kill you." Indeed, Larry,[5] a team member, made me look bad whenever possible. Without conscious thought, my values surfaced and I blurted out, "I can't kill him or anyone. I play win-win." It was clear that I value integrity and working with people who also value it.

Then the pivotal point occurred. My boss, not me, was sent to debut my product to the world. No one in management supported me. My inner voice spoke again: "After sacrificing your personal life for years for this delivery, you are not valued here." Feeling discounted and betrayed, I learned that I value an environment where all people can contribute and be rewarded to the fullest. Once more, my wiser self advised me: "If you are going to work this hard, get a piece of the action so you can establish the values, mold the environment, and have input on decisions. Make the change."

This time I followed my heart along with my head and left the company. Adversity was the positive force that encouraged me to change. Only later did I realize that the company was not standing in my way of getting all that I wanted in life—I was. By not knowing what I truly valued, not engaging all parts of me, and encouraging my workaholic tendencies, I was my own worst enemy. Fortunately, life kept repeating a wake-up call for change. Finally, I heard it and surrendered to its message.

I found that each significant event helped me determine what was important to me. I first had a long list of values, then consolidated them into five. These formed the personal foundation I contributed to the founding of Radish:

1. *Whole,* healthy, authentic *Self* on physical, mental, emotional, and spiritual levels, living with integrity, true to my highest convictions.

2. Loving *Connections* with self, fellow beings, God and spiritual forces, and nature.
3. *Meaningful Work* where I can contribute and be rewarded to the fullest.
4. *Prosperity.*
5. *Flow* or enjoying life in a joyful, passionate, optimistic state.

Discern and Probe into Your Values

You can get a pretty clear idea of your values by observing the way you spend your two most valuable currencies—time and money.

RICHARD LEIDER, *The Power of Purpose*[6]

Ask yourself, "What is important to me?" Values are the source of meaning and the spark for passion.

Use your life experiences to clarify your values. By looking back at critical incidents in life over time, values become apparent. If you are unsure of your values, spend some time to create a list of the things that are important to you.

Analyze your list to fully explore what those words mean to you and why. Let's look into integrity, which my study shows is a core element of the whole self and of Passionate Pursuers.

What Is Integrity?

Dictionaries define *integrity* as the state of being whole, of having a steadfast adherence to a strict moral or ethical code. Synonyms include *truthfulness, honor, authenticity,* and *uprightness.* According to Erik Erikson,[7] human development expert, integrity is acceptance of responsibility for one's own life cycle.

How do you know what integrity means to you? The foundation is laid early on from family, school, and church. Life experience is the true teacher of what any value means.

A work colleague insisted that we call her "Doctor so and so." When the company attempted to verify her degree and couldn't, she was terminated.

A friend of mine noticed that a restaurant bill was wrong. He told the waiter that a charge needed to be *added* to the bill. The owner later said, "Thank you for mentioning it. Most people would not." My friend's integrity impressed me.

Integrity of Effort Is Important

Success in the pursuit of purpose is typically defined as accomplishing the goal. But some people believe a pursuit that does not reach the target can still be successful if you maintain integrity of effort and do the best you can. Jim Collins, best-selling author whose story is shared later in this chapter, distinguishes between failure and "fallure" when rock climbing or in life. He defines fallure as falling before reaching the climbing goal while still maintaining integrity of effort. Integrity is trying with 100 percent commitment—no wavering whatsoever. He considers both fallure and reaching the goal as success.

This definition helped me reinterpret some of my own past failures as fallures. It is *integrity of the pursuit,* and *not only the attainment* of the goal, that brings success as well as satisfaction and meaning to life.

Do You Have Standards for Your Life?

Typically, we define standards for ourselves, and test them against the standards of others. For Jim Collins, "Living to integrity means feeling comfortable having everything you do, think, and say—your decisions and the way you thought about the decisions you make—shared with everybody in the world."

Most organizations and governments have policies that set clear standards to help employees do the right thing. There is also an international standard. The Rotary 4-Way Test,[8] a widely quoted statement of business ethics developed by the worldwide organization of business and professional leaders, asks:

1. Is it the truth?
2. Is it fair to all concerned?
3. Will it build goodwill and better friendships?
4. Will it be beneficial to all concerned?

In high schools across the nation, this 4-Way Test is being introduced in an interactive workshop to help students clarify and strengthen integrity.

How Do You Strengthen Integrity?

Not meeting the standards can have external consequences with a big price tag. On the other hand, you may be the only one who knows whether you are meeting your standards. In not living up to them, you deny a part of yourself. You must determine how to retrieve your wholeness.

Just as exercises build muscles, challenges to values make them stronger. Karen Bernardi, an award-winning realtor whose story appears later in this chapter, asks, "When you are squeezed, what comes out?" When the self is squeezed, true spirit usually comes out. Life's challenges help us determine what we stand for. Most people do not perceive adversity as a gift and want to move beyond hard times as soon as possible. But, it is the difficult times that clarify and strengthen us.

What Helps You Live True to Your Integrity Standard?

It helps to be surrounded by people who live by your standard and who give you genuine feedback. My women's group did an exercise in which we prioritized our own life values. Then, to compare others' perceptions with our stated intentions, we told each other what values we saw in each other. What I learned was shocking. I ranked authenticity as my highest value, with connections to others next in line. Based on my behavior, the others perceived that I most value work and recognition. Actions speak louder than words. This wake-up call has helped me live more consistently with what I truly value.

How Do You Measure Someone Else's Integrity?

Words are not enough—you must see a person in action. Our Radish team established a set of "values to live by." The highest on the list was integrity. Interested in attracting employees who shared these values, we asked candidates, "What are the values *you* live by?" We hired a key staff member who said he valued integrity. Later I challenged him to stop behavior in the workplace that, in my opinion, lacked integrity. He refused, because, in his opinion, it did *not* lack integrity. I learned that people have different definitions of integrity and determining integrity through interviews has its limitations.

Knowing yourself starts with discernment and deep probing of your values. It also includes uncovering your gifts.

Determine Your Gifts

How can you best serve your values? Eileen Joseph, philanthropic consultant, tells us, "We are given the gift of life for a purpose. We need to honor that gift by knowing ourselves, and loving those around us." Use your unique self in a meaningful way. Like every other human, you have a unique set of gifts—talents, aptitudes, abilities, personality, and strengths—

that you distinctively do well and enjoy. Accessible resources such as your education, growth experiences, and life circumstances expand your gifts and help you determine and develop them.

You can deliberately strengthen and deepen your gifts. But first you need to discover them. Take time to list your talents, experiences, abilities, aptitudes, and education. Ask trusted friends for inputs. See what insights about your gifts life brings. Let's look at three factors—growing up experiences, life events, and adversity—that may not typically be considered gifts.

Growing Up Experiences Are Gifts—Margaret Hansson's Story

It has been said that your past is not your future. Yet your past influences your future because it helps form the person you are today. The growing-up experience builds your whole self.

It is never too early to open children's eyes to passionate purpose. Before Hansson was 10 years old, she started her first business by selling soda pop to thirsty kids roller skating on the newly paved street in front of her house. Opportunity knocked, and with her mother's help, she seized it. "Mother said, 'I'll lend you the money for supplies, but you need to pay me back.' At Christmas that year, I sold plum puddings to everyone I knew. I made lots of money and caught the entrepreneurial bug. My mother encouraged me from the beginning to start and run a business. She taught me how to look carefully at the finances. It has stayed with me all these years."

Margaret Hansson went on to establish eight start-up ventures including Gerry Baby Products Company, now a division of Evenflo with annual sales over $160 million. As a mother with four young children, she invented its original products, Gerry Baby Carriers, which created a huge industry and new freedom for parents.

Life Events Are Part of Divine Order—Carol Grever's Story

Grever wrote her first book at age 7, but she didn't know until much later that she would be called to use her writing talent for a greater cause. Only in searching for answers to recover from her own trauma did she discover how to align her gift with helping other people through their traumatic times.

Growing up in Oklahoma as the only child of supportive parents, Grever developed a healthy self. Little did she realize how important this would be for her long-term survival. "I had an extremely happy, sheltered, loving home life. My parents provided values, discipline, encouragement, work ethic, and self-esteem. I grew up thinking that there is nothing that I can't do. And I still believe that."

Grever married her high school sweetheart, Jim, and they had two sons. Her career evolved over the next 30 years from teaching as an English professor to building, with Jim, a successful company in the staffing industry.

Then catastrophe struck. After more than 35 years of marriage, Jim finally broke the news, "I'm gay." If this was not enough to break her heart, Grever's father died suddenly two months later. Her life was shattered like a pane of glass.

Over the next few years, as the couple told their family, separated, divorced, and sold the business, Grever got clear on her purpose. "Even before I left the business, I knew intuitively that writing a book was my purpose. There was a strong sense that my own complete healing was dependent on it. And, I knew others needed this."

She pursued her purpose. "I wrote my story four times, but it was not substantive. The turning point came when I turned away from me to the entire recovery process and to other people—the shift was away from my inward working to outward looking. The thesis of my book *My Husband Is Gay* is: Happiness, on the other side of this kind of experience, is possible for all partners. Learnings come through the process. There is a way to heal the hurt. We have everything we need within us to live the life we choose. Attaining authenticity brings wholeness. Healing is not possible without forgiveness. . .

I believe there is a divine order in the world, which we can't really understand. But many times an event that seems like the greatest disaster turns out to be another piece of your life's work.

CAROL GREVER, author

Grever then assessed her progress. "In other words, I had to go through Jim's coming out in order to write the book that millions of women need. I couldn't have written for them if I hadn't experienced the anguish myself. Now I see this project as one of the greatest contributions I can make to the world—a legacy. I've come to believe that such occurrences are not random. Indeed, they help shape our lives."

Grever explained how events could open opportunities. "Yet this is not 'predetermination' at all! Rather, these events give us options, choices, through which we determine our own outcomes. Some of the straight spouses I met crashed and burned. They became alcoholics, committed suicide, or got stuck in anger or grief. But others emerged triumphant through their courage and wisdom. My advice is to be open to the possibilities in every seeming disaster. Ask, 'Why is the teacher here? What am I supposed to learn from this teacher?' This is a source of wisdom."

From her trauma, Grever discovered how to meaningfully use her gift. "It isn't what we get, it is what we give that makes life worthwhile. Service to others brings meaning to my life."

Adversity as a Positive Force—Karen Bernardi's Story

Adversity often serves as a positive force to encourage the pursuit of passionate purpose. The well-known refrain, "When the going gets tough, the tough get going"[9] reflects that truth. Many people who encountered great misfortune were highly motivated to change the situation, although few of those people recognized the positive role that hardship played in their lives.

It takes wisdom to view difficulties as a positive force. Too often, when times get tough, the afflicted person believes "God has forsaken me" or claims "the Universe is out to get me," instead of seeing difficulty as a gift from which to learn and grow.

In Bernardi's opinion, hard times are a positive force encouraging your real self to emerge. As an alcoholic, single mother with a young daughter, she was living in a tent and barely existing. Then the pivotal point arrived. "A good friend of mine was killed on Good Friday by a drunk driver. I got sober right after that. God must have a big purpose for me, because I am alive."

A friend lent Bernardi the money to get her real estate license, and she got to work. Today as an award-winning realtor, Bernardi uses the team approach to reach great heights in customer satisfaction. She insists, "Adversity has been a positive force in my life. People and purpose rise out of adversity."

"Would there have been Gandhi without oppression, would there have been Nelson Mandela without apartheid, would there have been Martin Luther King Jr. without discrimination?

"My mother resented my daughter's father for getting me pregnant, not marrying me, and paying no child support. He did me a big favor. I wouldn't have been so driven toward these goals otherwise. Being so poor made me so motivated."

Discover Your Traits

The most effective Passionate Pursuers are whole, healthy individuals who know how and when to employ the success strategies. Similar to sunflowers, they have personal traits of confidence and self-esteem, curiosity, energy, integrity of effort, optimism, passion, regeneration, and wholeness.[10]

We are born with the potential to live true to these characteristics at the highest level. Once you understand the traits, use the Self Inventory to assess how you are doing with these attributes. The Self Inventory (Table 3.1, page 54) and suggestions for nurturing yourself are provided later in this chapter.

Confidence and Self-Esteem

As the core foundation for human development,[11] full trust in self and others—confidence—is the most important element of the healthy self. Oakleigh Thorne II, environmental educator, tells us, "The key to finding and pursuing a worthwhile purpose is developing self-esteem. Nature is a builder of self-esteem."

Confident people generate high self-esteem. People with high self-esteem know their own worth; they have a favorable impression, respect, appreciation, and belief in themselves. Thus, Passionate Pursuers pack high self-esteem, with confidence, for their journey. Follow Goethe's advice, "Just trust yourself, then you will know how to live."[12]

People in my study report that early responsibility during the growing-up years, supportive inputs from external sources, banishment of self-doubt, and use of positive feedback loops strengthen self-esteem and self-confidence.

It is encouraging that people can take steps to create more confidence.[13] Pursuit of a passionate purpose in itself stimulates assurance. No one says it better than Mark Plaatjes, 1993 world marathon champion. "Believe in yourself. The one who wins is the one who wants it the most—the one with the most self-confidence."

Curiosity

Curiosity to learn, explore, and discover propels Passionate Pursuers forward. People who are curious actively bolster interest, attention, and desire to know. Albert Einstein[14] said, "I am no different than everyone else. I just have great curiosity." Exploration strengthens curiosity.

Jacqueline Frischknecht, divorced from a disastrous marriage and the sole supporter of her children, decided at age 29 that she was severely unhappy and completely bored with her life. What she needed, for her own sake and that of her children, was to be better educated. Not sure if she was smart enough to get a college degree, she decided to try a night school class in Art Appreciation. Two and a half years later, she had finished a four-year degree while working 20 hours a week and caring for her daughters. "A major force encouraging me to find and pursue various purposes in my life has been curiosity about the world and a desire for knowledge. Once my mind was made up, nothing really held me back. Finances were usually difficult, but they were overcome." Jackie eventually completed her PhD and now is an accelerated learning consultant, author, and former professor.

Energy

The capacity to do work—energy—is a habit of vigorous activity and forceful expression. Your head, heart, and hands are your energy centers. There are simple ways to increase your energy level. David Hawkins, MD, PhD, explains in *Power vs. Force: The Hidden Determinants of Human Behavior*[15] that energy levels can be calibrated into a map of consciousness. Low energy levels manifest as shame, guilt, grief, and fear. Courage, acceptance, love, and enlightenment align with high energy levels. Positive jumps in energy are possible through intention, will, choice, and motivation. Many spiritual disciplines of the world are interested in approaches to ascend these levels. Meditation is one such useful technique.

Optimism

Norman Vincent Peale in *The Power of Positive Thinking*[16] popularized and humanized the importance of a can-do outlook using examples of real people. People with a positive attitude carry a hopeful, upbeat disposition with the belief that good ultimately overcomes evil. Johnny Halberstadt, professional runner, footwear inventor, and entrepreneur, has such a winning personal philosophy. "There's no such thing as can't. If you want to do something passionately you will find a way."

Integrity of Effort

Passionate Pursuers have a strong inner drive—a determined willingness and ability to work hard to get what they want. They harness this initiative and maintain a strong work ethic. This "industry" concept, also a fundamental element in the progress of human development,[17] is defined by Erik Erikson as an ability to "eagerly work and produce to completion by steady attention and persevering diligence."

Passion

When you are passionate, you have intense zeal, fervor, and devotion. Passion reflects interest, enthusiasm, and excited involvement. This attribute, the fuel of the pursuit, is explored throughout this book (see Chapter 4). As explained earlier, you will find what you are passionate about at the intersection of your values and gifts. Passionate Pursuers have clearly defined convictions based on their core beliefs, morals, ideology, and ethics. They know who they are and what is meaningful to them, and they align their values with their talents to spark passion.

Regeneration

A regenerative nature allows Passionate Pursuers to revive, renew, and produce again despite adversity, setbacks, and obstacles. With the ability to bounce back, recover readily, and rise from the ashes, they possess the Phoenix factor described in Chapter 6. As a process of human development and reinforced through life,[18] generativity is indispensable in all pursuits of passionate purpose. Such resilience appears to be interdependent with the traits of confidence, optimistic attitude, and integrity of effort.

Wholeness

When you are whole, you appreciate and unify all aspects of your nature especially head, heart, and hands; you are connected to your inner self. The internal and external worlds are coalesced into oneness to create stability and strength. This concept is so significant for Passionate Pursuers that it is included here as well as in the Polarity Strategy (see Chapter 7) and in the Connections Strategy (see Chapter 11).

Assessment of Self

You cannot easily build a healthier self until you know who you are now. Start with an inventory of how well you are doing with these traits. Completing the Self Inventory (Table 3.1, page 54) will take only a few minutes. Use it to understand where you are now and what aspects you need to nurture.

To Build or Not to Build

Everyone, regardless of overall scores, has the potential to develop. All these traits can be strengthened. How? Make the choice to begin. Start with where you are. Then use the approaches that follow. (Also see Chapter 12.)

Table 3.1 Self Inventory

Based on *your* perception, indicate how OFTEN each statement describes who you are today. Using a 1–5 scale where 1 is rarely and 5 is most of the time, write the appropriate number of points in the corresponding column. Sum all the numbers to get your Self total points.

Consider now, the present—not yesterday or tomorrow. Do not over-analyze; mark your initial reaction to the statement.

Trait	Rarely or Never	Seldom	Sometimes	Frequently	Most or All of Time
Number of points per response in this column	1	2	3	4	5
1. I believe in my own ability, power, judgments, and decisions.					
2. I respect myself.					
3. I live true to well-defined values.					
4. I approach situations with an optimistic attitude.					
5. I am curious about different things.					
6. I have the ability to be intensely absorbed, passionate, or devoted.					
7. I am willing to work hard to maintain a high standard.					
8. When faced with challenges, I revive and produce anew.					
9. I have the energy to do what I need to do.					
10. I unify aspects of my self—head, heart, hands—into a balanced whole.					
Total points = _____					

Scoring

50–41   You have a robust and healthy self with the attributes needed to get all that you want in life. Pat yourself on the back and keep it up!

40–31   You have a solid foundation and many healthy traits. Some fine-tuning will help.

30–21   Your self is shaky and needs nurturing. It is time to explore and take care of yourself.

Below 21 Immediate attention is needed. You have lots of room for improvement. Focus, as your passionate purpose for now, on building a healthier self.

Now look at individual statements. If you scored 1 or 2 on any one, some tweaking is needed. Focus on these elements as you nurture yourself.

"Failure" versus Failure—Jim Collins's Story

Life brings both good and bad luck. For Jim Collins, author of *Good to Great* and coauthor of *Built to Last,* it was bad luck when his "incompetent and indifferent" father chose to die of bladder cancer at the age of 48 rather than cure it. "It was absolutely horrific growing up."

A few years later the pivotal point arrived and he found a worthwhile purpose. "Mom remarried when I was in eighth grade and I knew I wanted to escape. I had good luck with what I got in my brain. I decided, just out of the blue, that I could use my brain as a vehicle to build a bridge of independence and not have to depend on other people."

Collins knows himself. "My top values are enjoyment, respect, climbing mountains, commitments and integrity, and a meta-value of relationships. I truly believe that a life spent in unenjoyable activities is not worth living." Self-described as "a productive neurotic," Collins says, "I was born with hot coals in my stomach—with a relentless, driving passion."

Collins matches his values with his gifts to define passionate purpose. "I have a level of passionate drive that is always on. So then the question becomes simply, 'Where do I channel it?' Number one is that which I just enjoy doing. The second lens for external achievement is the need for distinction, to be truly superior at what you do."

For Collins, the most meaningful purpose in life is to maintain integrity of effort by climbing to fallure rather than failure. Fallure is success, regardless of whether the goal is accomplished. "If you make a commitment to somebody, there are only two alternatives: Fulfill the commitment or you are dead. Fallure, 100% commitment with no wavering whatsoever, is integrity."

The "Good to Great" purpose came when a colleague planted the seed of a really great question with Collins: Can a good company become a great company and, if so, how?[19] "I did not pick it; it picked me. All of my best projects are questions that come from elsewhere and won't let go. I just knew that I had a question and I had a project."

Then he pursued the purpose. "Like any other project, you break it up into pieces, you complete the study, mark down the data, get great people on the team, write the book, launch it. Doing a gigantic project like Good to Great is like walking across the United States, from San Diego to Maine. You just get up in the morning, and you walk 10 miles, and then you stop. There's the whole process. It's that simple." In effect, his tracking of progress by moving a little tag across a U.S. wall map stimulates the operation of the Attraction Strategy (see Chapter 8) and the "10 miles each day" is the divide-and-conquer component of the Persistence Strategy (see Chapter 9).

Eventually it is time to let go and allow. "There is a cycle. That is the beauty of projects—projects come to an end. The easiest way to let go is to carry things through to completion, to the nth degree plus one. Letting go is usually defined as starting the next piece of work."

Collins balances his heart and head using, in effect, the Polarity Strategy. "My passion or drive is primal; its trajectory is shaped intellectually. It's a duality. Think of going to the moon. The fuel, or passion, propels the rocket ship. The real driving force is the thrusters with the explosive fuel in the engines that drive the ship off the launch pad. The guidance system, the mind part, is simply how you guide it so somehow you keep it from crashing. The rocket ship doesn't go anywhere without the primal drive of the engines and the fuel and the explosion. But at the same time, if you just had all of that without the guidance system, who knows where you would go? They play with each other without tension."

Besides good luck, the right people who help along the way are the most positive, encouraging force in Collins's life. Bad luck is a negative force. Unless misfortune stops him flat out, Collins does not let bad luck halt or discourage him. He successfully packs energizers and removes hindrances by using the Pack and Connections Strategies.

PRACTICAL POINTERS

What helps you live true to your values, determine your gifts, and discover your traits?

- *Inquire.* Probe deeply into your values, gifts, and traits. Ask for feedback.
- *Explore.* Consider how your values and gifts help define what you are passionate about.
- *Test.* Strengthen your sense of self by putting your values, gifts, and traits to work in hard times. Interpret adversity as a positive force.
- *Interpret.* Define being true to your own integrity of effort standard as success, even if you don't achieve the envisioned outcome.
- *Surround.* Encircle yourself with trustworthy people who are good examples, give you honest feedback, and live true to your standards.

For those taking on a passionate purpose, Collins has this advice:

- Only do stuff that in the big picture you really enjoy.
- Only do stuff for which you can be truly distinctive.
- Be careful about big projects you undertake, but when you undertake them, always fulfill them completely. Completion is very important.
- Pick the right people with whom to do things. In fact, you may want to let *what* you do be determined by *who* you are doing it with.

Collins sums it up, "I am very satisfied with my life, but unsatisfied with my achievements. My life is a perpetual dissatisfaction and that's what drives me."

NURTURE YOURSELF

The second part of the *Know and Nurture the Person* stage is: Nurture your whole self. How do you nurture yourself into the person you want to be? People in my study report that it requires deliberate effort using these approaches:

- Explore internally and externally.
- Take care of yourself.
- Integrate all of your polarities.
- Rise above hindrances.

My Path—Uncovering the Real Me

Having quit my job, I felt that I would find the real me through travel. Exploring the South Pacific during a two-month adventure trip with no itinerary, I went in-between and reconnected with my self. I decided to change the words of that *South Pacific* song to, "I'm gonna wash that *job* right out of my hair." Everywhere, I saw cute babies, families, love, and marriage.

I started to reawaken one rainy day in New Zealand when I volunteered to help the hostel hosts shear their sheep. Actually you can't shear sheep in the rain because the wool is wet. So instead, another volunteer and I sat in a tiny trailer with our hosts drinking tea, eating scones, and laughing until our sides ached. My inner voice whispered, "Yes, I remember now. I do value friends and having fun."

Perhaps I found my sense of self at a wedding in a tiny village in Fiji. Diving 90 feet deep to marvel at a wall of rare, soft white coral by day, I was invited, along with everyone else in the village, from big-eyed babies to the talkative elders, to attend an elaborate Indian wedding at night. The voice was louder now, "Yes, I do value family and commitment."

Returning to the United States, I embarked on new pursuits—the Man Plan, Baby Plan, and Family Plan—to complement my career aspirations. My new plans required taking on the Wholeness Plan—moving beyond the domination of my head to integration of my whole self—head, heart, and hands—into a balanced person.

Yes, there were detours. It wasn't quite that easy. My head convinced me to start a doctoral program and start my management consulting practice, while giving my heart just a few free moments to find the man. Was this sabotage?

The path to wholeness was not easy, but it brought lessons on how to rise above hindrances. Even with my daily meditation practice as a helpful balancing aid, my head continued to dominate as my heart struggled for attention. Learning and persisting along the way while using the Pursuit of Passionate Purpose formula, I completed the Degree Plan and then moved on to pursue the entrepreneurial dream through the Business Plan.

Explore Internally

The exploration of life is inward as much as outward.

MARSHA SEMMEL, museum director

People agree that internal as well as external exploration is needed to know and nurture yourself. The more curious you are, the more inviting the exploration may be. The more you investigate, the higher your level of curiosity.

Establish rituals to practice exploration regularly. To encourage a natural rhythm and allow your inner self to speak, use simple procedures on a daily basis. Experiment and try different methods until you settle into a nourishing tradition. Here are a few of the most effective ways people, regardless of age, undertake this expansive, exciting venture inward.[20]

Get Still

Have you ever just stopped and stood completely still, while the rest of the world rushed by? Doing so requires discipline, but you may become aware of amazing things. We tried this experiment during a short autumn hike with our troop of 7-year-old Brownie Girl Scouts. Once settled, children and leaders alike became aware of another reality. We experienced the gurgle of the trickling stream; smell of the fallen, golden leaves; warmth of afternoon sunshine on our shoulders; and view of squirrels jumping between trees within the colorful forest. Incredible. It made us wonder what other parts of life we are missing because we are too noisy, talkative, and busy to notice the moment-by-moment unfolding of existence.

Stop everything for a moment. Be quiet. Let your mind calm, while opening your sense gates. Listen and learn what you have been missing. Stephanie Nestlerode, management consultant, has this suggestion, "Slow down and be conscious in each moment. Be a psychic warrior."

Journal

Moving thoughts from your head onto something tangible—paper or into a computer file—allows you to get a different connection to your inner self. I have a file on my computer called "head," and most mornings this is the first file I open. As my hands begin to move, they unlock my heart and head to pour into this safe haven.

You may want to journal in a spiral notebook that you can easily carry around. You might, like me, have assorted journals with different themes located in several places. My dream diary is next to my bed; a log for consulting, coaching, and speaking clients is in my briefcase; the parenting chronicle about my daughter is near the kitchen phone; a writing and meditation journal sits by the computer; and my head file is on the computer. Sean Redmond, finance manager and writer, uses the following routine: "I arise at 4 A.M. to spend a few precious hours writing and thinking. Then, the magic comes, and my thoughts and my poetry flow like a silent stream, stealthily plodding a course seaward. My writing helps me focus my perceptions."

Make sure your journal is in a private place so that others will not violate you by reading it. There are many techniques to open a dialogue with yourself. My women's group spent an entire weekend retreat trying dozens of creative journaling procedures. You can write to yourself, others, or a greater spiritual force. Find what works best for you. There is no right or wrong. Just begin today.

Dream

Invite your dreams, both while sleeping and daydreaming, to speak to you. Dreams are sacred glimpses into your subconscious. Carry a journal to record precious memories before they fade—this engages hands energy. Activate head energy by looking for patterns and connections. Do not let your head overanalyze, bring in your heart and allow emotions to surface. Carlos Aguirre, opera singer, put this idea in simple terms: "Ask yourself what do I want? Let yourself dream about it. To dream is not expensive."

If your dreams are confusing, request your inner self to provide more clarification and better retention. Ask and you shall receive. Before you fall asleep, affirm, "I remember my dreams with vivid clarity and understand their meaning." There are many sources on interpreting dreams (even entire graduate courses).

Pray

If you believe in a higher power, enter into a spiritual communion with God or your own form of goodness. Most major religions believe that some form of God is within each person. Praying is, therefore, communicating with your inner self and beyond.

Madame Chiang Kai-shek[21] reflected, "Prayer . . . is more than meditation. . . . In meditation the source of strength is one's self. When one prays he goes to a source of strength greater than his own."

You can use standard prayers or your own words, based on your own experience and heartfelt feelings. Prayers take many forms—they may ask for something concrete or intangible, inspire and help us be the best we can be, give thanks, honor the holy, chant rhythmically or musically, open a discussion, or convey other sentiments.

There is an ancient contemplative practice from the Catholic Church called Centering Prayer that can be useful in reaching out to God's presence and opening to the healing power within you.[22] Monks and nuns traditionally used this approach as a means of direct connection with God. A Centering Prayer session lasts about 20 minutes and begins by sitting quietly with an intention to be present with God, the life force. As you still your mind, pick a word to represent your intention. This is a simple word, perhaps love, peace, spirit, flow, be, or whatever works for you. Let go of thoughts and everything else—just allow them to gently flow without interference. If your mind clings to thoughts, ever so gently say your word and put your attention back on your intention of listening and being receptive to the Holy Spirit.

Lee Hogan, management consultant, finds that "Prayer and meditation help immensely." Perhaps it is time to revisit and bring back into your life this sacred practice.

Move

Movement is a vehicle to involve more of your body (hands) in inward and outward exploration. Walks, dance, and exercise stimulate oxygen flow. Stand up, stretch, close your eyes, and take a deep, calming breath. A minute of deep breathing may be as effective as a 20-minute workout. Listen and flow to music. Free your energy and encourage your inner self to take over. Give movement a try. You may be delighted at the joy and insights that surface.

Plan

Planning gives the head a chance to use rational, logical analysis. It may be an appropriate way to organize yourself, but it doesn't need to be linear or written. Use what works for you. Do you need a map, a diagram, a flow-chart, or a to-do list? I am a planner at heart. With my Day-Timer in hand, I arrange my year, months, weeks, and days. Perhaps it is because I love the feeling of crossing off completed activities.

The most important part is taking the time to focus your head energy and create the plan. Then use it to reaffirm and direct your efforts.

Meditate

There is a subtle, yet significant, difference between meditation and silence. Meditation involves observing what is and then accepting it. Mindfulness[23] meditation, weaves together two basic concepts to produce a remarkable end product. The first element is mindfulness, being extremely attentive to ordinary sensory experience. The second concept is equanimity, which means letting the sense gates flow without resistance. Shinzen Young,[24] mindfulness meditation teacher, pinpointed the value of this technique: "Subtle is significant."

One of the effects of meditation is that you can acquire deep understanding about the nature of experience, yourself, and universal issues. Blockages to intrinsic happiness are cleaned away. You may directly experience the underlying spirit of life unifying all fellow beings. This can be powerful.

There are additional tangible results to meditation such as improved concentration, energy, relaxation, and more positive emotions. Andrew Weil, MD, reports,[25] "Meditation may not only make you happier, but also keep you healthier. It can benefit health concerns ranging from stress and anxiety to atherosclerosis and chronic pain."

Learn and practice meditation, yoga, tai chi, relaxation techniques, or another form of contemplation. Find a beginner's course. Consider joining a practice group, working with trained teachers, reading books, and attending retreats. Build support for and commit to a daily practice.

Meditation teacher Shinzen Young, whose story is shared in Chapter 4, developed the Core Practice[26] as a simple way to help people benefit from meditation. You divide and conquer by systematically contacting, observing, and accepting your body sensations, mental images, and internal talk. Try the basic session provided in Appendix B.

Explore Externally

External exploration, or searching outside yourself, is another way to nurture the self.

Learn

Learn all that you can. Take in information from everyone and everything. How do you learn best? People learn in many ways—they read, watch movies, TV, or videos, do research in the library or online, attend lectures and presentations, listen to the radio or audiotapes, or play challenging games that encourage thinking and feeling. Many observe and use their other senses to absorb information. Fred Ramirez Briggs, foundation director, has this advice: "Learn as much as possible. Knowledge is power."

The next step is to process information in some way by organizing, sorting, categorizing, studying, analyzing, questioning, and talking to others. Then decide to store, use, ignore, further process, or discard it.

As soon as you think you are mastering a subject, go a little deeper. You will discover how much more there is to learn. The learning journey is infinite. Take entrepreneur Margaret Hansson's advice to heart, "Do not stop learning."

Change Your Environment

A different environment may expose you to new ways of living, thinking, behaving, feeling, working, entertaining, having fun, and more. It provides a great opportunity to question how you have always done things. Brooks Preston, philanthropic consultant, commented, "I took six months to travel and talk to people. My idea matured."

Travel and vary your surroundings. I can attest from personal experience that travel works. Change your job, discover a new set of people, culture, procedures, and language. Experiment—go from rural to urban, civilized to uncivilized, cold to hot, wild to domesticated, land to sea, sea to air, stable to unstable, rich to poor. Shake things up a bit to stimulate your growth with new experiences.

Talk to People

Get people, of all ages and perspectives, involved in your exploration. Follow the advice of Linda Shoemaker, attorney and community builder: "Talk to everyone. Hire the best people." Let people show you and teach you. Then listen. Find a mentor, coach, or role model. Strategically make proper connections (see Chapter 11). Marsha Semmel, museum director, suggests, "Work with someone to find more about yourself and your strengths and how to align them."

There was a time in growing up that I thought it was best to do things alone. After all, you could have more control and ensure that things were done your way. Then, thank goodness, I learned another easier and more enjoyable way. Explore and learn with others. We have much to teach each other.

Take Care of Yourself

Now that you are building and nurturing your self, what is next? How are you going to maintain that strength? It takes continual care. Just as muscles grow weaker if you do not use them, your strength will diminish without attention. Here are a few ideas that people have found helpful.

Pamper Yourself

Ellie Sciarra, tap dancer, tells us, "Go to the bathtub and places that nurture the soul. Go to the beach. Do things that support you and your vision."

What nourishment are you providing yourself? After we started Radish, I lost track of caring for myself. My energy was directed toward caring for the company. Then the day before the big trade show preannouncing our product to the media, I looked in the mirror. I took a double take. Was that really me? If I didn't take care of replenishing myself, I wouldn't have any energy left to care for the company.

The Universe provided—luckily my hairdresser quickly squeezed me in and transformed me. When I came back to the office, our new president noticed. "Wow, you look different," he said. What he really meant was, "What an improvement!" I felt revived, ready to pull off the greatest show on earth, and recommitted to taking care of myself.

After making sure everything was ready, Dick and I flew out a day ahead of the opening. Arriving at the hotel that night, I attended to the next most important piece of my care plan—sleep. After sleeping 15 hours, I was a recharged woman, more like my true self, and ready to make the show successful.

Put some self-care into your plan. Whatever the elements, don't let them fall off the to-do list.

Take a Break

Respite can be a one-minute power break, a long workout, or a two-week vacation. If you are like me and get totally absorbed, you lose track of time as you enjoy the pleasure of progress. I set alarms in other rooms. Getting up to shut them off mobilizes me. Another tactic is to drink lots of water and let nature call you to move. Breaks make way for new inputs to keep you going longer. Discover tactics that are most effective in forcing you to take a break.

Hang Out

As Anne Quindlan[27] notes, doing nothing is important. Try a different kind of break. One of my most precious photos was taken when my daughter was just two. Snuggled in our backyard hammock, we looked at some of her favorite books. Swinging gently in the summer breeze, we watched the puffy clouds float by, the golden aspen leaves shimmer, and hummingbirds dart to the feeder. Here our head, heart, and hands touched as we read stories, shared some of our own, and giggled. The photo, shown on page 219, captures our smiles in these moments of delight.

I don't remember what project I was working on in that period of time or what business phone calls I missed to hang out with my daughter Annie.

While it is difficult to do nothing at work, take a few minutes to just sit and gaze out a window. Look at clouds or snow or rain while letting your mind drift. When was the last time you just hung out? Is your soul calling? Where is your beloved place to hang out, for a moment or a month, without a care in the world? Give yourself, and others, permission for a refreshing reverie.

Integrate Polarities into Wholeness

Nurturing of self to wholeness is such an important concept that it is embodied in the Polarity Strategy (see Chapter 7). Combining disparate elements into a strong, united entity allows the head, heart, and hands to operate in harmony. Recognize polarities and allow dynamic movement between them.

Rise above Hindrances

The environment may provide internal and external obstacles that block your best traits, thus hindering you. Often the internal blocks are learned, and therefore you can unlearn them. Likewise, you can remove external blocks with intentional effort. Use the Pack Strategy—remove the hindrances from your pack and replace them with energizers using suggestions in Chapter 12.

Embrace the Journey—Kevin Streicher's Story

Kevin Streicher, advertising salesperson, was 26 years old. He smiled pleasantly as he sat surrounded by pine trees and calmly strummed his guitar. You would never have realized that he had locked himself out of his car while camping. As he waited for help, he shared his story of transitioning from a stressed out, unhealthy advertising salesperson for rock and sports radio stations to a man committed to real meaning in his life. Relaxing in his folding chair with sunshine around him at Yellowstone National Park in Wyoming, he was enjoying the process of reconnecting with his true self.

Just four months earlier, Streicher had been 50 pounds heavier and was holding a stressful job in a fast-paced industry that was eating his soul. "For about a year, I knew I needed a change. My lifestyle was work, work, and more work. Work had negatively affected my health.

"Fear and anxiety held me in the job. Through role playing, I asked myself, 'What would you do if you had no fear?' Finally I told myself, 'You just have to do it! Stop the insanity. Go and do what's in your heart!' "

"I had the strength within me, as well as the education, family, and supportive friends, to help me land on my feet. Realizing that my life would not end, I found the courage to allow myself to fail. I discovered faith in myself."

Streicher went in-between. "So I left to travel for three months and put myself in an optimal environment—outside with enough time. I believe in the energy from nature—it puts things into perspective. The immediate purpose was to see my country, improve my health, and get clarity on what to do next. By removing myself, I have centered within."

As he traveled, Streicher asked significant questions, "What is important? What do I want? Am I giving anything to future generations?" He found answers, "Life itself gives meaning—experience, travel, learning, people, walking barefoot, brushing teeth in the morning. It also comes from the bad parts of life—feeling sad and losing love."

He started to know and nurture the self. "I have traveled and my health has improved. I realized that I used unhealthy things for emotional deficiencies. Don't use food as a filler, go and find where you are missing something and fill it.

"My biggest worry is income and stability. I want to be able to provide for a family. Acceptance of change and challenge help me overcome these discouraging forces. I know that change is for the better."

Streicher, getting more clarity and confidence, continues, "I had a vision that I was on top of a pole, tenuously rocking back and forth, between nothing and everything to worry about. I got the message to embrace life as fragile and that I will eventually land."

He has this advice. "Put yourself first. Don't leave people in the dirt, but take care of yourself. Be true to yourself and have confidence—don't let anyone tell you differently. Smile more and laugh at yourself. Be nice to everyone. No one is better than anyone else.

"Coming out of college, I knew music and people were part of my passion. Now, I want to be a catalyst for people's experiences. I am seeking new goals, exploring options. I still revel knowing that it is the journey, not the destination, that is the real part of life. Embrace it!"

Postlude: Today, three years after sharing this story, Streicher reports that he just finished his first year of teaching in the Chicago public schools. He is pursuing passionate purpose.

PRACTICAL POINTERS

Try some of these tactics to nurture yourself:

- *Intuit*. Strengthen your intuition and relationship with your inner self.
- *Explore*. Provide time and space to explore internally and externally.
- *Build*. Take proactive steps to balance various parts of yourself, overcome hindrances, and build yourself.
- *Care*. Take care of yourself and keep healthy.

SUMMARY

- The initial stage of the process is "Know and Nurture the Person."
- Begin to get to know who you are. Understanding revolves around discerning and deeply probing your values, determining your gifts, and discovering your traits.
  —Values define meaning. Values when aligned with gifts spark passion.
  —Meaning is important to people.
  —Purpose is a source of meaning.
  —Meaningful purpose unleashes passion.
  —Passion fuels the pursuit.
  —Passion along with other personal traits determines how effectively you pursue your purpose.
  —Pursuit of passionate purpose, not only its attainment, brings satisfaction.
- Values can be strengthened. Tough times or adversity are gifts in disguise that help you determine who you are and what matters to you. They develop your sense of self and your values.
- Traits of effective Passionate Pursuers include high confidence and self-esteem, curiosity, energy, integrity of effort, optimism, passion, regeneration, and wholeness.
- Nurture yourself into the person you want to be by using certain procedures—explore internally and externally, take care of yourself, balance all parts of yourself, and make a deliberate effort to overcome your hindrances.
  —The Self Inventory helps you determine how well you are doing with these attributes.
  —Explore internally by getting still, journaling, dreaming, praying, moving, planning, and meditating. Shinzen Young's Core Practice, in Appendix B, is a valuable meditation technique for deepening connection to your inner self and for providing many other benefits.
  —Explore externally by learning, changing your environment, and talking to people.
  —Pamper yourself, take a break, hang out.
  —Integrate all the aspects of yourself—head, heart, hands—into a unified whole by using the Polarity Strategy.
  —Rise above your hindrances by overcoming internal and external blocks.

4  Find Passionate Purpose

Premise: People have values that define meaning.

Path: Align values and gifts with the needs of the world thereby defining a worthwhile purpose.

Outcome: Clarity of, and commitment to, passionate purpose.

During this stage, you answer the questions "What do I want and what do I not want?" Your response comes from understanding how to use your values and gifts—what you are passionate about—to address the wants of the world. The intersection of world needs with your passion is your passionate purpose. Thus, the second stage of the process enables you to foster passion, align it with a worthwhile purpose, and commit fully to the passionate purpose.

WHAT YOU CAN GET FROM THIS CHAPTER

You cannot pursue purpose until you find it. Passionate Pursuers may get ideas to help reaffirm why they are committed to a cause and make midcourse modifications to their pursuit. Seekers may find this stage the most important part of the process.

In-between'ers may receive validation that their passionate purpose, for now, is to be in the neutral zone. When the time is right, they can use the approach in this stage to determine what to do next.

FOSTER PASSION

We may affirm absolutely that nothing great in the world has been accomplished without passion.

GEORG WILHELM FRIEDRICH HEGEL[1]

Passion releases tremendous energy that propels people forward toward their purpose.

My Path—Discovering the Passion behind the Dream

"Free at last, free at last, thank God Almighty I'm free at last!" The words of Martin Luther King Jr.[2] echoed in my mind. Yes, I was free and flying as fast as safety permitted in Dick's midnight blue Porsche 911. We were headed toward Ohio, and I didn't have a care in the world. I had just handed in my 386-page dissertation to the University of Colorado's graduate school. I was "*PhinisheD* at last," as they say, with the Degree Plan behind me. During the program, I came to realize that academia was not for me, and I had clarified what I valued. Now, I was on to bigger and better things—back to the real world to find my next purpose.

Dick and I started this trip with the goal of simplifying our lives so that we could finance "whatever it took" to follow our dream—our new, yet-to-be conceived venture. If it required selling the Porsche, selling our houses, and cutting expenses, we were ready. Little did we know what it would take to found and fund Radish. And we certainly did not anticipate that it would be almost two years from the time we started until we received our first paychecks.

With the wind on my face and my hair blowing without restraint, I gripped the steering wheel and pressed down on the accelerator. That precision automobile easily opened up and so, too, did my own energy. As the speedometer moved higher, I wondered how fast she could go. Did she have limits? Did I? Now was the right time to purge the tensions of the past few years to celebrate and to open myself to the next phase of life's journey. With that last pursuit behind me, I would never do anything that I did not absolutely love doing. It was time to pursue the entrepreneurial dream.

An Ohio family friend was buying the Porsche so Dick could provide his share of the founder's funding. While driving across country, we talked about the possibilities for a business venture. When we stopped for lunch, we excitedly scribbled telecommunications product thoughts on napkins. We didn't know which one of these ideas would be good enough.

Part of preparing for the next passionate purpose was selling Dick's Porsche 911 for founder's capital. As we drove to Ohio to sell it, we discussed possible ideas and the values on which to base the venture. Soon thereafter Radish was conceived.

What we both truly loved, in addition to each other, was successfully bringing useful new technology to the marketplace to help people. Knowing that the values of a company emerge from those of the founders, we began to clarify the venture's values:

- *Integrity.*
- *Stakeholder delight* that would produce financial rewards and satisfaction for all involved.
- *Innovative solutions* that would contribute to the world in a way that would outlive us.
- *Environment* that would allow an empowered team of people to contribute and be rewarded to the fullest.
- *Community service.*

We were passionate about making a difference in the world through innovative technological solutions and living by our values.

How Pursuing Passionate Purpose Feels

It is important to know what the pursuit of passionate purpose feels like so you will recognize it when you find it. Think back to when you were passionate about pursuing something. How did it feel?

Most people say that it feels wonderful. When pursuing passionate purpose, they have tremendous energy and get lost in time. Hours may have flown by, but it feels like minutes. Pursuing passionate purpose stimulates pleasant body sensations. The body (hands) communicates this state of bliss through goose bumps, a tingle up the spine, or even tears of joy.

Matthew 6:21 tells us, "Where your treasure is, there is your heart." The heart feels delight, satisfaction, emotional responsiveness, and other gratifying sensations. The head is engaged with planning, analyzing, and creating. In the optimal pursuit, your entire self is fully absorbed and you experience flow.[3]

It is extremely helpful to recognize passion, so you can connect, flow, and nurture it. *Jonathan Livingston Seagull,*[4] is the story of a bird with a passion to learn and serve. The other gulls did not understand him. But when Jonathan was flying fast and high, when he was learning, surpassing all limits, and helping others, he felt wonderful, happy, alive, and trembled with delight. A part of each of you is like Jonathan. You must find your passion and let it be the wind under your wings. Then you will soar to a rewarding life.

What Makes a Purpose Passionate

Sometimes you may not know why a purpose is passionate. Perhaps you do not even think about it. That is fine. Knowing the reasons is useful, however, because then you can more easily find passion in other parts of your life.

People report that their purpose is passionate because it:

- Allows them to make a difference or do something meaningful.
- Helps others or the self.
- Feels good.
- Is their calling and provides a journey.
- Offers other things, such as an outlet for creativity, connection, and change.

It is not surprising that most of these reasons tie in with what brings meaning to a person's life. Values define meaning. Meaning defines what you are passionate about.

How to Nurture Passion

Passion is the fuel that drives the pursuit of a purpose. Many feel that enthusiasm is essential. Some feel that the ability to be passionate originates with a strong sense of self, especially high self-esteem. That is why a critical stage of the process is *Know and Nurture the Person*. Through this stage, you clarify your values and gifts, which define what you are passionate about. People use many approaches. Whether you have a purpose or not, you can cultivate passion. Here are four techniques.

Clarify Values and Gifts

You can find what you are passionate about—your passion—in the connection between your values and gifts. If passion is lacking, revisit what is meaningful to you. There might not be deep enough meaning behind the use of your gifts. If so, determine ways to increase their meaningfulness.[5] Alternatively, probe into your gifts. Are you doing something for which you lack talent because you value the outcome? If so, go back to the *Know and Nurture the Person* stage to explore your gifts further or see if there are ways to increase your sense of competency with the appropriate skills.

Jim Collins in *Good to Great*[6] recommends getting the right people on the bus, the wrong people off the bus, and the right people in the right seats. Using this metaphor, consider a company that hires the right people—those perceived to have productive Passionate Pursuer traits—then spends considerable time and resources training these workers. Studies[7] show that within a year more than 25 percent of these employees are no longer engaged. Getting them in the right seats may mean providing projects in line with their values and gifts, so employees have a greater sense of meaningfulness and competency from their work. Being in the right seat therefore fosters passion, and ultimately brings more engagement, progress, and productivity.

Develop One-Pointedness through Meditation

Shinzen Young, mindfulness meditation teacher, explains that meditation increases your ability to focus and concentrate. With that single focus, or *one-pointedness,* comes intense interest or passion: "When you become one-pointed, your object of meditation becomes an object of fascination. This produces pleasant, joyful body sensations, which encourage you to pay even more attention. This becomes a feedback loop. This does not give you purpose, but it gives everything more focus. It gives a moment by moment purpose of fully participating in life, and from this you might get a sense of your life purpose." Use the Core Practice in Appendix B to develop one-pointedness. You can transfer the skill of being single-focused to many activities.

Transfer Passion to Other Experiences

Visualize yourself with more intense passion. Here's how. Vividly recall a time when you were passionately pursuing some purpose. How did it feel? Remember and reconnect with the pleasant body sensations, mental images, and talk during that pursuit. Connect with all parts of that feeling. It feels good. You are energized and alive. You are so involved in the activity that nothing else seems to matter.

If you were passionate then, you can be passionate again. Transfer your passion from one pursuit to another. Visualize yourself doing some activity for which you desire to feel more passion. Recall your earlier experience. Imagine yourself in detail doing the new activity and experiencing all the same gratifying sensations.

Gordon Gamm, 62, attorney and humanist movement leader, shares his approach to this concept. "We have a capacity to create passion in our lives. I recommend the use of Neural Linguistic Programming (NLP) to take the ordinary and make it special. Much of the way we experience life is based on the choices we make of our feelings. Realize how much control you have over your emotions. Transport yourself into a time of passion, a special experience, from the past. Reexperience it with your entire range of senses. For example, I find passion in spiritual experiences such as nature, music, dance, poetry, and walks in the woods. We can transfer emotions to other experiences. Realize that you can make what you're doing fulfilling and exciting."

Remove Hindrances Blocking Passion

Consider what might be hindering your passion. Control, fear, impatience, desire, societal influences, and other hindrances are possibilities. Once you identify the obstacle, take the actions mentioned in Chapter 12 to remove this block from your bag.

Meditation Cultivates Passion, Clarifies Purpose— Shinzen Young's Story

"I can characterize my life as a series of love affairs of purposes," says Shinzen Young, nationally renowned mindfulness meditation teacher. Starting at age 11 when he was passionately interested in studying insects, Young evolved to learning everything he could about Asian languages. He then focused on the intellectual aspects, and later the practice, of Buddhism. Now his goal is to help people. To find his purposes, "I just followed my bliss and did what felt good and what gave me pleasant body sensations.

"After completing my PhD course work in Buddhism, I went to Japan to do research on the Shingon School of Buddhism. Shingon is Japanese vajrayana Buddhism, a practice related to that of Tibet. They wouldn't tell you anything, unless you really take on the practice. So in 1970, I became ordained as a Buddhist monk and trained for three years in the practice of meditation. They had me do menial, simple physical tasks and would not allow me to do any intellectual work. I hated it—it seemed meaningless. Finally one of the monks clued me in, 'The simple tasks *are* the meditation. Stay with the sensory experience in the moment—the sound, sight, and touch of your physical labor. To focus on anything else is wandering.' As I continued, it became fun. I reached states of one-pointedness and samadhi—or high concentration—that didn't go away."

Through meditating, Shinzen Young learned to generate passion. "If your purpose of life is to live fully in each moment, meditation delivers. . . . My first lesson as a Buddhist monk was that passion in an activity does not have to be related to the activity. You can generate passion from inside, with one-pointedness."

He also learned that meditation lights the path to helping others. "As you go beyond the states of concentration and bliss, you get insights into your sense of self. You experience oneness of inside and outside, self and the world. This is called enlightenment. From enlightenment, you get your overall purpose of life. You realize that you are one with everyone you see. Then you want to do something to help. The way you help people will depend on your personality, culture, and more.

"In this life we really have two goals: to be fulfilled for the self and to be a source of fulfillment for others. Psycho-spiritually mature persons understand the complementary nature of these two. If you try to serve society without working on your self, you will get burned out, bummed out, or freaked out. If you only work on your self, you will not achieve a balanced, spiritual life."

This philosophy guides Shinzen Young's purpose: "This is what brings meaning to my life—to use my intelligence to find new and effective ways to help people reduce their suffering, elevate their fulfillment, and give them a sense of who they are as spiritual beings. My mission is to bring the scientific method to the study of meditative states with the vision of making classical enlightenment available to anyone who wants it."

PRACTICAL POINTERS

- *Clarify.* Probe further into your values and gifts. Look for ways to increase your sense of meaningfulness and competency.
- *Experiment.* Try things that are worthwhile for which you have some interest but not necessarily great passion, and experiment with stimulating passion. Passion can be developed.
- *Cultivate.* Nurture and intensify passion with any activity by concentrating with more and more one-pointedness on an activity.
- *Transfer.* Remember pleasurable sensations, images, and talk associated with a pursuit of a passionate purpose that was on track. Know that you can rekindle that passion and transfer it to other experiences.
- *Remove.* Determine what blocks your passion and find ways to reduce the impact of this hindrance.
- *Ask for help.* Surround yourself with people who will provide support.

ALIGN PASSION WITH PURPOSE

Passion needs a purpose. Together they move your life from success to significance.

FRED RAMIREZ BRIGGS, foundation director

After fostering passion, the next task in this stage is to align it with a worthwhile purpose by using the following techniques:

- Preparing.
- Finding the overlap of your passion with needs of the world.
- Creating a Purpose Proclamation.

My Path—Attracting the Idea

We were visualizing, feeling, and saying affirmative statements about our intended outcome. Dick and I remembered the words of George Bernard Shaw[8] "You see things; and you say, 'Why?' But I dream things that never were; and I say, 'Why not?'" We actively sought to attract the right purpose. But it was Dick who received the creative inspiration. Months earlier, Dick's mother had gone into an irreversible coma after a sudden cardiac arrest. As she lay month after month in a fetal position on the hospital bed, Dick felt he got a message from his mother. "Live your life to the fullest. Grab a good idea and run with it. Don't be afraid to act with courage. Bring love into your life."

A few weeks after she died, a lightbulb went on for Dick during a telephone call with a travel agent. As he asked questions, the agent brought information up on his computer screen and read it to Dick over the phone. "This is stupid," Dick thought to himself. "Why can't he just share the visual information with me in real time rather than reading. I know the technology is available to make this happen." And so came his vision for a better way to communicate: Share visual information as easily as making an ordinary telephone call.

We knew that this simple idea had great potential. It was a grand idea. Grand companies are built from grand ideas. Grand ideas are both simple and elegant.

In one sense, the genesis of Radish Communications Systems was a gift from the Universe. As Coelho[9] explains in *The Alchemist,* "The Universe aligns to help you fulfill your destiny. The Universe wants you to succeed. You only need to listen to your heart and follow your dreams."

Prepare for Passionate Purpose

Oprah Winfrey reminds us, "Luck is a matter of preparation meeting opportunity."[10] Do you find your purpose or does it find you? Many would say that purpose comes when *preparation meets possibilities.* There are ways to prepare to find your passionate purpose.

My Path—Groundwork

Laying the proper groundwork was important in the founding of Radish. For Dick, the preparation included giving up his Porsche, selling his house, and leaving his full-time job with Bell Laboratories with enough resources in place to support the endeavor until it could support itself. Part of the preparation for me had been completing one purpose, the PhD, so I could say yes to the next. Another part was selling my house in New Jersey; buying a more affordable house in Colorado, where we would live and initially run the company; and organizing finances to survive and fund our dream.

Although we might not have realized it at the time, we had spent decades preparing. By working for technology companies, we gained experience in successfully bringing technology-based innovations to market. We acquired all the formal and informal education possible on the business, technology, and industry aspects. We built a network of people to support us. We saved enough money to use as founder's capital and personal support until the company was funded. We consolidated our households to minimize expenses. We quit other jobs so we could focus on the birth of Radish. All this and more went into the preparation. It paid off.

Proper Preparation

Successfully pursuing passionate purpose takes many resources. Each situation has different requirements. Your values, gifts, and traits such as curiosity and integrity of effort are essential. Without optimism and a belief that you can garner these characteristics, you are doomed from the onset.

Sometimes you won't know until later what you really need. The requirements typically evolve over time. Ask yourself what contingencies are available if necessary resources are not available. Experienced advisors play a priceless role here. Expect to call for more help than you initially anticipate. Understand the importance of prioritizing. You may find that you cannot have everything up front that you will ultimately need.

Find the Fourth-Fold

Passionate purpose resides in the *fourth-fold*. Although people use different terminology in explaining this phenomenon, passionate purpose is often found in the overlap of three elements:

1. *Your values:* Your underlying beliefs unleash the fire in your belly.
2. *Your gifts:* Your gifts mold how you can uniquely contribute.
3. *Needs of the world:* Here you define what is required to help make this world a better place. Businesses traditionally call this the *market need*. Include here your wildest dreams of what you would like to have in Utopia. Societal influences, an important part of this element, are based on people's opinions and prejudices of what is or is not a worthy cause. Many people believe the best and most enduring purposes are those that serve a greater cause, not just personal desire. Out of this yearning or hunger will surface the purposes through which you can make a difference and contribute.

At the junction of your values and gifts is passion. What do you get when you overlap passion and the needs of the world? In the intersection of these elements, you may find, when the time is right, your passionate purpose. This fourth-fold is shown in Figure 4.1.

My Path—Vision in the Fourth-Fold

The Radish vision came from the intersection of our values, gifts, and market need. Sharing visual information as easily as making an ordinary telephone call was an important market need. Our experience, education, and knowledge of the telecommunications industry were gifts that aligned with our value of finding an innovative way to allow people to communicate more effectively. By holding the intention of finding our passionate purpose and through direct effort of thinking, feeling, and doing, the fourth-fold appeared as an insight.

How to Find Your Fourth-Fold

People report that they found passionate purpose through great need, desire, and dissatisfaction. Another route was by being open to the Universe or following their hearts. Some found it takes time, through searching and trying, with the influence of people. Others found purpose by accident.

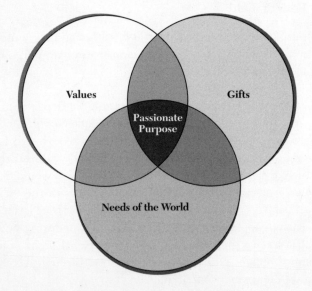

Figure 4.1   The fourth-fold.

Some fortunate people, even from an early age, don't know how they found it, "it just was." Try these suggestions:

- *Use your head* by creating lists of your values, gifts, and market needs. Analyze the lists, with the help of others, while searching for the right intersection.
- *Use the Attraction Strategy,* once you have a general sense of what the fourth-fold may represent (see Chapter 8). First, set a broad intention of wanting to discover your passionate purpose. Then open to the possibilities that are everywhere and let go of attachment to a certain outcome. Create a vision and imagine what it will be like when you connect with your purpose. Engage all your senses so you believe it is possible. From belief comes strength and conviction, and the ability to pull what you want toward you. Envision that you are successfully completing a long race. See yourself crossing the finish line. Hear the crowd's roar of approval. Feel the pats on the back and the supportive hugs of your comrades. Taste the victory champagne or sparkling water. Smell the congratulatory bouquet of roses. Feel your internal delight. Hear the positive self-talk. This race is a metaphor for whatever passionate purpose you are embracing.
- *Experiment with your hands and heart*—physically put yourself in real and visualized situations that represent alternative fourth-folds and see how you feel. Give yourself time to explore—be patient, but persistent.

Create a Purpose Proclamation

A man should conceive of a legitimate purpose in his heart, and set out to accomplish it.

JAMES ALLEN,[11] *As a Man Thinketh*

Remember Alice when she was lost in Wonderland.[12] She came upon the Cheshire Cat and asked, "Would you tell me, please, which way I ought to go from here?" "That depends a great deal on where you want to get to," said the Cat. Alice said, "I don't much care where." The wise feline then responded, "Then it doesn't matter which way you go." If we want something, we must be clear on what it is and be able to communicate it succinctly to others.

What would you say if someone asked you to describe your core purpose? Do you have a short, clear, and distinguishing explanation of what you want as your desired outcome? Think of being on an elevator and having 30 seconds to describe your reason for being. It would be useful to have a polished statement ready to share at a moment's notice.

My Path—Defining the Purpose

We held a strong intention to find our passionate purpose and were well prepared. We opened our hearts, along with our heads and hands to possibilities; and used visualizations, affirmations, and active planning to pull the creative forces out like a magnet.

From this effort, a *purpose* emerged that integrated our heads, hearts, and hands:

- Build a company (the hands goal).
- Based on the core values where all people could contribute and be rewarded to their fullest (the heart goal).
- That was financially successful delivering innovative technology-based products that significantly improved the way people communicate (the head goal).

We were passionate about this purpose. It was meaningful because it aligned with our values.

The Radish *mission* was to develop and market communications products designed to increase the efficiency of telephone computer transactions. Radish aimed to advance the widespread proliferation of VoiceView®, facilitating its acceptance as the de facto standard for integrated voice, data, and graphics communications over the existing switched telephone network.

Purpose Proclamation

A Purpose Proclamation is a positive declaration asserting what you want to do. It is a description of your intentions. Optimally, it has three *characteristics:*

1. *Brevity:* It is easy to understand and remember.
2. *Distinctiveness:* It differentiates you and your cause.
3. *Flexibility:* It provides room to evolve and will last a long time.

A Purpose Proclamation provides many *benefits*. It will:

- Communicate who you are and what you are about. Other people then realize how they can support you or how you can help them.
- Provide direction and motivation to you and others around you.

- Reinforce what is important.
- Offer focus to make decisions.

Here's my example: "I, Theresa Szczurek, am the catalyst for others' extraordinary results. I help organizations and individuals succeed on their path to fulfillment." Try building your own.

Environmental Passion Aligned with Purpose— Oak Thorne's Story

Dr. Oakleigh Thorne II's passionate purpose is connecting kids with nature. As the founder of the Thorne Ecological Institute, he believes that kids who grow up environmentally aware are one step closer to saving the earth, humanity, and themselves. "The key to finding and pursuing a worthwhile purpose is developing self-esteem. Nature is a builder of self-esteem. Kids can be successful in nature. The typical education system kills passion and self-esteem." Founded in 1954, Thorne Ecological Institute has touched over 100,000 lives in nearly 50 years. Its mission is to offer hands-on environmental education for young people along the Front Range of Colorado.

Thorne grew up in rural Long Island living close to nature, loving it, and establishing values of treasuring this environment. By the time he was 14 years old, he was on his career path in conservation. "Your life is your career," Oak shares. His high school biology teacher was an early role model, the first ecologist in his life. In the process of completing his education, he found his purpose.

Thorne's passion was ignited during the summer after his first year in college. "I went to the New York American Museum and asked the curator if he had a project for me. He gave me the goal of 'saving the Sunken Forest on Fire Island.' " Thorne quickly determined that $15,000 was needed in six weeks to purchase an option on the Sunken Forest. He researched the situation, established a nonprofit organization, created a 10-minute film, and got publicity. The *New York Times* editorial on the project started the calls offering help. The night before the deadline, he received a call from the Old Dominion Foundation, which provided $15,000. The eventual result was the creation of the "Fire Island National Seashore."

Life is not about success or failure, it is all about learning. Follow your inner voice, your intuition, and allow life to unfold.

OAK THORNE, environmental educator

Thorne advises, "Life will be an exciting, ever-changing journey. Don't be afraid of risks. If you don't take risks, you won't get anywhere. You learn always by taking risks. Fear holds people back. Just do it. There is nothing wrong with planning, but don't think too much, just try it."

When asked how to keep passion alive, Thorne suggests, "It is a life philosophy. Wake up. Keep a positive attitude of life. Keep your passion going, by following your dreams or your stars. Ignore the negative people who question what you are doing. Believe in what you are doing and just try it. Connect with the right people."

Not everyone has the good fortune to discover the right path so early. For people who may not have found their passionate purpose, Thorne suggests using the *three-sheet method*. "Create lists on three sheets of paper. On one, put all of your experience, education, and training. On another, list your hobbies, interests, and talents. On the third, list your wildest dreams and everything you would like to have happen. Then review this with a trusted colleague and see if a thread emerges which might suggest a path." This three-sheet method uses slightly different terminology but really represents the fourth-fold formula.

Dr. Oak Thorne, 73, has an important message. "If you don't go for your dream, you will never know. If it doesn't work out, try something else."

PRACTICAL POINTERS

- *Prepare*. Purpose comes when preparation meets the possibilities. Nurture yourself and your passions by continuing to learn, grow, and try new things. Do things that will build your true self, including high confidence and self-esteem. Tune your attitude. Test different situations and see what stimulates your head, heart, and hands energy. Be action-oriented.
- *Decide*. Ask yourself what you need to get the intended results. What useful knowledge do you have from similar past experiences? Determine the groundwork you need ahead of time. Along the way, check your gut. Are you getting what you need in your preparation? If not, what needs to change?

- *Be patient.* Give yourself time and be kind. Trust that when the time is right, you will know. Don't set a timetable. Surrender to the natural process. Persevere and don't quit. Keep trying. Be open to the possibilities. Let serendipity and synchronicity emerge. Make it easy for your purpose to find you.
- *Take action.* Create lists of your values, gifts, and world needs. Look for the fourth-fold intersection.
- *Connect.* Build a support system, with proper people and others in the web of life. Ask for feedback on your lists and perceptions of your fourth-fold.
- *Test.* Create a Purpose Proclamation and check it out with your friends, family, and colleagues. What kind of feedback do you receive? In their opinion, is it brief, distinctive, and flexible? If not, modify it. Next time you see these people, ask them to restate your Purpose Proclamation. If they can remember some or all of it, then you have an understandable and distinctive statement. If not, modify it again.
- *Use.* Share it in your communications. Say it daily to yourself as an affirmation. Reexamine it on a regular basis. Does it need to be adjusted to represent your authentic self? How?

COMMIT TO A MEANINGFUL PURPOSE

I didn't think it took courage. I just did what needed to be done.
MARTHA ARNETT,[13] retired university secretary

Having a good idea is not enough. Thousands of people have fabulous ideas and never pursue them. They waver, cannot make a decision, and don't take action. They lack the courage to commit, because commitment requires a pledge, devotion, and obligation. The Universe finds another conduit somewhere for this creativity.

Passionate Pursuers have the courage to seize the idea and then commit to it fully. The dictionary defines courage as mental or moral strength, firmness of mind and will to venture, persevere, and withstand difficulty. Pledging yourself to a pursuit takes courage and more.

My Path—My Heart Broke Through

Dick and I both knew in our guts, there was potential here. The idea could be the foundation for a great company. Dick was the one who first knew it was right, perhaps because he was the one who received the gift of the idea. In contrast, I thought about it (head), started doing preliminary planning work with the business concept (hands), and then talked to close confidants for perspective. Where was my heart? As usual, my head dominated with its rational, logical approach, while my heart yearned to be heard.

Finally, my heart broke through so that all parts of me could come together in harmony. With this idea for simple voice/data transactions as the foundation for the company, I realized that we had found a worthwhile purpose that aligned with our values and gifts. In trusting my inner voice, the courage came. This breakthrough brought me to the point of commitment.

We devoted ourselves fully to this passionate purpose—with our heart, head, and hands; with everything we had. And so our first baby, Radish, was conceived.

Know When a Purpose Is Right

When asked how they knew a passionate purpose was right for them, many people said the answer typically came from inside. Carol Grever put it this way: "If it is your purpose it won't let you alone, just like Jonah and the Whale." Others received positive feedback from outside or from the pursuit of the purpose itself. A few did not know it was right, but took the leap and gave it a try anyway.

From Inside

Your inner self may communicate messages via a mixture of head, heart, or hands energy as well as through intuition or insight:

- *Head:* You might conduct a logical decision analysis or use other cognitive approaches.
- *Heart:* Most people in my study, however, know a passionate purpose is appropriate because of their feelings and emotions. Some people shared, "It just feels right and good." They agree with the little prince in the book by Antoine de Saint-Exupéry,[14] who said, "Listen to your heart, because it is only with the heart that one can see rightly. What is essential is invisible to the eye." Shinzen Young[15] teaches that "juice" of emotion lies in your body sensations. So the

heart really does communicate through the gut with pleasant or painful sensations.

- *Hands:* Some people listen to their gut, or physical body sensations. Others try pursuing the purpose without knowing if it fits, and wait to see if things flow. By listening to the gut, taking action, and thereby engaging hands energy, supportive signals may encourage continuation.
- *Whole self leads to insights:* Still others look for an alignment that "there is harmony with head, hands, and heart," which can lead to direct insights and intuitive knowing. A number of people report that they know the purpose is right because: "There is a direct or intuitive knowing."

From Outside

Positive messages from others indicate that the purpose is right. In the early Radish days as we sought seed funding from friends and family, their financial support was a sign that we should proceed. When we conducted the earliest market research to test the concept, interest from prospective customers and industry opinion leaders propelled us on. Later when the venture capitalists decided to invest millions of dollars to fund our fledging start-up, we knew we were on the right course.

Direct Knowing in Action—Wendy James's Story

Wendy James, 29, thought she wanted to be a psychologist until the doors for that career would not open. But she kept patiently trying other things while keeping her head and heart open to the possibilities. "It wasn't easy finding the right purpose for me. I tried a lot of locked doors, before one swung open. One day I saw a movie with a female FBI agent. Things just clicked for me. I knew I could do this. Then I recalled being interested in this in Junior High. I realized I wanted to be a Secret Service agent. It was as if disjointed pieces of my life suddenly came together and I knew what I wanted to do. I'd found my purpose."

Others who knew her well were able to provide feedback that this was a good fit. After completing her master's degree in Criminal Justice, persisting through a yearlong application process, and keeping her optimism by visualizing the optimal end result, James became a Secret Service agent stationed at the White House.

When everything is aligned correctly, good things happen. James also met the love of her life in boot camp. She married less than a year later and is now Wendy Desmond.

Find the Courage to Commit

Once you know the purpose is right, it's time to commit to it wholly. Mary Daly,[16] *Minnesota Women's Press,* points out, "You become courageous by doing courageous acts. . . . Courage is a habit." Here are suggestions on finding courage.

Align with Values

Many people have remarkable ideas, but they never take on a pursuit because they cannot find the courage to act. Courage is a word with a French root, *corage,* that means "having heart." If you are clear on your values and the idea serves your spirit and values, the courage comes. With courage to commit comes more passion, zeal, and fervor. This is the energy essential for successful pursuit.

When my boss advised me to "kill Larry," I didn't have to think before leaping. My values were strong and took over. "No, I can't kill Larry. I play win-win." I spoke courageously in alignment with my values.

When you know and nurture yourself, you clarify who you are and what you stand for. Understanding your values—core beliefs, morale imperatives, and ethics—provides the courage.

Make Your Own Choice

There is more intrinsic motivation, when a person chooses whether to embrace a certain purpose.[17] Motivation brings courage and commitment. Make your own choices of what to pursue. Take the lead so it is your dream, and not someone else's.

Just Do It

Often people find a worthy purpose, but do not commit to it. Perhaps there is not enough alignment with values, or perhaps you need to jump in regardless of fear and just do it (see suggestions in Chapter 12 on overcoming doubt and fear). "I have always felt fear. Sometimes you have to jump in and do it even if it hurts or is uncomfortable." So says Phyllis Postlewait, financial consultant and vice president of investments for a large brokerage firm, who was previously a teacher of newly blinded adults.

"When I worked with the newly blinded, I just handed them a cane and said, 'We are going for a walk.' Once they experienced even the smallest success, they were able to keep moving and learn. My mother coined the phrase 'Just Do It' long before Nike."

Push Past Fear and Commit—Ann Cooper's Story

Ann Cooper, a successful realtor who was born and raised in a small town in Georgia, remembers acting with courage even at the young age of 8. "My mother was a domestic who worked in a uniform. The woman for whom she worked picked Mom up every day. Mom sat in the back seat of the car. Everyday, I would say to her, 'Sit in the front.' 'No, I can't sit in front,' Mom would say."

"So I created a mini plan to achieve my purpose of getting Mom to sit in front. At least I had to try. I was out sweeping the sidewalk by the curb so that I would be there when the car came. When the car stopped, I opened the front door of the car and said to Mom, 'Get in.' She got in. She never talked to me about it, but Mom sat in the front from then on. It was such a victory."

A critical experience in her early childhood allowed Ann to push past fear and take appropriate action to pursue her purpose. This fear may surface as negative self-talk and self-doubt. "All of us in life have gone through negative energy that wants to not make what we want happen. One must say—I know this is fear. I will push past it and go through it."

"Every night as a very young girl I would dream about a big monster in the doorway blocking me from my mother's room. One night I said, 'I will go past you to my mother's room.' I made it and I never saw that monster again. Push past it. Push past those monsters, your biggest fears. Everything will be okay. I now know there are other monsters in life and I can use this same approach with them."

Cooper has advice for others pursuing a passionate purpose. "Keep going and forging on. Don't stop. Remember your passion, do it in the best way possible with respect, and enjoy the process. Don't be vested in the outcome you think it should be. Pay more attention to the process than the outcome."

PRACTICAL POINTERS

- *Listen*. Tap your intuition. Be receptive. Look inside for messages from your head, heart, and hands. Learn to trust yourself.
- *Ask*. If the internal messages are not obvious, request clearer guidance.

(continued)

- *Connect*. Find supportive people who will be by your side or who will gently "kick you in the butt." Be open to inputs from outside yourself.
- *Align*. Know your values and make sure your purpose is consistent with them.
- *Choose*. Realize that you have options. Be sure to make your own choices.
- *Do*. Push past your fear and just do it. Do not try, do.

SUMMARY

- During this stage of the process, Passionate Pursuers foster passion, align it with a worthwhile purpose, and commit fully.
- Pursuit of passionate purpose feels wonderful. You can get into the flow—a state of delightful concentration where nothing else seems to matter.
- There are ways to nurture and strengthen passion. Passion is important because it fuels the pursuit. Meditation is an effective technique. Others include clarification of values and gifts, visualization, and removal of hindrances.
- Many would say that purpose comes when "preparation meets possibilities."
- To align your passion with purpose, start by defining your passion. The first step is to know yourself, your values, and gifts—what you are passionate about. Next look at the intersection of your passion with the hungers of the world. This junction, or fourth-fold, holds your passionate purpose.
- To find your fourth-fold, create lists of your values, gifts, and market needs. Analyze the lists, with the help of others, while searching for the right intersection.
- Use the Attraction Strategy to naturally attract opportunities that are everywhere into your fourth-fold.
- Create a Purpose Proclamation, a brief, distinctive, and flexible declaration asserting what you want to do.

- Inner messages and feedback from outside yourself help you know that a passionate purpose is right for you. Internal messages come from your head, hands, and heart as well as your spirit or intuitive self.
- Commit to a meaningful purpose. It takes courage to commit. There are approaches to strengthen courage:
  —When you align purpose with your values, courage more easily comes.
  —Make your own choices on what to pursue.
  —Push past your fears and just do it.

5

Pursue Purpose

Premise: Passion fuels the persistent pursuit.

Path: Develop and implement a plan, while performing persistently and enjoying the process.

Outcome: Make progress.

Once you have found your passionate purpose, the next stage of the process is to pursue it while you keep your fire burning. The *Pursue Purpose* stage answers the question "How do I get where I want to go?" This effort requires:

- Development of a focused plan—saying no to other things in order to say yes to this purpose.
- Persistent implementation with engaged resources and effective internal and external communications.
- Enjoyment of the process.

WHAT YOU CAN GET FROM THIS CHAPTER

Passionate Pursuers get an explanation of what you have been already doing, as well as practical pointers to help you along the way. Seekers, who have defined your immediate purpose as finding and nurturing your true self, learn about what is next for you in the process. You can still benefit from planning, engaging the right resources, and promoting. In-between'ers validate what you have done or not done while pursuing previous quests and realize that you are now preparing, perhaps indirectly, for the next pursuit.

MY PATH—PURSUE THE ENTREPRENEURIAL DREAM

After getting to know who we were and what we wanted, we found and committed to our passionate purpose. Radish was born. Well not really. It was not that quick and easy. In reality, Radish was barely conceived. You could say that after finding the vision, we had an embryonic idea that we needed to nurture during the gestation phase. It was probably a high-risk pregnancy with a grave possibility of miscarriage. Key elements would determine whether the venture would be born healthy, survive, and thrive. These elements included a plan for building a viable business, funding, proper people and partners, and promotion. Persistence, while enjoying the process, was also a key strategy.

Our experiences in creating and building Radish illustrate fundamentals needed to successfully pursue any purpose.

DEVELOP A PLAN

A legendary study of graduates from Harvard University showed the importance of goal setting and planning. People with a plan outperformed those without one. The 3 percent with a written plan greatly outperformed all the others, who only had a mental plan. Having a written plan is a key factor in effectively pursuing your passionate purpose. Deborah Myers, freelance writer, learned to do this with great success: "Once I planned my writing like a business instead of only like a passion, I could put those tedious business thoughts to bed and get back to the creativity and passion for my purpose."

My Path—The Plan

Our business plan was a living document that continued to evolve with the changing market conditions. Radish initially developed a business model based on designing, manufacturing, and marketing proprietary VoiceView® systems.

The plan clarified our approach so we could explain it and attract the support of others. At first it was the magnet for essential resources—investors, consultants, employees, and partners. Later, it helped us stay the course and say no to some opportunities in order to focus on those with the highest potential.

What Is a Plan?

A plan is a road map that guides you to where you want to go. In a recent panel discussion, two successful entrepreneurs and a seasoned venture capitalist[1] stressed planning as an essential step in getting funded and driving the business. They recommended being flexible, making changes along the way, and using the plan as an evolving document to guide operations.

Connect to Your Values

Why are you doing this anyway? Make sure that your plan incorporates your values, since they are a source of meaning. Remember—meaning ignites passion. Passion provides energy for the pursuit. Ensure that you build your plans to support your beliefs.

A Plan to Create the Plan

Whether you are pursuing a personal or professional, modest or grand purpose, you need a plan. Some plans are lengthy; Radish's business plan that raised the first $3 million in venture capital funding filled over 40 pages, and the detailed operating plan with budgets was even larger. Other plans are short, and if they include the essentials, shorter is better. A plan should include the following critical elements:

- *Overall purpose:* The Purpose Proclamation is a statement of what you want and why.
- *Values:* Your underlying core beliefs act as the foundation for your pursuit.
- *Goals:* Direct your effort to reasonable objectives that are written, measurable, feasible, and easy to understand.
- *Plan strategy:* Find creative approaches to meet your goal given the strengths, weaknesses, opportunities, and threats of the situation.
- *Tactics:* Identify specific items and steps to implement your plan's strategy and achieve your goal.

Do you have a written plan? When was the last time you reviewed and updated it? Make sure your plan is feasible and motivates you.

I created my annual business plan last January. A few weeks later, I started having chest pains and could not sleep at night. After ruling out anything serious, the doctor asked, "What kinds of stress are you under?" Then I realized my plan was not achievable. The standards were so high that

I knew, in my heart, they were not attainable. My inner self was giving me a message. That night I revised the plan by cutting the goals in half. The chest discomfort disappeared and I was even more motivated to work with this realistic plan.

Radish's Business Plan

Here is part of a plan we created for Radish's second year of operation. The Purpose Proclamation is geared toward the firm rather than any individual in the company.

- *Overall purpose:* Based on values in harmony with the founders' deepest convictions, build a financially successful company that improves the way people communicate.
- *Purpose Proclamation:* Radish Communications Systems is a profitable company leading the market in the development of integrated voice/data telephone applications.
- *Values:* These include integrity, stakeholder delight including financial performance, innovative solutions, environment where all can contribute and be rewarded, and service to the greater community.
- *Goal 1:* Ship Release I VoiceView systems by September 30 to real customers.
- *Plan strategy A:* Attract adequate financing to keep the company growing.
  —Tactic a: Write a convincing business plan.
  —Tactic b: Obtain seed funding by selling convertible debentures through the Private Placement Offering.
  —Tactic c: Secure $3 million in VC funding by March 30.
- *Plan strategy B:* Develop, test, manufacture, and ship VoiceView by September 30.
  —Tactic a: Complete first prototype and controlled introduction Release I system.
  —Tactic b: Finish system requirements, protocol specification, and production design.
  —Tactic c: File patent and trademark registrations.
  —Tactic d: Pass all FCC and UL testing, secure tooling, and manufacture Release I products.

　　—Tactic e: Deliver Release I system to real customers by September 30.
- *Plan strategy C:* Manage marketing efforts to announce and sell VoiceView.
　　—Tactic a: Conduct preliminary market discussions and analysis.
　　—Tactic b: Sign first and second strategic marketing partners.
　　—Tactic c: Announce company and VoiceView at May 1 major trade show.
　　—Tactic d: Close first sale for September 30 delivery.
- *Plan strategy D:* Handle supporting administrative responsibilities.
　　—Tactic a: Acquire larger facilities and additional equipment.
　　—Tactic b: Convert consultants into employees, including executive staff.
　　—Tactic c: Hire and train additional staff as planned.

Another View

Plans do not need to be logical, linear, and detailed. Plans can engage the whole range of senses with a creative drawing. Participants in Pursuit of Passionate Purpose workshops often draw an image of their vision and the process for getting there. Drawings have a powerful impact because they open the heart and involve more of the senses. The quality of the artwork is not as important as the meaning of the image. Figure 5.1 represents the high-level Radish plan.

Focus—Say No to Say Yes

One purpose of a plan is to focus efforts. While the earlier stages are expansive and explorative, the *Pursue Purpose* stage requires setting boundaries and saying no to many things in order to say yes to priorities. "Say NO!" is handwritten on a note attached to my PC monitor and phone. Pursuit of passionate purpose requires focus and cutting out extraneous things to keep time and attention on the most important elements.

> *The secret of success is concentration; wherever there has been a great life, or a great work, that has gone before. Taste everything a little, look at everything a little; but live for one thing.*
> RALPH IRON,[2] *The Story of an African Farm*

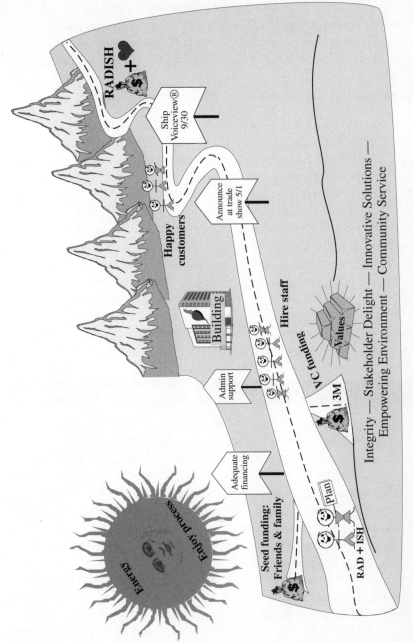

Figure 5.1 The high-level Radish plan.

There are ways to strengthen your ability to focus. Studies[3] show that experienced meditators have exceptionally strong concentration skills. Just as exercise strengthens physical muscles, meditation strengthens the mental attention muscle and it becomes easier with practice. Use the Core Practice meditation, described in Appendix B, to train your concentration.

Say No to Say Yes to Passion—Margot Zaher's Story

When Margot Zaher was 12 years old, she met an exchange student who ignited her desire to live and work in France. Determined to reach her goal, she developed a plan. She studied French and focused.

"I said no to cheerleading and many other things so I could earn enough money to travel." After trips to France at age 16, 17, and 20, she took a job with a U.S. company. "I felt dead and unfulfilled. I quit the job and went to Paris, earned a master's degree in business there, and landed an impressive job with Procter & Gamble in that country. It took many small steps. Perseverance is key. You need a support system. It's like an incubator that helps your dream grow. My mom and my other French connections were this support."

After seven years in France achieving her purpose, she assessed progress and decided to come home. Margot Zaher, today, is a life coach who helps people live their passions.

PRACTICAL POINTERS

- *Produce*. Create an annual written plan. Shorter is better. Consider making a visual plan, which engages all the senses.
- *Review*. Are you being realistic? Have you unobtainable goals? Perhaps you need to adjust and make it workable. Get feedback from your advisor, coach, or supportive colleagues. Often when you make a plan public by sharing it with someone, you are more committed to making it happen.
- *Use*. Allow your plan to focus your efforts on an ongoing basis. Stay focused on your plan by saying yes only to priorities.
- *Revise*. Keep the plan alive by modifying it as conditions change.
- *Look*. Identify times that you said no in the past. Think of examples when you successfully said no to say yes. What helped or hindered you?

- *Inquire*. Ask yourself what is blocking you from saying no. "The answer lies within you," *The Alchemist*[4] said. In reality, many of us have been unable to hear that answer from our internal, wiser self. Stay open so you can hear the message and take appropriate action. You might be surprised at what you hear.
- *List*. Make a list of all the good reasons to say no.
- *Practice*. Try saying no to the easy, unimportant things.
- *Meditate*. Try contemplation to strengthen your ability to focus.

IMPLEMENT THE PLAN

Winning the prize [1963 Nobel Prize in physics] *wasn't half as exciting as doing the work itself.*

MARIA GOEPPERT MAYER, in Barbara Shiels,
Women and the Nobel Prize[5]

Once you know what your purpose is, then implement your plan with unremitting willpower. Perform while involving people in partnership, resources, and communication.

Connect to People

Who are involved and what roles do they play? What additional players or partnerships can help? Connections play such a crucial part in the successful implementation of your plan that they are explored in Chapter 11.

My Path—Web of Support

Many key people participated during Radish's various phases of growth. A web of people supported the venture and brought positive contributions. Others were naysayers or tried to discourage us. We needed to evaluate and strengthen supporters while not letting the others pull us down.

Each player contributed his or her own values to the overall Radish mix. Some, based on their roles, had a bigger influence than others. The CEO, board of directors, and executive staff had the most power. We did not realize until later the consequences of having them outweigh the founders. The bottom line is that people are the most important resource; they make or break a venture.

Find Money and Other Resources

How do you find the resources to successfully pursue passionate purpose? Resources include money as well as time and other means needed on your pursuit.

My Path—Finding the Funds

It takes money to make money, even when operating frugally. Where would we get the funding for Radish? It started with founder's capital—initially we each put in several thousand dollars and then convinced Dick's father to become a founder, too. This amount grew over the first 12 months to $60,000. We cut corners when appropriate—operating out of my home and using pro bono advisors wherever possible.

Knowing which corners to cut and which ones not to cut was not always easy. Radish spent money wisely on protecting the idea through patent applications, designing its professional image, developing a prototype, and assessing the market's reaction.

We had a big idea and big ideas take big money. After the first six months of operation, it became clear that this technology had great potential and we needed more funds. Based on the counsel of advisors, Radish sold $250,000 of unregistered securities to friends and family through a Private Placement Offering (PPO). During this period, Dick and I got married. The weekend of our wedding, we raised enough money, in lieu of traditional wedding gifts, to support the company for another six months. Our friends and family helped us achieve our dream.

We wrote a strong business plan, began talking to venture capitalists (VCs) and responding to their due diligence questions, moved product development forward, began selling to selective accounts, and carefully managed the cash flow. Proactively responding to the concerns of prospective VC investors, we broadened our management team. Finally, after almost two years of gestation, we closed on a $3 million financing with two VC investors, and Radish was born.

We charged ahead with the pursuit. Radish quickly moved into larger facilities, converted selected consultants into employees, and hired additional staff. Radish and VoiceView were announced at a major telecommunications conference, and we launched an aggressive sales and marketing effort. Consistent with our value of having all employees contribute and be rewarded to their fullest, they received stock options commensurate with their contributions to the firm. Within six months, Radish manufactured

Pursuing passionate purpose takes funds. We got married just a year after founding Radish. What a strategic funding decision! The weekend of our wedding, we raised enough money from friends and family, in lieu of traditional wedding gifts, to carry the company for six more months.

and shipped its first release of VoiceView to customers. The company was off and running in its early childhood. Over the next three and a half years as its business model evolved, Radish raised millions of dollars through financings from current and new investors.

Resource Tactics

People in my study recommend a variety of approaches:

- *Be appropriately patient.* Consider Joe Rush whose story is shared in Chapter 12. To support his family during the Great Depression, Rush worked for seven years at an unchallenging job as a radio technician and delayed completing his education to become a physicist. Patience paid off, and he achieved his dream to become an atomic research scientist.
- *Be creative and carefully manage resources.* Merc Mercure, a seasoned entrepreneur, venture capitalist, and corporate board member with extensive university experience, leveraged all of his contacts and creativity, when founding CDM Optics with only

$500. He bootstrapped the company with government and corporate grants until revenues from product licensing and sales could support it. The firm, which enhances the performance of conventional optical systems, manages its cash flow carefully and retains earnings to fund company growth and technology development. With a wide range of potential applications that resolve serious problems, CDM Optics evaluates projects based on their ability to produce cash.

- *Multitask.* To preserve his cash flow during the start-up phase, Mike, a technology entrepreneur, had to consult part-time at a local hospital while cofounding his first venture. That company grew to employ 3,000 employees with annual revenues of over $300 million. Sometimes, with persistence, it is necessary to support your passionate purpose with other work.
- *Focus.* Mark Walker had to make the difficult decision to close one of his two fledgling companies since financial ruin was looming. He was just not able to build two ventures and support his family. As difficult as it was, he closed one venture and took a full-time job as a sales executive with an established firm that paid a salary. By focusing, Walker was able to survive and thrive.

Communicate

Communication informs the world of your passionate purpose, gives you feedback, and provides other forms of supportive energy. This helps you affirm progress, stimulate more passion, build intrinsic motivation, connect with the web of life, attract needed resources, and guide the pursuit.

Sometimes the intended receiver is you. Other times, the value is the feedback from others. Or, its worth may be in the resulting actions that others take or that you embrace. What kind of messages would help keep your fire burning? Let people know what you need; ask for specific inputs, or tell people the reaction you would like. Design communications to bring your desired response:

- Validation that your work is meaningful.
- Confirmation that you made the right choice and should continue.
- Evidence of progress.
- Proof of your competency.
- Recognition and exposure.

- Information from the marketplace to guide your pursuit.
- Something else?

My Path—Drop "Technoinfo" Babble

The communication started, for us, with a distinctive name that stood out from the technoinfo babble. Why name a company Radish? Because it was a zesty complement to the communications platter just as a radish spices up a salad. Radish was fast growing and down to earth. And, of course, there was the tie into the founders' names. With a distinctive logo and promotional materials, the name communicated professionalism, innovativeness, and quality.

We immediately began to communicate with the marketplace to gauge their reaction to the VoiceView concept and determine how best to meet market needs. Through confidential discussions with hundreds of opinion leaders and potential customers, we reaffirmed the worth of the idea, tested applications, and verified interest. This information, and other data collected through ongoing market research, became an essential part of our business plan that convinced investors and guided operations.

When Radish announced VoiceView at our first industry trade show just a month after receiving VC funding, we were voted "best at the show." As a giveaway, we passed out packets of radish seeds proclaiming Radish as the "hottest idea in the field."

As a priority, we sought media exposure. There is nothing like a feature article in an important trade publication to reconfirm to all stakeholders that you are on course. We posted awards and press coverage to demonstrate tangible evidence of results. Promotion proved to be an important factor that paid off.

We recorded the pursuit with photos and a scrapbook. Regular company meetings communicated the vision and our progress, and helped keep the fire burning.

Perform and Persist

The pursuit takes effort, doing, performing, and taking action. This, however, is where you find great, enduring satisfaction. People in my study were more satisfied with life when pursuing a purpose, then before identifying one. Attainment of the goal brought even more satisfaction, but this faded over time. The pursuit itself is one of the real rewards.

Promotion helps the pursuit and differentiates you from the crowd. As we an-nounced our company and product at the industry's leading trade show one month after receiving VC funding, we handed out packets of radish seeds declaring that Radish was the "hottest idea in the field."

How do you persist while not being overwhelmed by a large, daunt-ing goal? Using the Persistence Strategy, apply the *divide-and-conquer* tac-tic. Partition the path to the purpose into smaller pieces. State what you optimally want to have as the end result for each subgoal. Then focus on each subgoal, one at a time, until you achieve it. This approach, described in Chapter 9, is useful in all stages of the pursuit of passionate purpose.

My Path—Never Say Never

Growing Radish took lots of hard work and perseverance. Our mantra became:

> **Never quit. Never say never.**
> **Continue with unremitting will toward the vision.**
> **Persist. Get up and go in.**
> **Find the strength within and carry on.**

As obstacles surface, it can be hard to keep going. In Radish's first six months, AT&T announced its ScreenPhone. It received major coverage in the *Wall Street Journal*[6] and other business publications. With our experi-ence working for AT&T, we knew the financial power and human re-sources behind that effort. How could our tiny start-up compete? To survive, we had to maintain our confidence and nimbly charge forward. In-stead of looking at this market leader's action as a death knell, we embraced a different perspective. Surely, this superpower would not enter into this space unless there was a real market. We used this announcement to verify our business plan. Since many of our engineers were the best and brightest retirees from Bell Laboratories, we knew our technology was at least as ele-gant as theirs. We also were fast moving and entrepreneurial. We pressed on to rise above this hindrance. Our persistence and optimism paid off. A few years later, AT&T dropped its ScreenPhone and their chip division licensed Radish's VoiceView.

A Plan for Justice through Business—Tom Chappell's Story

Tom Chappell, an entrepreneur who cofounded the personal care products firm Tom's of Maine, has an overall purpose to build a financially success-ful business that is accountable to society.

Chappell and his wife Kate started a business built on core values that makes "products that are good for people, environment, and society and creates wealth. I wanted a life of justice by using the life of business. We know it is a worthy purpose, good for others and self, because we continue to get positive feedback from people that it is working.

"The best part of growing a business is learning about self. As you face challenges, you realize that what makes it work is 'knowing yourself.' Know what you care about deeply."

Chappell found that it is important is to seek advice. "I learned that I was audacious and not listening to others. It has taken me a while to want to listen and hear others. It is important to bring people with more wisdom in many areas into the business. I also learned how to listen to consumers so that we can live true to our values while meeting the needs of the customers. Many entrepreneurs make the mistake of putting themselves in the place of the consumer and then building a product for themselves."

PRACTICAL POINTERS

- *Connect.* Get the proper people involved. Be open to building strategic partnerships.
- *Identify.* Recognize and prioritize the resources you will need. Sometimes you will not know until later what they are, because the requirements typically evolve over time. Experienced advisors play a priceless role here. Expect to call for more than you initially anticipate. Make sure you have the minimum set of resources to survive.
- *Be creative and ask.* Be open to all the possibilities. Let others know what you need.
- *Plan.* Determine with whom you need to communicate. Consider what feedback you want and the appropriate means to get the desired response. Develop a communication plan.
- *Experiment.* Send and receive messages through various media. Send e-mail messages. Mail a postcard. Write a media release. Post on your web site. Put your message on your voice mail system. Use word of mouth and spread the good news. Schedule a face-to-face meeting. Present to a group.
- *Post it.* Show off the tangible evidence of your progress so that you and others can appreciate it.
- *Persist.* It takes perseverance to implement the plan. Don't quit.

In his first book, *The Soul of a Business,*[7] Chappell recommends the use of a "creative talking circle" as a place for open give-and-take among interdependent members of the company. "Take caution if there is one prevailing spokesperson in leadership. Wisdom comes from a circle of people who are all involved in creating the future. It requires diversity of perspectives."

Communication is the vehicle to build trust and connection. "We changed our name to Tom's of Maine so we could relate to the customer on a one-to-one human level, not as an institution. We, thereby, create a relationship with the customer around the product and the values behind the product."

In his recent book *Managing Upside Down: The Seven Intentions of Values-Centered Leadership,*[8] Chappell explains further how communication extends to the greater goodness of the Universe. "I believe strongly that you can pursue good and material wealth. One leads to the other. Goodness must be held all the time as you pursue wealth."

For someone pursuing a passionate purpose, Chappell recommends, "Know yourself and be true to your values. Integrate the rational and creative into an effective process. Understand the vision and hold on to it. Be intentional. Say no to some things in the near term that look tempting. Have patience. Be open to how others are thinking. Do not let go of your purpose, but let go of the process of how to pursue it."

ENJOY THE PROCESS

The more you can enjoy the journey, the more productive and satisfied you will be as a Passionate Pursuer. After all, it is the *pursuit* of passionate purpose, *not only its attainment,* that brings meaning and satisfaction to life. In *The Reinvention of Work,* Matthew Fox[9] has this to say: "To sustain our work, we must experience deep elements of joy and goodness."

I asked author Jim Collins how to take pleasure in the process and not overly press for completion of a long project. How does he overcome impatience, the desire for shortcuts, the pain and boredom of some of the project pieces, and other hindrances? He said, "There is nothing more blissful than having a huge project that will take years. It is the very definition of fun. Being done—well, that is really not fun."

Passionate Pursuers take pleasure in the process. However, this can be a challenge for many of us. When asked, "How do you enjoy the process of getting where you want to go?" people shared several tactics. It helps to recognize that there is a natural gestation period for projects; accept that it will be easier, based on personality, for some people and more difficult for others. Resolve the tension between being driven and going with the flow; open to the possibilities; play more; smile a lot; cultivate a sense of humor; be in the moment; and surround yourself with the proper people.

My Path—Play along the Way

Even though we experienced typical start-up challenges, we were having fun and it showed in the motivation and energy we generated. The passion was contagious. Many bright people chose to jump on our bandwagon because they found meaning in aligning with our core values. In addition, people saw potential for success, perceived progress, and felt competent.

People worked and played hard. We held parties to celebrate milestones. One day the engineering team started the day with a bungee jump. Our annual company photo showed our growth. People proudly wore t-shirts and buttons showing off the Radish logo. Radish was more than a company; it was a family and a community.

Recognize the Gestation Period

Pursuing passionate purpose is similar to having a baby. There is a minimum gestation period after conception. Nature takes its course and moves things along at its own pace. If you try to force a baby's birth in less than the required time, you risk the health of the infant.

> *It's about the process, not the goals. Don't focus on the end result or outcome. No matter what ever came in the end, the learning itself along the journey was the payoff.*
>
> WENDY JAMES, secret service agent

Pursuits have a natural gestation period. Goals have a point of diminishing returns. At first, if they are reasonable while still aggressive, they provide motivation. But when they become unrealistic, they become a source of stress and slow you down. Just as with pregnancy, being too aggressive can actually hurt the outcome. For me, and perhaps for you, this can be difficult to accept. I am naturally driven to see the finished product and like crossing off a goal from my to-do list.

To enjoy the process, respect and have faith that the journey and the knowledge it brings are the rewards. Don't be vested in the outcome. Be flexible along the way and let the process unfold. Recognize that pursuits take time.

Accept Personality Differences

Whether you can easily enjoy the process may be a function of personality. Some of us prefer closure and getting to the goal. These people are characterized as "J" or judging using the Myers-Briggs Type indicator.[10] Others, characterized as "'P'" for perceiving, seem to have a play ethic and want things to be open-ended. P's are more likely to seek an enjoyable work process.

There certainly are differences in personalities, and these differences change the journey for each of us. Appreciate the differences. J's, especially, can experiment with new behavior. Because the more you can enjoy the journey, the more effective you will be as a Passionate Pursuer.

Balance Polar Opposites

The tension between going with the flow and being driven are polar opposites that can hinder the enjoyment of the journey. How can we bring persistence with the pursuit in harmony with letting go? Perhaps the persistence is "walking the 10 miles each day" in the direction you believe you need to go, but the letting go is venturing into the side valleys to explore. This requires accepting both poles as valuable and working to resolve the tension between them (see Chapter 7).

Open to the Possibilities

During a trip to Europe in my late teens, I wanted to see every tourist site on my list. This I did, walking miles each day. But I did not really see it all. The sites are now a blur because I did not smell the flowers, see smiles on the children's faces, or sip tea slowly in a café. I was not open to spontaneous possibilities and neglected the important parts of the journey to cross off more names from my to-do list—sites that I cannot even remember today.

In contrast, I went to Europe years later without much of an itinerary. Being open to the possibilities, I really experienced the country and people from the laughter of locals traveling together with me in crowded trains to the hospitality of families who invited me into their homes and on to the inspiring natural wonders of the Alps and the Mediterranean Sea.

These and many more spontaneous experiences emerge when you are open to the possibilities and free of a set agenda. By letting the journey unfold, you find the real spice and joy of life. The underlying premise is trust. To just let life emerge as it will, you need to have faith that the "invisible hands will come."[11]

Play

Are you having fun yet? Has your pursuit become a grind or is time flying by as you wonder how you could be so lucky? How often do you smile while you are pursuing your dreams? Are you playing or drudging?

As O. Fred Donaldson, PhD,[12] defines it, "Play is a process of trust in the unknown . . . a common and ever-characteristic phenomenon of human nature." Children typically indulge in this spur-of-the-moment activity better than grown-ups. Adults often cut themselves off from their will to play and from the inborn natural state of ecstatic wonder. Society's message is that we are supposed to grow up and move out of this magic place. Yet, the benefits of maintaining a playful attitude are great:

- More creativity, since play allows for experimentation.
- Less stress, since play reduces psychic tension, provides a safe outlet for aggression, and uses up excess energy.
- More wonder and awe, since play introduces various aspects of culture.
- More confidence, since play develops competency.
- Greater awakening and connection to all parts of the self and thus more wholeness, since play provides opportunities to develop a strong ego and open the heart.
- Support from playmates, since play develops cooperation along with competition, and provides practice in social functioning.

Sometimes it just takes an attitude adjustment and different perspective in pursuing your purpose to view what you have to do as play. Entrepreneur Nathan Thompson suggests, "To accomplish great goals, you need to get gratification out of things that seem like work."

Smile a Lot

When we feel joy in the process, we smile more. Dr. Allen Konopacki, behavioral scientist and president of Incomm Research,[13] reports that people smile less as they age, due to a fear of not being socially accepted. While children under age five smile over 300 times daily, teenagers smile an average of 30, and adults a mere 21 times a day. Smiling releases endorphins and makes you feel better. And, this positive feeling easily transfers to other people.

Be more childlike and smile more often. Use the Smile Monitor—regularly check in on how often you and the people around you are smiling. Use the number of smiles as your monitor of enjoyment.

Cultivate a Sense of Humor

Humor moves us out of our head and into our heart. It helps us be more balanced and whole. Since the rational, logical thinker can dominate many parts of the *Pursue Purpose* stage, if we let it, it is even more important to lighten up. Laughter increases muscular activity, heart rate, and oxygen exchange, and stimulates the production of endorphins.[14] Viktor Frankl[15] in documenting his experiences in a Nazi concentration camp reported, "Humor was another of the soul's weapons in the fight for self-preservation. The attempt to develop a sense of humor and to see things in a humorous light is some kind of a trick learned while mastering the art of living."

Josephine Heath, whose story is shared in Chapter 11, has dealt with many stressful situations including losing a U.S. Senate seat after winning her party's endorsement in a difficult primary. She recommends maintaining a sense of humor and also keeps this quote by Katharine Graham[16] in mind: "To love what you do and feel that it matters—how could anything be more fun?"

PRACTICAL POINTERS

- *Discern*. What is important on your journey of life? Ask yourself, "What can I learn from this?"
- *Affirm*. Say the following affirmation every day, "I enjoy the process of life and let it naturally unfold. I am open to the opportunities that are everywhere and embrace the ones that are right for me."
- *Accept*. Appreciate who you are. Be patient. It might be a long road. Don't kid yourself that the journey will be easy. Accept that

(continued)

obstacles and adversity exist. Have a good attitude and take action to turn "lemons into lemonade." Adversity can be a positive force in the end. Keep forging ahead.

- *Emulate*. Surround yourself with people who know how to play. Ask supporters to assist you in lightening up.
- *Experiment*. Try new behaviors. Spontaneously take a break. Take some time to play.
- *Meditate*. Use the Core Practice (Appendix B) to become mindful when you are being driven and when you are letting an enjoyable process unfold. Be in the moment.
- *Play*. Make the pursuit fun and playful. Smile more. Maintain a sense of humor. Especially, laugh at yourself.

SUMMARY

- Passion fuels the pursuit. Yet how do you keep that fire burning through all the ups and downs of the journey? The answer, which varies from person to person, comes from using all these tactics along the path:
  —Create a plan of how to get where you want to go, but allow it to be a living document that changes as circumstances evolve.
  —Keep connected with the meaning in the pursuit of your passionate purpose. Why are you doing this anyway? Allow your values to be represented and act as the fuel for the pursuit.
  —Keep focused and concentrated. Diffusion of energies can easily dissipate passion and progress on the pursuit.
- Implement your plan.
  —Surround yourself with and connect to the supportive web of life.
  —Ensure, to the extent possible, that the necessary resources are available as energy to sustain the journey.
  —Communicate and promote.
  —Use the Persistence Strategy to divide and conquer (see Chapter 9).
- Play and have fun along the way so you are enjoying the process.

6

Assess Progress

Premise: There is a beginning, middle, and end in everything.

Path: Evaluate progress, recognize success, appreciate, and determine what's next.

Outcome: Celebration, continuation, modification, or transition.

During this stage of the process, you assess "How are things going?" And depending on the answer, you determine "What's next?" Your perceived progress will help you determine if it may be appropriate to:

- Recognize success and move on.
- Continue pursuing this passionate purpose, with or without mid-course adjustments.

In this stage, effective Passionate Pursuers evaluate progress, recognize success, appreciate, and then make necessary adjustments.

WHAT YOU CAN GET FROM THIS CHAPTER

Everyone can benefit from assessment. In-between'ers may determine whether it is the right time to get back on a pursuit. Seekers can assess how their search for a meaningful purpose is going and decide if they need to make alterations. Pursuers can evaluate and appreciate progress and take appropriate next steps.

ASSESS PROGRESS

What is progress? It is maintaining your integrity of effort standards, while moving toward or attaining the goal. Although assessment offers many benefits, it is typically the most neglected part of the four-stage process. People do not have enough expertise using assessment tools.

My Path—Pain Is the Signal

After we diligently pursued our dream, Radish was born and survived the newborn stage. We were on our way.

Radish's Assessment

Good things were happening for Radish, yet when we did an honest assessment, we found that our business model was not sustainable. As with many start-ups, we were not meeting our revenue targets, cash was burning quickly, and investors were hesitant to provide additional funding. Radish was in pain.

Our business model was based on designing, manufacturing, and marketing proprietary VoiceView systems composed of hardware, software, and the protocol. Although users liked the ease of use and the benefit of transferring data during a phone call, other factors held the technology back from wider adoption. Parties on both sides of the phone call needed to have specialized VoiceView products. More people needed to have VoiceView to grow its use as the standard for voice/data communications. We hadn't found the "killer application" with enough significant benefits to persuade business customers that outfitting a critical mass of users would be profitable.

We found that the negative forces outweighed the positive forces when we analyzed our initial model.[1]

Positive Forces Encouraging Diffusion	Negative Forces Discouraging Diffusion
Ease of use	Specialized VoiceView products
Benefits from using technology to see and hear during business transactions	Limited population of users Question of whether Radish would survive
	Limited applications for product VoiceView was not the industry standard

VoiceView callers could see and hear information during a normal telephone call by using the VoiceView set, or by using a PC with unique hardware and software. (Photo by Geoffrey Wheeler)

From here, there were three possible approaches—live with it, change, or accept/move on. Our leadership was astute enough to realize that it was change or die; there was no living with this situation. We needed to let go of the current business model, but asked, "What approach could we embrace that would turn the negative forces into positive forces, get rid of negative forces, and produce more positive forces?"

As a company we went back to the *Know and Nurture* stage to revisit our core values and distinctive competencies. One of our clever employees proposed that Radish could evolve to a revised business model. Rather than manufacture proprietary hardware, we would license the VoiceView Protocol to major manufacturers to embed it in off-the-shelf products such as modems and PCs. There would be millions of users with VoiceView provided as a free component on standard devices. With this user base, it would become the de facto standard.

If we could implement this revised business model, positive forces would greatly outweigh the negative forces:

Positive Forces Encouraging Diffusion	Negative Forces Discouraging Diffusion
Ease of use	Limited applications
Benefits from seeing and hearing	
Embedded in off-the-shelf products	
Huge population of potential users	
VoiceView as de facto standard	
Embraced by major industry players	

There was one catch. This business model required the right partners—original equipment manufacturers who would build VoiceView into their products. How would we attract them?

Personal Pain

Radish had a lot of potential with the new business model, yet something was not working for me anymore. I was working harder than ever, yet progress had faltered in building the kind of company environment I envisioned. As we changed the business model and brought in more players to implement it with different backgrounds, expertise, and values, I found myself in greater and greater pain. This discomfort was escalated into tremendous suffering, as I resisted the inevitable.

I saw a real change in some employees who were not living by the original values of the company. Our culture was changing in the wrong direction and I was no longer in a position to handle the situation directly. By making the decision to keep Radish alive with venture capital funding, Dick and I had lost control of the company and its values.

My pain came from a tension between values: Could the firm build an environment where all people could contribute and be rewarded to their fullest and create outstanding financial performance? How could we bring the heart and head goals of the firm into harmony?

Why People Do Not Assess Progress

People and organizations need and want feedback in their pursuits of passionate purpose. Yet, they typically neglect this part of the process. Why?

- Perhaps people don't have enough practice with assessment. They may not know how to assess and so they just continue doing the same old thing.
- Evaluation takes time and people are so busy that they cannot find the time for thoughtful reflection.
- Assessment may lead to change. People prefer the status quo, even if painful, to an unknown outcome.
- In the frantic frenzy of life with constant time pressures, there is a need to cut something out and, on the surface, assessment seems the least important. People do not always value the outcome of the assessment.
- Instead of all parts of ourselves being balanced, one element such as the head or heart overpowers with a biased message, "You are on course. You don't need to assess."

Benefits from Assessment

Evaluating progress offers the following benefits:

- Provides information to put you back on track so that you can more easily get what you really want.
- Saves time because you do not keep doing the wrong things.
- Affirms when you are on course and motivates you.
- Allows for appreciation and rewards for your progress, letting you feel good about your efforts, and frees more energy for the pursuit.

How to Assess Progress

Here are ways to evaluate how things are going in your pursuits. Assessment includes both internal as well as external factors. The best review involves all of you—head, heart, and hands.

Pleasure and Pain

When you are pursuing your chosen purpose—your passion is intense and purpose is clear—you generally feel good (see Chapter 2). When you are indifferent and confused about your purpose, you do not feel as good. People generally prefer pleasure to pain. These emotions provide a simple way to evaluate how things are going. Through them, your heart and hands speak to you.

When something feels good, you are getting a message from your inner voice that you are on course and should continue. When something feels bad, it is a call for change or growth. We all try to avoid pain, but pain is very helpful. Feeling good does not mean that there is no room for improvement. Feeling some pain does not mean you should automatically drop the pursuit; it is a message to take action.

Deliberately assess whether your pursuits are bringing pleasure or pain. Ask your inner voice to speak more clearly through feelings, dreams, coincidences, and even understandable thoughts. While doing the Core Practice (see Appendix B), hold an image of passionate purpose pursuit. Ask yourself, "How do I feel while pursuing my passionate purpose? Good, neutral, or bad?" If you feel bad, some change may be necessary.

My Path.   During my last year at Radish, my pain from the values conflict grew until it was greater than my pleasure. My resistance escalated that pain into great suffering. The bottom line was that I did not feel good, and there was a call for change.

Intrinsic Measures

Do you have ongoing motivation for this passionate purpose? In *Intrinsic Motivation,*[2] Kenneth Thomas explains that four rewards ignite internal enthusiasm—a sense of meaningfulness, choice, competency, and progress. These four elements coincide with the four-stage process of passionate purpose. Use the Thomas Intrinsic Motivation model to assess progress with pursuing passionate purpose:

- *Know and nurture the person.* In getting to know yourself, you discern your values. These values, along with your gifts, define what you will be passionate about and what has meaning for you. Ask yourself, "Do I get a sense of meaningfulness from this pursuit? Is my level of meaningfulness low, medium, or high?" When there is a high level of worth, you will have intrinsic motivation to continue the pursuit. When meaningfulness is lacking and you seem to be wasting your time, there is a call for modification. What can you do to increase your perception that the pursuit is worthwhile?
- *Find passionate purpose.* This stage includes determining a way to align your passions with a worthwhile purpose, and then making the decision to commit to it. Ask yourself, "Do I get a sense of choice for this purpose? Is my level of choice low, medium, or high?" When there is a high level of flexibility and you are driving

the effort, you will have intrinsic motivation to continue. When choice is lacking and you feel constrained, there is a need for change. What can you do to allow more selection and variety?

- *Pursue purpose.* During this stage, you relentlessly work toward your end goal. Ask yourself, "Do I get a sense of competency from this pursuit? Is my level of competency low, medium, or high? When you are meeting high standards and feel proficient, you are more motivated. When you are not meeting your own performance criteria, you should make alterations. What can you do to produce high-quality work?"

- *Assess progress.* The more advancement you perceive toward the destination, the more motivation you have for continuing the journey. Ask yourself, "Do I get a sense of progress from pursuing this passionate purpose? Is my level of progress low, medium, or high?" Significant forward movement spurs continued effort. Monitoring progress toward the purpose tells you whether you are on the right path. If you are stuck, make adjustments. What can you do to stimulate progress? Perhaps you need to change your definition of the purpose and how you are pursuing it.

My Path. I used this model to assess my situation at Radish. Initially, I found tremendous meaning from pursuing this entrepreneurial dream. We were pursuing our head and heart purposes, thereby providing an environment where all people could contribute and be rewarded to their fullest. Over time, circumstances changed and a significant values conflict developed. I could no longer live true to my highest convictions in this environment. As much as I tried to resolve the discord, it ultimately brought my meaningfulness from the work to a low level. The more I pushed toward the end I desired, the more resistance I received, and this began to erode my personal sense of competency in bringing about my dream. As investors took over control of the company, they restricted my choices. Even though my sense of progress with the head purpose of the firm was relatively high, a low sense of meaningfulness, unstable level of competency, and constrained choice in important matters impeded my ability to feel good about staying at Radish.

Sigh and Smile Monitors

Chapter 5 introduced the Smile Monitor to determine how much fun you are having along the way. The Sigh Monitor measures the number of noisy exhalations to establish how much you are dreading the process or feeling stressed out by it. A sigh is an unconscious, natural means by which your body releases tension and takes in more oxygen. Become aware of how frequently you smile or sigh. This monitor uses your hands (physical body) to tangibly measure the pleasure and pain that you are experiencing.

My Path. In the early days of Radish, I couldn't stop smiling. At the end of a day, my cheeks often hurt from smiling so much. Things changed. By the end, I was sighing and internally crying.

Health and Sleep Monitors

Another way to assess your progress is to note your health and sleeping patterns. Since pursuing your purpose, how have you been feeling? Are you healthy or do you get sick often or stay sick for a long time? What is your energy level?

How well are you resting at night? Do you feel energized and refreshed in the morning? Do you have an easy time falling and staying asleep? Do not ignore these physical signs as you move through the stages of your pursuit.

My Path. As tension escalated due to my weakened sense of meaning, choice, and competency, my health suffered. It was extremely difficult to fall asleep and get a good night's rest. I had severe headaches and worsening backaches. Ignoring these signals, I continued my relentless drive. To make deadlines, I worked until two in the morning for weeks without taking a day off. My expectations for my staff and myself were unreasonably high. Meditation helped replenish some of my energy, but I was on a collision course to get very ill. Could I stop before crashing?

Force Field Analysis

As highlighted in this section, a force field analysis is useful for both personal and organizational situations. Conduct an analysis by determining the positive and negative forces impacting the current situation. Use this information to better understand what needs to change.

Feedback from Others

People, both supportive and unsupportive, can provide useful information to help in assessment.

My Path. To cope with the unbelievable stress, I saw a personal therapist who helped me see my situation as a train on a deadly collision course.

Others, including my staff, women's group, a professional group of organization development consultants, the management team, and especially Dick, offered helpful feedback and suggestions. Knowing more than anyone the challenges in the situation, Dick said that he would support me in whatever decision I made.

Life Circumstances

For some people, life events or uncontrollable circumstances bring the messages needed for assessment. David Hofmockel, a professional engineer, was recently laid off from his technical position with an established firm. It was not unexpected as the economy and company had signaled this possibility. Having prepared properly by taking the Pursuit of Passionate Purpose workshop before the pink slip arrived, Dave was open to opportunities and ready for change. He enrolled in massage therapy school and is happier than ever, pursuing a new passionate purpose as a certified massage therapist. Life brought him the circumstances to assess and then change. Now integrating his engineering gifts into his new work, he expanded into developing of products for the massage industry.

A Tracking and Instant Feedback System

There are ways to show progress and determine whether you are on track. Many organizations and people use graphs, charts, or lists. It is hard to miss the progress you have or have not made when you post it on the wall or see some tangible representation.

As described in Chapter 3, author Jim Collins tracks progress with large projects by moving a tag across a U.S. wall map using the metaphor of a journey across the country. The tracking system provides instant feedback of "walking 10 miles each day," and making progress. For my projects, I use a graphic image of a circular journey, much like the four-stage process, to provide assessment of forward movement.

My Path. At Radish, we used standard project management tracking charts to represent progress and keep everyone informed. We also shared monthly financial comparisons of planned to actual operating projections during team and board meetings.

Other Methods

Perhaps you have another method that helps you determine how things are going. Everyone is different. For one person, the best method is the number of anxiety attacks or nightmares. For another person, it is the number of arguments with significant others or compliments received. Whatever method you use, be aware and willing to listen to the message.

Using the Progress Inventory

So how do you assess progress with your purpose? One way is the Progress Inventory, shown in Table 6.1, which combines the various approaches to provide an overall assessment. Use it to assess how your pursuit is going.

Depending on the total points, you must then decide what standard feels right and what elements of assessment are the most relevant. Only you can decide what the assessment means for your pursuit.

You may want to complete the instrument again, reflecting on how often the statements would have described you during a different stage in the project. Is there a downward trend, upward trend, or is it the same? What made the difference between then and now? This can provide insights into areas that need attention.

Now look at individual statements. If you scored 1 or 2 on any one of them, focus on improving these elements as you continue the pursuit.

When to Assess Progress

Build assessment into your plan as an ongoing task. Schedule it for certain times of the year such as New Year's Day, the end of a quarter, your birthday, or at other critical points.

The material for assessment is present all the time. Yet, it is difficult for people to see, hear, and feel the internal and external messages without bias. The information for assessment comes to us through a natural escalation process. At first, messages are subtle. Then communication becomes louder. Even if you conduct regular assessments, you may have sudden wake-up calls that require you to make changes.

Pivotal Points

Assessment and the call for change can happen instantly like a lightning bolt. Pivotal points are wake-up calls that you cannot ignore like earlier quieter and gentler messages.

If we do not hear the escalating messages for change that come as we move along our journey, pivotal points are inevitable. We do not have to wait for them to put us back on track to pursue the top priority passionate

Table 6.1 Progress Inventory

Identify a purpose you are pursuing: _____

Based on your perception of pursuing this purpose, indicate how OFTEN each statement describes who you are. Using a 1–5 scale where 1 is rarely and 5 is most of the time, write the appropriate number of points in the corresponding column. Sum all the numbers to get your Progress total.

Don't overanalyze; record your initial reaction to the statement.

Purpose I am pursuing: _____ _____	Rarely or Never	Seldom	Sometimes	Frequently	Most or All of Time
Number of points per response in this column	1	2	3	4	5
1. Pursuing this purpose makes me feel good.					
2. I have choice in this pursuit.					
3. I feel competent.					
4. I have the energy to do what I need to do.					
5. I smile more than sigh.					
6. Compared with my normal sleep patterns, I am sleeping well.					
7. I feel physically healthy and strong.					
8. I am making good progress.					
9. My time is spent on something worthwhile.					
10. Messages from people I trust and from life in general encourage me.					
Total points = _____					

Scoring

The maximum score possible is 50, as a result of giving yourself a 5 on every statement. The minimum is 10. What does the total score mean?

50–41   You are making great progress. Appreciate and keep it up!

40–31   There is forward movement and good indications that you are on track. Some modifications may be in order.

30–21   Progress is limited. There is a call for growth or change. It is time to make some adjustments.

Below 21   Immediate attention is needed. You may be stuck and at a pivotal point in this pursuit. Don't wait—start figuring out what you can do to change the situation now.

purpose in life. The beginning of the year, end of a quarter, or key passages in life are natural times to stop and evaluate.

Wake-Up Call—Jonathan Sawyer's Story

Sawyer was passionately pursuing his purpose in life through the entrepreneurial company he had started with innovative technology. The business was extremely profitable, but required tremendous focus and energy. His life was a stressful juggling act to balance an extensive workload, time with his two young children and wife, his passion for airplanes, and political interests for causes such as alternative energy sources as a way to save the planet. Then he received a loud wake-up call. Over and over again, he had severe chest pains and went to the emergency room. Finally, during the last episode, he learned about his enlarged aorta and dangerously skyrocketing blood pressure. The cardiologist asked him, "Do you want to see your children grow up and eventually marry? If so, you need to make some big changes."

This was a pivotal point in his life. His priorities became clear. He changed course to focus on what was truly meaningful to him—health and family. He sold his airplane, because proper preparation to stay current and fly safely was a big source of stress. He ended his involvement in political debates and arguments, as they only caused his blood pressure to rise. Through

PRACTICAL POINTERS

- *Recognize that assessment is valuable* and provides great benefits.
- *Plan assessments as part of your pursuit.* Write evaluation to-do items into your calendar.
- *Choose one simple measure,* such as the Smile and Sigh Monitor, to use frequently.
- *Tell others, especially your kids and people with whom you work, what progress you see.* This allows them to see movement toward their goals and helps them assess how things are going. Feedback is precious.
- *Recognize the progress you have made and how things are going.* Open your eyes and see it. Notice the small as well as the big movements toward the goal.

an eight-week health program, he changed his diet to lose 40 pounds, began tai chi as a stress reduction technique, and started an appropriate exercise program.

His heart diagnosis was a pivotal point that led him to reevaluate who he is and what he values. He refined his passionate purpose to "healthy living."

RECOGNIZE SUCCESS

What does success look like in the pursuit of passionate purpose? You can choose how you define success. It is helpful to know what it looks like so you will recognize it and move on. Some Passionate Pursuers are so skilled at persistent performance that they need help knowing when to stop and say they are finished. Then they can go in-between and evolve into the next stage of their overall life purpose.

My Path—Defining Success

During this period at Radish, I maintained my integrity of effort. Outside recognition helped boost my sense of progress and self, yet it was difficult to let go of my attachment to a certain definition of success. Only now, as I look back with a clearer perspective, can I recognize the situation as success.

Define Success

André Pettigrew, public administrator, offers a fresh perspective on success: "People need personal victories each and every day. These can be the things that build your endorphins—a smile on a face or a satisfied customer. Some people are only measuring success by home runs. Look at base hits and outs whereby you maintained integrity of effort as victories also."

It is extremely constructive to define success as maintaining your integrity of effort, whether you make your objective or do not make it. Integrity of effort is doing everything possible in the pursuit until there is absolutely no other option. Then in either case, you must move on.

As one trait of effective Passionate Pursuers, integrity of effort strengthens your whole self. Consider James Allen's wisdom,[3] "Even if he fails again and again to accomplish his purpose, the strength of character gained will be the measure of his true success, and this will form a new starting point for future power and triumph."

If you maintained integrity of effort and did everything possible in reaching the purpose, then moving on is not a failure. It is success. As explained by author Jim Collins's story in Chapter 3, his victory comes from maintaining integrity of effort, whether or not he has realized the intention. Fallure is not failure. Both fallure and making the goal are success. Collins also chooses to define success in life in his own terms,[4] "The ultimate definition of success in life is that your spouse likes and respects you ever more as the years go by."

You have a choice in how you define success. Moving on may just be the next step in your process.

PRACTICAL POINTERS

- *Review.* Look back and revisit the joys and sorrows. What did you learn? What will you do differently next time around?
- *Appreciate.* Make sure you celebrate, reward, and recognize before moving on. Celebration provides a sense of completion and frees energy for the next pursuit. Honor and thank all those who have helped you with this pursuit.
- *Create an ending.* Determine what and when is the best way to stop. Then say, "The End!"
- *Go in-between.* Give yourself a change to renew by going into a neutral zone before embracing the next part of your life journey.

APPRECIATE

Appreciate the progress you have made in your pursuit and the people who have supported you. Again André Pettigrew, public administrator, has wise advice: "Don't lose sight of the little things—the photos, thank you notes, and awards—that remind you of a personal victory. Be prepared to go back and review these, if necessary. They might be the fuel, or spark, for the next effort." As the cliché describes it, it is far easier to see the glass half empty than to see it half full. Even when you have made significant forward movement or succeeded, there is a tendency to focus on what you still need to do or on the next goal. You may lose a great opportunity to replenish, reenergize, and reaffirm the purpose toward which you and the people around you are working.

My Path—Reap Real Rewards

Seeing the fruits of our labor, the delivery of a quality VoiceView solution to real customers, was one of the best rewards. Our users' delight in the product demonstrated our competence as well as progress toward our bigger goal, building a financially successful company that would help people communicate more effectively.

We chose to reward every employee with stock options. While salaries and bonuses were constrained as the company struggled to become profitable, each employee received a piece of the action. There were many other nonfinancial rewards such as being part of the Radish family, building strong relationships with all the players, and making a difference in growing something special. The real rewards included meaningfulness and choice.

In addition to big rewards such as signed sales contracts and recognition in media coverage, smaller forms of acknowledgment were also gratifying. The annual company photographs displayed on our facility walls showed how we had grown from two cofounders to over 60 dedicated employees in just a few years. Our building, designed and built especially for Radish, was quite an improvement over where we started in my house. In our entranceway, we displayed with special care, the awards we received from a wide variety of publications and trade shows. Each of these and many more symbols acknowledged that we were making noteworthy progress on a daily basis.

We were blessed with much to celebrate. We found ways to enjoy ourselves—regular Friday after-work happy hours, parties after the release of a new product, and annual family picnics.

Reward, Recognize, and Celebrate

Keep in mind the advice of Rachel Snyder[5] in *365 Words of Well-Being for Women:* "Celebrate anything you want. Celebrate the start of something, the end of something. Celebrate early, celebrate late, and celebrate often."

Rewards

Material items such as bonuses, gifts, and financial compensation are not the only rewards, yet we are programmed through society to use them as the measure of success. You can feel appreciated from feedback, compliments, and being involved in decision making.[6] *The 1001 Rewards & Recognition Fieldbook*[7] provides many other suggestions to keep workers happy with their jobs.

The Radish management team celebrates receiving the first payment from a real customer.

126

As discussed under Intrinsic Measures, the most important rewards are typically internal and come from work that offers a sense of meaning, choice, competency, and progress.

Recognition

Most people thrive on acknowledgment. Being appreciated feels good. Whether a voice mail message of gratitude or a public thank-you, people like to receive credit and praise for their contributions. Recognition helps energize you for the pursuit and keeps the fire burning.

Celebration

To celebrate means to commemorate with appropriate rites and ceremonies, honor, make known publicly, proclaim, rejoice, and make merry. There is no limit to how your creativity can run wild in commemoration.

Appreciate Those Who Helped

Who, in the foreground or in the background, helps you follow your dreams? It may be time to send thanks and appreciation to many fellow beings, spiritual forces, and yourself. Progress is not possible without the efforts of others. You don't do it alone. Acknowledge the help from yourself and others. Send gratitude.

You

The hardest person to appreciate can be you. Too often, you ignore your own effort. For me, a yearned-for reward is a long, uninterrupted night of deep sleep followed by exercise outside. Another prize is time to pamper myself with a facial or massage, a date with my biggest supporter, and moments with my closest friends. There are no nasty to-do items during this period; instead I set aside time to cuddle with my daughter Annie, read a special book, and play a duet on the piano. How do you reward yourself?

Do you take time to reward yourself? Are you like me and delay the gratification too long? Delayed gratification is learned through decades of completing work projects and college assignments. My trip to Africa during the Radish days was an overdue reward for completing the previous purpose. So yes, as Nathan Thompson tells us in Chapter 9, "learn delayed gratification," but also fulfill your promises to yourself and deliver on the hard-earned rewards.

Tested Technique

Try the Appreciation Meditation in Appendix B, which is a variation on ancient loving kindness meditations,[8] to express gratitude to self and others. Incorporate it or some other form of appreciation into your daily practices.

PRACTICAL POINTERS

- *Reaffirm* the value in appreciating progress and smooth going.
- *Reward your progress.* Determine ways to justly remunerate. Especially incorporate intrinsic rewards for yourself, and when possible, support others in receiving these rewards, too.
- *Appreciate fellow beings, spiritual forces, and yourself*—all those who helped you achieve progress. Don't delay gratification too much. Try the Appreciation Meditation.
- *Be creative* and acknowledge progress in a variety of ways.
- *Celebrate every success and turn failure into opportunities.* Be your own scorekeeper and cheerleader.

MAKE ADJUSTMENTS

God, give us the grace to accept with serenity the things that cannot be changed, courage to change the things which should be changed, and the wisdom to distinguish the one from the other.

REINHOLD NIEBUHR, The Serenity Prayer[9]

After assessing your progress, use this information to make adjustments, if needed. Consider what's next. Either you recognize success and move on or continue pursuing this passionate purpose, with or without some changes. Either way, adjustments are necessary.

Follow your heart, along with your head and hands. Trust that you will know when the time is right to continue or move on. Just like the cycle of life, each pursuit has a natural beginning, middle, and end.

My Path—Unresolved Conflict

My assessment led me to the painful conclusion that the situation was intolerable.

Try to Change the Situation

I tried everything I could to change the situation, it was that important to me. I confronted the values issue directly in subtle and not so subtle ways. I escalated it to the very top of management and the board of directors. This just caused more stress for everyone. The people who could make changes, chose to ignore the situation because they did not agree that the behavior violated critical standards. It was a matter of values definition and priority.

Influence Where Possible

Since I had limited influence in the bigger matter, I focused on my own department where I had authority. I got involved in the smallest decisions. My constant oversight made staff feel that I did not trust them or their work. It didn't matter if my efforts might make a better final end product, I was killing their motivation and drive with my overzealous management.

I realized I had to take positive action for change and hired an organization development consultant to help. At an off-site retreat, we dealt with building trust and open communications. I promised to back off and give staff room to do their work—I could at least make some personal changes. Things seemed on a better track in my department.

Live with It

Although I tried to change the values situation, I had not resolved the conflict to honor both the head and heart purposes. I felt my only option was to live with it for Radish's sake. Then a different opportunity knocked.

Continue

Assessment may indicate progress is being made and continuation is appropriate. When you continue, there are two situations. Either all is well and you carry on as is or things are not okay and there is need for some change. When not okay, there are two options:

1. First, try to change the situation with some midcourse modifications.
2. If that does not work, maintain your integrity of effort and live with the situation as it is.

Change

You are still committed to the purpose, but changes are required to get you there and perhaps in what is an acceptable outcome. Flexibility is key.

Pain in itself is not necessarily bad and does not mean giving up. It just sig-
nifies the need to alter how you are getting to where you want to go. The
most difficult challenge is figuring out what and how to change. Often
the only thing you can change is yourself—your attitude and behavior.

Making change may not be easy. To this end, there are entire graduate
courses on change management. One approach is to conduct a force field
analysis, as shown in this chapter, and then use this information to determine
how to alleviate the negative forces hindering progress. Another approach is
the Polarity Strategy, which honors opposites and allows dynamic movement between two or more options (see Chapter 7).

Live with the Situation

Sometimes the best course of action is to hold on and to live with the situation. Perhaps you have tried everything you can think of to change the
situation to no avail, but you are not ready, willing, or able to let go completely. So you let go of some of your resistance to the situation and find a
way to hang on. Try living with the situation:

- When the pain is bearable and you still anticipate a meaningful outcome.
- When the end is in sight and the goal is attainable, if only you continue. In other words, there is some progress and you have hope of
  finishing.
- When some part of the pursuit is providing some nourishment, motivation, or meaning. Perhaps it is not deeply meaningful, does not
  provide you choice, shows little progress, and you are not meeting
  your own performance standards, but you are still getting a pay-
  check. This can be meaningful when the bills are due and other employment options are limited (see Joe Rush's story in Chapter 12).
- When there is no other available option.

Use the Allowing Strategy to more easily allow yourself to live with a difficult situation (see Chapter 10).

Move On

If you succeed or if you cannot change it or live with it, eventually it will
be time to move on and let go further. This may call for refining the overall general intention and the specific purpose you are pursuing. This may

allow you to progress to the next purpose or to take a break in-between. It is just the cycle of life and of everything in the Universe.

How Do You Know When the Time Is Right?

Think of the cycles of life. There is a beginning, middle, and end to each day, year, and life itself. So, too, there is a cycle with pursuits of passionate purpose. Even if you learn how to pursue a purpose, there still comes a time to allow yourself to move on to the next stage of the purpose or life. Depending on the cause, the work may be complete or the time may be right to move on.

> *Letting go comes from the heart. As long as there is a spark in the heart and the vision feels right, stay with it. Once the spark in the heart dies and it feels heavy, like duty or an obligation, you may need to evolve.*
>
> MARGOT ZAHER, life coach[10]

Most people feel that it is sometimes required but difficult to do. You will know that letting go is necessary when:

- You have achieved your purpose, intention, or goal.
- You have tried everything else and the assessment still comes back "not okay."
- The passion is not there, you have exhausted 100 percent of the options and all of your energy, and you are not making progress. You try, try, and try some more, but receive no positive feedback and see no progress.
- Your head and heart, speaking through your body, tell you. Using intuition and insight, you just know.
- You reach the pivotal point.
- It stops being fun.
- Life circumstances close this door.

Figure Out What's Next

Eventually moving on from Radish helped me to have a vision of my next passionate purpose—the Baby Plan. Author Jim Collins noted that finding the next project, helps him let go. Bridget Jeffrey, management consultant, advises, "It is easier to let go when you have the next thing figured out, and this is easier to do in jobs than in relationships."

For some people, moving on to something else may not be feasible, but if it is possible, a change can help. Select something, even if it is not your do-all and end-all purpose, and let that occupy you. Having something else on which to focus your attention helps you realize that there is more in life.

Follow the Phoenix Factor

Moving on from one purpose, when the time is right, does not necessarily mean that your passion dies. Just like the Phoenix, the unique mythical bird fabled to have lived 500 years or more, you can choose to rise from the ashes and live through another passionate pursuit of purpose. Eventually after taking a break in-between, you can move on to reaffirm who you are and find another purpose. Josephine Heath, stateswoman and community leader, recommends, "Read about and listen to other people who have successfully moved beyond difficult situations."

There are times when life slams a door shut. In hiring to fill a certain position, only one person is likely to be selected. In elections, one person wins and others lose. While there is always tomorrow and the next election could be a possibility in some situations, the dream of winning is shattered for now. Josephine Heath, the community leader and former politician who lost her bid for the U.S. Senate, has suggestions for moving beyond. "When should you let go? If it feels bad and you 'don't have the stomach.' Rely on good instinct. Be practical. It is the hardest to let go when there is a principle behind the pursuit. In running for the U.S. Senate, I realized that you either end up on the cover of *Time* magazine or in a dark basement forgotten. How can you be resilient and land on your feet? It helps to think of Eleanor Roosevelt's[10] comment, 'No one can make you feel inferior without your consent.' And then redefine yourself."

PRACTICAL POINTERS

- *Determine.* If you are continuing, envision the optimal outcome. What do you want to change? Start by discerning, if possible, from where the change needs to come: inside you, outside you from the situation or other people, or both.
- *Analyze.* As one method to understand what adjustments might help, conduct a force field analysis[11] or Polarity Map® (see Chapter 7) of the current situation.

- *Broaden.* If you are living with it, take hold of a bigger purpose or larger intention. Find something meaningful in continuing.
- *Divide.* If you are living with it, do what you need to do "a day at a time," knowing you will make a change as soon as you can. Take it in small chunks, day by day. Use the Persistence Strategy's divide-and-conquer tactic.
- *Allow.* If you are continuing, living with it, or moving on, drop resistance and attachment to the exact outcome. Use the Allowing Strategy.
- *Find.* Nourish your passions from other parts of your life. Give yourself and others options. Have something else to embrace. Follow the Phoenix Factor—there is a life beyond this passionate purpose. Determine what's next.

APPLY TO REAL PURSUITS

Is it time for you to assess your progress? Do not wait too long. Here's an example of one business woman's assessment and subsequent response.

From Frying Pan into Fire—Liz Valles's Story

Liz Valles thought she had made it. As a finance executive of a Fortune 500 company, she had arrived—or so it seemed—with designer suits, gold watches, and other symbols of success. Yet, something wasn't working. The stress from long workweeks along with the lack of a personal life took their toll. Accidents and illnesses told her that she was on the wrong path. So she quit and became the controller for a growing entrepreneurial venture. And she began hiking again. Surely this would provide more balance and satisfaction in life. But it didn't; she had simply exchanged one stress for another.

Not until Valles fell off a 17-foot cliff, did she wake up to how miserable she was. She survived the fall and realized that she needed big changes in her professional and personal lives. Her head had dominated her decisions to this point. Finally, her heart broke through crying out to be heard, "Follow your heart. Live your passions."

Although she didn't know it, Valles started the *Assess Progress* stage when she fell off the cliff. Realizing that she was not happy, she let go of her frenzied corporate life. She embarked on the *Know and Nurture the Person* stage. She stopped working, healed physically and, through travel, explored who she was and what was important to her. She had neglected an important part of herself—her love of music and singing. But how could she pursue that and make a living? During the *Find Passionate Purpose* stage, she found the answer. Valles started Calico Consulting that provides accounting and financial management services to firms that only need a part-time controller. In addition, she became the manager and lead singer in her band, Deji Blu. Immersed in the *Pursue Purpose* stage, she followed her heart to live her dream.

Had Valles arrived? Her journey brought her back around to the *Assess Progress* stage. How could she run two businesses and maintain balance? Valles made some midcourse corrections. By letting go of doing so much herself, she found a way to sustain the pace.

SUMMARY

- This chapter explores the *Assess Progress* stage of the process: Evaluate progress, recognize success, appreciate, and then make necessary adjustments.
- Assessment is an important, often neglected part of the pursuit of passionate purpose. Benefits from assessment include saving time and efficiently getting back on track.
- Assessment methods rely on both internal and external factors.
  —Internal assessment approaches include monitoring:
    - Pain and pleasure.
    - Intrinsic measures of meaningfulness, choice, competency, and progress.
    - Smiles and sighs.
    - Health and sleep.
    - Force field analysis.
  —External assessment is based on:
    - Feedback from others.
    - Life circumstances.
    - Tracking systems with immediate feedback.
- Use the Progress Inventory to assess forward movement in your pursuits.

- Once you recognize success or some progress, then appreciate it. Rewards, recognition, and celebration are ways to appreciate progress and reenergize the pursuit. Appreciate yourself, other people, and spiritual forces that helped you along the way.
- Assessment may indicate that you should recognize success and move on or continue the pursuit, as is or with changes. When the situation is not okay, your options include continuing with midcourse adjustments, living with it, or moving on.
- All pursuits have a beginning, middle, and end, just like all cycles of life. Sometimes it is necessary, albeit difficult, to move on.
- The time is right to let go if you have reached your purpose, there are no other options, you are in a doom loop with no positive progress, your inner self tells you to let go, you reach a pivotal point, you are not enjoying the process, or life circumstances slam the door.

PART THREE

APPLY SUCCESS STRATEGIES

Premise: Universal strategies help things work more effectively.

Path: Use of the strategies.

Outcome: Progress and knowledge of how things work.

Use six success strategies to help you flow smoothly through the Pursuit of Passionate Purpose process. These strategies, called Polarity, Attraction, Persistence, Allowing, Connections, and Pack, are principles of operation and lubrication that maximize your progress.

7

Polarity
Strategy

Premise: Polarities exist in all of life, including in ourselves.

Path: Honor opposites in life and allow dynamic movement between interdependent poles.

Outcome: Harmony, stability, and energy.

Polarities are part of everything in life, including ourselves. People mention tensions between their head and heart, between making a living and making a difference, between family and work. Effective Passionate Pursuers can balance opposing parts of themselves, organizations, or systems. Instead of seeing a polarity as a problem to solve, honor opposites in life and encourage dynamic movement between interdependent poles. The synergy of two or more poles working together in harmony is stronger and more stable than that of one side working alone.

WHAT YOU CAN GET FROM THIS CHAPTER

Whether we know it or not, we all experience polarities and can benefit from using the Polarity Strategy. As Passionate Pursuers encounter challenges in their pursuits, they can more effectively discern when polarities exist and can use alternative approaches for managing them. Seekers will find the Polarity Strategy useful in resolving conflicts in values or in possible purposes. In-between'ers can experiment with these techniques and be ready to apply them to future pursuits.

My Path—Natural Rhythm in the Right Environment

"You promised," my heart cried out. It was nearly four years since I had finished my degree and promised myself to travel to Africa as a reward. I was totally engulfed in running Radish, yet the pledge was still unfulfilled. The heart does not forget such agreements.

Then the Universe delivered the opportunity. Friends who were going to East Africa to climb Kilimanjaro asked me to travel with them.

"Yes!" my heart sang out in glee. "You will meet the gorillas, see all of the animals, and climb Kili, too."

"But how can you leave Radish for three weeks just as we are updating the business plan and getting ready to attract more funding?" my head insisted.

Like the tensions at Radish, the battle between my head and heart was getting more intense. Perhaps because my head was so tired from constant professional conflicts, my heart triumphed.

As I lingered savoring our last hug, Dick gave me a farewell card with the message from the *Little Prince*,[1] "It is only with the heart that one sees rightly. What is essential is invisible to the eye." It is really with the head and heart in harmony that one sees rightly, but for now, I was following my heart.

Before long, I stood in the open-topped safari jeep, speeding along, and sang "Born Free" as loudly as possible while the wind raced through my hair. The wild animals of Kenya encouraged me, thousands of beasts for as far as you could see. The gentle gorillas of Rwanda touched my soul. I connected with the calm zebras, drinking from a lake. Coyotes howled as a full moon rose and the campfire danced, as did my spirit. Fulfilling this promise replenished me. As my heart began to trust my head again, I moved toward wholeness.

Preparation met possibility, and I committed to climb the tallest peak in Africa. I used the 50-mile, 5-day trek as a minipursuit of passionate purpose. My spirit companion, as usual, guided me to the top as I meditated on body sensations, mental images, and internal talk. Bitterly cold from the frigid winds, yet warmed by the thrill of making the goal, I rediscovered my integrated self at the summit of Kilimanjaro (see page 4).

By rediscovering my inner rhythm through this physical activity and meditation in the right environment, I rebuilt confidence in my integrated self. However, it only provided temporary balancing of my head/heart polarity. When I returned to the workplace, I again found uncontrollable obstacles blocking this balance. This indicated that the right environment makes a big difference. If only I had such a direct way to bring the tensions at Radish into harmony.

ABOUT POLARITIES

You cannot live without recognizing opposites. Opposites create balance.

MARTHA ARNETT, retired university secretary

People have been aware of opposites, or polarities, in life for millennia, yet most Western educational programs teach little about this concept. Over 3,000 years ago, Lao Tzu wrote about the natural law of polarities in China's most loved book, the *Tao Te Ching:*[2] "Under heaven all can see beauty as beauty only because there is ugliness. All can know good as good only because there is evil." This timeless wisdom of how things work is still potent today.

John Heider in *The Tao of Leadership*[3] translated these ideas for Western culture. He explains, "All behavior consists of opposites or polarities. If I do anything more and more, over and over, its polarity will appear."

Polarity is healthy, unavoidable, unsolvable, indestructible, and omnipresent. Yet, too often people see difficulties as problems that they must solve by choosing either one or the other pole. There are many occasions when one pole is insufficient; the best solution is to manage the opposites as a dynamic system whose components are interdependent parts of the same whole. Managing polarities is an addition to problem solving, and not a replacement.

Examples of Polarities

Polarities are fundamental in our lives. Rahima Baldwin Dancy, in *You Are Your Child's First Teacher,*[4] describes their omnipresence: "We are surrounded by rhythm in nature: the phases of the moon, the cycle of the seasons, the ebb and flow of the tides. Our bodies are permeated by rhythm, in the beating of our hearts and the circadian rhythms of our metabolism."

In situations where polarities are balanced, a rhythm appears. Take the expansive and contractive breathing cycles in Barry Johnson's seminal work about managing polarities.[5] What's better—breathing in or breathing out? Neither is better. Both are needed to exist. Exhalation and inhalation are not static, but part of "an ongoing flow of shifting emphasis from one to the other and back again. Managing polarities requires choosing BOTH inhaling AND exhaling."

Consider other polarities within yourself:

- *In the head:* Left and right brain and control and letting go.
- *In the heart:* Pleasurable and painful emotions such as love and hate and joy and sorrow.
- *In the hands:* Beating of your heart making blood flow in and out and women's cycles allowing fertility and nonfertility.
- *As a whole:* Head and heart, Yin and Yang,[6] make a contribution and make a living, as well as the four pairs of personality preferences in the Myers-Briggs Type Indicator[7]—extravert and introvert, intuitive and sensing, thinking and feeling, and perceptive and judging.

Consider other polarities that surround you:

- *In relationships:* Caring for self and caring for others.
- *In organizations:* Centralization and decentralization, team and individual, and autocratic and participatory management.
- *In community and society:* Group and individual, equality and freedom, and capitalism and socialism.
- *In nature:* Day and night, ebb and flow of the tides, and wet and dry.

Some polarities are chosen, such as being at work and being at home. Other polarities are intrinsic, such as activity and rest. Since polarities are part of everything, expect to find them in the Pursuit of Passionate Purpose approach. In setting a purpose or intent, you need to consider the results or impact—this is the intent/impact polarity. Within the Persistence Strategy's divide-and-conquer tactic, there is the whole/part polarity. Within the Connections Strategy, there is a self/group polarity as well as the engage certain people/avoid certain people polarity. Within the Pack Strategy, there is the energizer/hindrance polarity. Persistence and Allowing Strategies are a polarity.

Benefits from Balance

As Barry Johnson notes in *Polarity Management™ Identifying and Managing Unsolvable Problems,*[8] when polarities are managed effectively, you "get the best of both opposites while avoiding the limits of each. The research is clear—leaders and organizations that manage polarities well outperform those that do not." The synergy of two poles working together in harmony results in improved effectiveness in managing complexity, change, conflict, chronic issues, and cross-cultural issues.

Virginia Corsi, management consultant, finds benefits in seeking balance: "My purpose in life is to find balance between both sides—my head and heart, my feminine and masculine. Following Gandhi's wisdom that 'my life is my work,' I strive to live my life as an example of my values, and to write a new script for women."

When the polarities are not stabilized in some rhythm that taps and utilizes the inherit tension, the tension leads to dysfunctional conflict. An enormous amount of human energy is wasted in unnecessary conflict. When you diminish the conflict, it frees up tremendous energy for more productive pursuits.

The Need to Balance Polarities

Polarities are everywhere. Balance between them can occur naturally without intervention as in breathing in and out. At other times, blockages impede the movement. Thus, balancing polarities really means removing resistance to this flow by incorporating the wisdom of each pole.

Many people in my study, both men and women, sense a tension between various parts of themselves. Conflict, or lack of balance, with polarities is real. Most people seek to balance these polarities. Some who were not balanced in earlier years, moved with experience toward improved management of polarities. The few people in this study who do not experience unnecessary conflict tend to be over 60 years old.

All of us at times get out of balance. Our education systems teach problem solving, and neglect polarity balancing as another option. People do not recognize polarities and do not know how to manage them.

If there is ongoing pain, discomfort, or tension, you are getting a message that some attention is needed. A continuing difficulty that does not go away may be a polarity to manage and not a problem to solve.

Are two or more interdependent alternatives both required over time to attain your bigger purpose? If the predicament is ongoing, there is a good chance there is an underlying polarity worth attention. With the breathing example, there is an interdependent relationship between the poles; you need both inhaling and exhaling to live. Barry Johnson explains,[9]

"In order to gain and maintain the benefits of one pole, you must also pursue the benefits of the other. The ability to inhale the greatest amount of fresh air requires that first you exhale as completely as possible." Although inhalation and exhalation are opposites, they are united into a whole.

HOW TO BALANCE POLARITIES

Resolving the polarity between left and right brain, head and heart, is the key to happiness in life.

NATHAN THOMPSON, data storage entrepreneur

Managing polarities is a continuous process of embracing both interdependent poles in a way that does not dilute either pole. To keep the system in balance, you must be able to dynamically and freely move between the poles. Balancing polarity really means honoring opposites in life.

When polarities are balanced, there is rhythm, a regular recurrence of elements in an action or function.

My Path—Balancing Head and Heart Polarity

A look at my head and heart during and after Radish days shows how polarities work. My head energy, as one pole, was the rational, logical thinker focused on accomplishment and outcome-oriented doing. My heart energy, as the opposite pole, focused on building relationships and nurturing a supportive culture.[10]

For the first few years, these interdependent poles operated in balance and were strong. My founding mother energy, in line with the heart purpose of an environment where all could contribute and be rewarded, encouraged a collaborative, workplace that felt like a family. My entrepreneurial drive at Radish, in line with the head purpose of financial success through innovation, brought extraordinary results and achievement through efficient, concrete, rational, decisive behaviors. The positive results of both poles were present. A Polarity Map representing the upside and downside of each pole for my situation is given in Figure 7.1.[11]

Things began to change with the new management's primary focus on the new business model and head purpose to the neglect of the heart purpose. As I overfocused on my head pole, the downside or negative result of this pole became more apparent. Some people perceived me as an overbearing, relentless workaholic who had to be in control. Even though

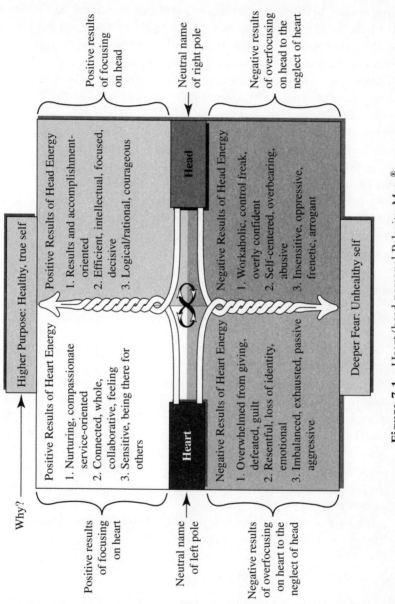

Figure 7.1 Heart/head personal Polarity Map.®

Why?

Higher Purpose: Healthy, true self

Positive results of focusing on heart

Positive Results of Heart Energy

1. Nurturing, compassionate service-oriented
2. Connected, whole, collaborative, feeling
3. Sensitive, being there for others

Positive Results of Head Energy

1. Results and accomplishment-oriented
2. Efficient, intellectual, focused, decisive
3. Logical/rational, courageous

Positive results of focusing on head

Neutral name of right pole

Head

Heart

Neutral name of left pole

Negative Results of Heart Energy

1. Overwhelmed from giving, defeated, guilt
2. Resentful, loss of identity, emotional
3. Imbalanced, exhausted, passive aggressive

Negative Results of Head Energy

1. Workaholic, control freak, overly confident
2. Self-centered, overbearing, abusive
3. Insensitive, oppressive, frenetic, arrogant

Negative results of overfocusing on head to the neglect of heart

Negative results of overfocusing on heart to the neglect of head

Deeper Fear: Unhealthy self

145

my trip to Africa allowed me to temporarily find balance between my head and heart, I was no longer in a situation at work to balance my head with corresponding heart energy. With my perceived movement to the downside of the head pole and the inability to move to the heart pole in the Radish environment, there was such conflict between the workplace and myself that I ultimately had to leave Radish to resolve the clash.

After leaving, I began to nurture my feeling side and moved, over time, to experience the upside of the heart pole with emphasis on the Baby Plan and then the Service Plan. As I became exhausted from giving in this mode, I moved into the heart's downside. Eventually, needing to reignite my whole spirit, my head called for more attention. I started consulting, speaking, conducting research, and writing again, and moved back to the upside of the head pole, while still being a mother and volunteer.

Signified by the infinity loop in Figure 7.1, a natural movement occurred between my poles once I reduced my resistance. The tension between my heart and head is not unique, but one that many people experience as a polarity.[12]

Practical Approach

Here are four practical steps to balancing polarities:

1. *Learn*. Acknowledge that polarities exist in life. Learn how polarities work.
2. *Question*. Consider whether you have a polarity to balance or a problem to solve. Is there ongoing conflict between interdependent poles? Can you move freely between the poles? If yes to both questions, then continue to balance polarities with the following steps. If no, you probably have a problem to solve, not a polarity to manage.
3. *Move*. Do what you can to encourage movement between the poles. Approaches vary with the circumstances and range from awareness to action planning.
4. *Monitor and correct*. How is it working? What have you learned? Refine your approach to encourage movement.

Ways to Encourage Movement

Try different methods to see what works best for you and your situation. Some of the following approaches may only be effective in certain situations, whereas "Analyze and Take Action" will work with all polarities.

Become Aware and Set Intention

Sometimes just becoming aware that a polarity exists and there is a need to embrace both poles stimulates ongoing movement between the poles. By setting the intention to give attention to each side over time, a natural rhythm can appear. André Pettigrew's story later in this chapter shows the results this method brought. Unfortunately, it is not always so easy.

Set a Schedule

Other times, schedules are needed to establish and maintain the movement between poles. The schedule is a means to recognize and honor rhythms and avoid getting stuck in one pole.

Some people find rhythm in a recurring personal schedule with regular times for waking, meals, exercise, work, family, quiet, play, part-time passions, and sleep. A daily, weekly, monthly, and seasonal rhythm stabilizes and strengthens your core. For me, if it is 7 A.M., breakfast calls. If it is Sunday morning, fellowship at church beckons. If it is the first Saturday of the month, it is time for the National Speakers Association meeting. Use calendars, reminder notes, or other scheduling devices to keep you on track.

We can coordinate and stabilize our work life with daily, weekly, seasonal, and other cyclical schedules. The fiscal year and tax periods are key for financial reporting. There are five-year business planning and annual operational budgeting cycles. Product development, market launch, and project management run on organized timelines as do team gatherings, board meetings, sales conferences, and user groups.

Analyze and Take Action

Often with complex, reoccurring difficulties, it is not sufficient to use the first two mentioned approaches: set intention or set a schedule. The Polarity Management method developed by Barry Johnson[13] provides a useful technique to understand the situation and determine the necessary interventions. Try these four steps:

1. *Involve.* Get the proper people from your support web involved. Especially include those who have some stake in the balance of the polarity—the ones affected by or able to balance the polarity. Don't work alone.
2. *Map.* Begin to analyze the difficulty or situation by writing it down. Divide a sheet of paper into four quadrants. Create a Polarity Map similar to that in Figure 7.1. What really is in conflict? What is the

nature of the struggle? Give yourself some time and realize this understanding comes through an iterative process.

- Identify left and right interdependent poles and give them neutral names. Try many alternatives, if the names of poles are not obvious.
- List in the upper quadrants the positive results of focusing on each pole. This is the upside of the pole.
- List in the lower quadrants the negative results of overfocusing on each pole to the neglect of the other pole. This is the pole's downside.

3. *Make an action plan.* Identify possible actions that allow movement between the poles.
- List action steps you can take to gain the positive results of each pole.
- List specific, observable, and measurable indicators, or Red Flags, that show you are in the downside of each pole.

4. *Take action.* When the negative results of a pole begin to appear, it is a sign to take action to move to the positive quadrant of the other pole. When you start noticing Red Flags on the downside of one pole, take the action steps for the other pole.

My Path—Balancing Radish's Head and Heart Purposes

A key Radish polarity revolved around the duality of simultaneous purposes. On one side was the heart purpose: to create an environment based on our core values where all people could contribute and be rewarded to the fullest. On the other was the head purpose: to create a financially successful company delivering innovative technology that improves the way people communicate. Figure 7.2 shows the Radish purpose Polarity Map with action steps from my perspective and presents the positive and negative results from a focus on either pole.[14]

Additionally, Figure 7.2 shows action steps that could have achieved the positive results of both poles. When Red Flags of the head purpose appeared, management could have taken action steps for the other pole. This would have encouraged movement between purposes allowing a dynamic balancing of the polarity.

Radish mostly operated in the upside of both poles. However, in my opinion, as the firm overly focused on financial results to survive, the Red Flags were raised from the downside of the head pole. In the unhealthy work environment, conflicts developed because a few employees behaved poorly, some attractive candidates chose not to be considered for employment, and rumors surfaced in the marketplace about not wanting to do

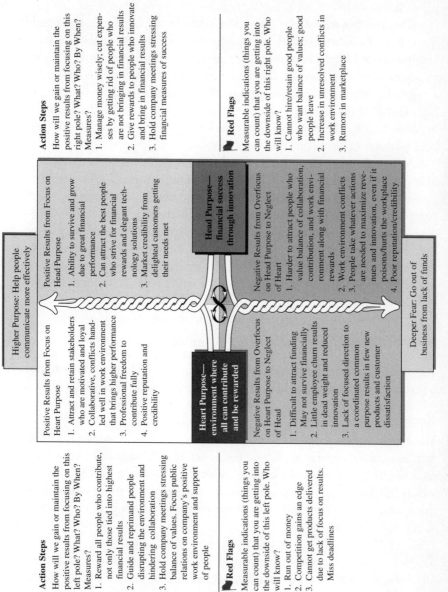

Figure 7.2 Expanded Radish Purpose Polarity Map with action steps.

business with Radish if it meant dealing with certain employees. For me, this was heartbreaking as I was limited in taking the necessary action to improve the situation.

Those in power did not take the actions of the heart pole that could have allowed a balancing with the upsides of both poles. Instead of the leadership stressing all the Radish values and helping employees build an environment where all could contribute to their fullest and be rewarded accordingly, they rewarded some noncollaborators who were bringing in high financial results. This hindered the oscillation that would naturally occur to balance the poles. In effect, those in power were saying only one pole was important to survival and success.

Although I did not realize it at the time, this situation is typical in many ventures where there is a change in management. The new leadership may not embrace the same purposes and values. One way to ensure continuity in such a transition is to retain controlling interest, or at least controlling management, of the firm. One side, thereby, ensures its pole dominates. Another way to lessen conflict from a polarity perspective is to embrace the old with the new—both sides see it as a polarity to manage and explicitly set the intention to empower the other pole. Without that, conflict is likely.

Try Action Steps to Encourage Movement

People in my study also recommend the following approaches, which may be especially effective action steps in balancing personal polarities.

Nurture Yourself

You may perceive the need to balance personal polarities within yourself, such as an imbalance between head and heart. Use the suggestions in Chapter 3 to nurture yourself. Build self-confidence and other traits of the whole self. Don't let one part of you dominate. People in my study recommend that you give attention and time to the part of you that is not dominant. When appropriate:

- Nurture and follow your heart, bliss, and passion. If something feels right, follow it. If it does not feel right, then make some changes.
- Nurture the head. For people with a more dominant heart than head, strengthen planning and other thinking activities.

Get in the Right Environment

Put yourself in an environment that allows attention to both poles. This worked temporarily for me during my African trip. Remember Kevin Streicher (in Chapter 3) who found balance by being in nature after leaving an unhealthy work situation. Surround yourself with people who are balanced. Ask for their feedback and help.

Meditate

Some people in my study use meditation to become aware of and integrate polarities. Carol Grever, author, recommends, "Use meditation to integrate mind and body. Then rest in the goodness." If you are like me, on most days your head easily dictates. Through most of our education, we are taught logical thinking. After head domination, your internal pendulum yearns to let other parts—heart and hands—get some attention. Experiment with the Core Practice (Appendix B) and intentionally move awareness among your head, heart, and hands as experienced in your body

PRACTICAL POINTERS

- *Start.* Develop your skills in balancing polarities. Experiment with some of the various methods by working on yourself. Use makes it easier to differentiate problems from polarities and to create and implement action steps.
- *Accept.* The movement between poles occurs naturally if you remove resistance that impedes the movement. If you are stuck in one pole, listen to and incorporate the values, fears, and wisdom of both poles.
- *Use.* Find teachable moments. When a paradox, dilemma, or resistance to an obvious solution keeps recurring, build a simple map to develop awareness in a group. Next, create possible action steps that allow movement between alternatives.
- *Expand.* Read the book *Polarity Management,* visit www .PolarityManagement.com, and learn more about this powerful technique.
- *Try.* Nurture yourself, change your environment, meditate, and use physical activities.

sensations, mental images, and self-talk. Over time, freely float your awareness and accept whatever you experience. The result may be a natural oscillation of these parts of you. Appendix B also offers an additional, meditation technique to balance a wide range of polarities.

Use Physical Activities

Simple physical activities can help your personal rhythm naturally balance certain polarities within yourself. *Kinesiology,* the study of muscles and their movements as applied to physical conditioning, offers us guidance. Brisk walking, cross-country skiing, certain dance and yoga forms, and other kinds of physical activity with oppositional movement also syncopate our left and right sides and balance various parts of self. With these activities, arms swing at your sides in opposition to the movement of your feet[15]—as the left arm and right leg go forward, the right arm and left leg go back. By physically moving, you can help regain your balance.

APPLY TO REAL PURSUITS

Perhaps you have never considered polarities and how to manage them. Here's an example of how one business leader resolved the conflict within a polarity.

Balance Work and Family—André Pettigrew's Story

Basketball was his passion and his ticket out of inner-city Detroit poverty. His goal, like that of many young people, was to be a professional athlete. André Pettigrew was on his way playing with the UCLA Freshman team when the door to his "passionate purpose" suddenly slammed shut with a career-threatening knee injury. Rather than wallow in the pain of this loss, he let go of sports, went back to his core values, and searched for a new passion. He found he could help other people with his business skills, and so he charted a course to pursue the entrepreneurial dream.

After completing his college education and getting some work experience, the time was right. Pettigrew met two partners with whom he started a management consulting firm that bridged the gap between technology and people. Over the next 10 years, it grew to a $14 million business with more than 200 employees. For three consecutive years, it was on the *Black Enterprise* 100 list of fastest growing African American firms in the country.

Pettigrew is like many people today who have received a call for change and are searching for more. André began the *Assess Progress* stage in the Pursuit of Passionate Purpose process when the injury occurred. Realizing that surgery could not reopen this door, he let go and embarked on the *Know and Nurture the Person* stage. He discerned that he valued "earning his way each day," continuous improvement, and working toward a meaningful purpose. How could he use his business skills to serve these values? During the *Find Purpose* stage, Pettigrew discovered the answer. As he opened to the possibilities, the right partners found him, and together they pursued the entrepreneurial dream. With confidence and commitment, he produced great results during the *Pursue Purpose* stage.

Had Pettigrew arrived? His journey brought him back full circle to the *Assess Progress* stage with the next set of challenges. He was paying a huge personal price for the success of his business because his family life was suffering. How could he balance it all?

He became aware of the work/family polarity and that he could not embrace both poles in the current work setting. "This has been a constant tension in my life. Tough jobs require passion, intellect, and hard work of 60 to 70 hours per week. I have a level of workaholism in me and it is easy to get out of balance. I knew I was disconnected from my family. There was a decision—family or business? I chose my family. I know I made the right choice. We wanted to raise our kids in a different style, and so we made a quality of life move without a job from California to Colorado."

Action steps helped him create a setting to manage this polarity. "Having kids helps because you want to be there. That can keep you balanced. I appreciate the simple things in life, quiet times, being with friends and family, and regular exercise."

Balance required letting go of the addictive parts of his behavior that were not allowing a dynamic shift between work and family. He could then embrace a more balanced life that included both poles. "Letting go is hard when it is your passionate purpose. There exists tunnel vision."

In choosing to balance his family and work priorities and supporting that decision with changes such as moving into the right environment, Pettigrew turned his life into learning experiences that have benefited his family and the business community, government, and education fields. Having served as an executive at the Boulder Chamber of Commerce and cabinet member for the state of Colorado, Pettigrew is now Assistant Superintendent of Denver Public Schools.

SUMMARY

- Polarities, or opposites, naturally exist in all parts of life.

- There are benefits from managing polarities as a whole, balanced system.

- There are ways to balance and manage polarities of self and situations, into an integrated whole.

- Use these four practical steps to balance polarities:
  1. *Learn.* Acknowledge that polarities exist in life. Learn how polarities work.
  2. *Question.* Determine if you have a polarity and if you have the flexibility to balance it.
  3. *Move.* Do what you can to encourage movement between the poles.
  4. *Monitor and correct.* Refine your approaches that encourage movement.

- Use various methods to encourage movement between poles:
  —Become aware and set the intention to move between poles.
  —Build a schedule.
  —Analyze and develop an action plan using the Polarity Management method as a continuous process allowing dynamic movement between the poles:
    - Get proper stakeholders involved.
    - Create a Polarity Map to understand the situation.
    - Identify action steps and measurable indicators, Red Flags, to help manage the polarities.
    - Take action.

- Try some of these action steps that may encourage movement between personal poles:
  —Nurture yourself and build confidence that you have the ability to find balance.
  —Get in the right environment
  —Use meditation to balance polarities.
  —Take physical action to integrate self into a whole person.

8

Attraction Strategy

Premise: Opportunities are everywhere.

Path: Think, feel passionately, and act to attain the purpose.

Outcome: Getting what you want.

Effective Passionate Pursuers attract what they want by holding a broad intention, while thinking, feeling, and taking action to get it. They direct their head, heart, and hands energy and encourage other people and resources in the web of life to direct their energy to help attain the purpose. When you know what you want, visualize getting it, believe you will get it, talk as if you have it, feel passionately about getting it, and take action to attain that purpose while remaining flexible and open to the possibilities, you are more likely to get the desired outcome. Believing, visualizing, and talking are all parts of thinking. Heart energy or feeling passionately about the outcome is the most vital. The Attraction Strategy means holding a broad intention and opening to opportunities that are everywhere, while thinking, feeling passionately, and taking action to get what you want.

WHAT YOU CAN GET FROM THIS CHAPTER

The Attraction Strategy is helpful in all stages of your pursuits, whether personal or professional and for everyone, regardless of profile. Seekers and In-between'ers can draw insights to help discern their values and gifts and attract their purpose. Passionate Pursuers can attract the means to effectively pursue their purpose. Everyone can pull toward them the necessary information to assess and take appropriate action.

USE THE ATTRACTION STRATEGY

The Law of Attraction—likes attract likes—is absolute.
                    LYNN GRABHORN,[1] *Excuse Me Your Life Is Waiting*

This strategy, to "power the pull," uses several tactics:

- Hold a broad intention of what you want.
- Be open to the possibilities.
- Think—believe, visualize, and affirm getting it.
- Feel passionately about getting it.
- Take action and engage others to get it.
- Allow and let go of attachment to a certain outcome.

More times than not when you are open to all possibilities, when the head, heart, and hands energy is strong enough to create a positive attraction, and when something is not blocking the effort, you receive what you want. How do you know if the energy is strong enough? When the energy is right, what you want comes to you with ease.

My Path—Attraction at Work

Radish offered many occasions to use the Attraction Strategy because it had become an unconscious part of me. At first we wanted to find the elegant idea and our purpose. Then we sought the right business model, funding, and talented consultants willing to work for stock options. We hunted for experienced advisors and economical facilities. The list goes on and on, and evolved as the firm matured. On all of these and more, the Attraction Strategy delivered.

Probably the most significant application was in attracting the right partners to help VoiceView proliferate. To accomplish this, we:

- Set a broad intention of having VoiceView become the de facto worldwide standard.
- Opened to the possibilities and were willing to license the protocol to original equipment manufacturers.
- Thought about how to achieve the new business model and believed it was possible to attain. We wrote the business case, talked to important industry players, and strategized about finding the proper

partners. We visualized, dreamed, and imagined VoiceView shipping in off-the-shelf modems and PCs. We talked to potential partners affirming why this was a great idea.

- Felt passionately about getting the right partners and implementing this business model.
- Acted like a partner of the biggest players in the marketplace, exhibited at the right trade shows, and promoted our capabilities.
- Let go of our original business model of being a proprietary systems provider.

And in the end, the right partners came on board to use the protocol.

Power the Pull

In *Power vs. Force,* David Hawkins,[2] explains, "In a universe where 'like goes to like' and 'birds of a feather fly together,' we attract to us that which we emanate."

Use your positive energy to attract what is intended.[3] Energy to attract the intention comes from your head, heart, and hands by thinking, feeling, and acting. The more energy you intensely focus toward your intention while being open to possibilities, the easier and faster you will attract what you want.

Margot Zaher,[4] life coach (see Chapter 5), wrote about the incredible power of intention:

> You are constantly attracting something to yourself. Attraction is based on an energy exchange. You are made up of energy, and so is everybody and everything around you. Your energy extends around you and touches the person next to you. Have you ever walked into a room and felt a heavy tense energy, and known that you have just interrupted an intense argument? Perhaps you could actually feel the intensity in the air. You attract that which mirrors the energy that you are giving out. When you put out negative energy, you tend to reap negative results or reactions.

Napoleon Hill[5] explains this further, "The human mind is constantly attracting vibrations which harmonize with that which dominates the mind. Any thought, idea, plan, or purpose which one *holds* in one's mind attracts a host of its relatives, adds these 'relatives' to its own force, and grows until it becomes the dominating, motivating master of the individual in whose mind it has been housed."

So how do you power the pull with your thinking, feeling, and acting? Once you set an intention and open to the opportunities, vividly imagine getting the outcome. Believe it is possible to attain it. Then talk to yourself in the form of positive affirmations as if you already have experienced this image. Talk to others. Journal and think about ways to get it. This engages more of your head energy.

But do more than just think about it. Engage all your senses. Infuse that vision with passionate feelings and intense positive emotions and thereby engage your heart energy. Experience what it feels like to get your intention. Foster passion for the outcome.

Do what is needed to attain this image. Share with and engage other people's energy to help attain this outcome. Create a physical representation of it, if possible. Act as if you have already received it. This is taking action, which physically engages hands energy.

HOLD THE INTENTION

What does it mean to hold a general intention? This broad intention is another term for your purpose. You state the optimal outcome in wide-ranging terms to yourself and then you put it in the back of your mind. It does not have to be at the front of your mind, but it can be. Even better, you write it down and you share it with others, which engages your thinking or head energy.

Virginia Corsi, management consultant, describes her approach: "I go on a hike and think of what I need. And I ask, 'How can I help serve?' I know if I help others, I will be helped. When I get home, the phone rings. The Universe is conspiring to help me. No matter what comes to me, I say yes. My entire consulting career has bloomed; money has just appeared."

Having a wide, rather than a narrow target, gives the Universe more room to maneuver. Be flexible and let the intention evolve. As is the case with many Seekers and In-between'ers, it is okay to not even know your intent; then your broadest aim is to find your intention. Your intent can be broad, but still clear.

My Path—Hold Intention in Your Unconscious

There was a time in my early twenties when I was heartbroken over losing the love of my life. At first, I cried and was terribly miserable. To allow myself the possibility that true love never dies, I promised myself to call him on his fortieth birthday. This promise freed me to finally move on from that relationship. I just set this intention, put it in my psychic background, consciously forgot about it, and went about my life.

Fifteen years later while working at my desk, I was overcome with thoughts of this long-lost friend. I couldn't understand why until I looked at the calendar. Could it be? That day was his fortieth birthday. Rest assured, you will not forget important promises that you put in the background with a sincere intention to remember. There is power in setting an intention.

Surrender and Intention Comes—Howard Selby's Story

Howard "Binx" Selby III, 58, is an eternally optimistic community leader, brilliant inventor, and creative entrepreneur who has started over 15 companies. He successfully pursues broader goals as a result of his contemplative practice. Whereas he used to define a specific purpose, write a detailed plan, and go after it with an aggressive, pushy style, Selby's approach has evolved over time to going with the flow toward a general intention. "It is essential to get in touch with the whole self, while getting away from domination of just what the mind thinks. Intention flows out of what is right for you. Do subtle work first. The proper intention surfaces as an insight, rather than as an intellectual product. Now, I surrender in the present moment to what is and a general, broad intention comes. Rather than being rigid, surrender opens more opportunities. Successes come out of this. The intention is always moving; there is no end point.

"Insights arise out of one's core, one's heart. Intuition is the insight facility. The more we quit being intellectual, the more the insight facility is useful. Once you get an insight, then use your thinking mind to do 'due diligence' on the insight.

"Finding purpose is a process of going with the flow. Surrender moment by moment and you can take advantage of opportunities along the way. I let an intention sit there and ferment in the background while I have discussions with lots of people."

Selby had a specific goal to build a Meditation Center. He encountered resistance. This experience helped him discover a formula for overcoming discouraging forces. "If you find resistance and push against it, the best thing to do is let go. Out of the present moment, you will find another way to achieve what you desire. Detachment is related to surrendering in the moment. If you accept the moment, you let go of fixation to the outcome. Go away from polarity and more into flow. It's really just expansion and contraction; it's really change. Neither one is good. Be aware of it, watch it, and travel from opportunity to opportunity without resistance."

After starting dozens of technology-based entrepreneurial ventures, some of which were tremendously successful, and then trying unsuccessfully to build the Meditation Center, Selby was called to use his talents to help start a Community Montessori Charter Public School in Arizona. "The broader intention is to provide an environment where kids get the sense that they can do anything, that they have choices. The others involved didn't have the courage to file the school charter. It didn't seem like such a big thing to me. It made sense. I'm used to stepping off a cliff. We had two weeks to do it. We just had to work hard. We pulled all-nighters, assembled it, drove to Phoenix, and got it in two minutes before the deadline. The opportunity came and I did not have resistance, so I was able to go with it. Now, I have been able to manifest the intention of building community. The intention flows more and from this comes more passion for life. The passion leads to joy and fulfillment."

Selby has this overall advice. "Work at being a personal optimist. Look at anything and find the optimistic outcome. Success comes from being in the moment. Be here and now and not too fixated on the end goal which can lead to burn out. Burnout is the signal that you have lost touch with the self in the moment. For those who can not find an intention or purpose, get connected to yourself and it will arise."

PRACTICAL POINTERS

- *Allow.* Allow the intention to emerge from your inner self as intuition or insight. Shut off the dominance of the mind so your heart has a voice. Do subtle work first. Use meditation as the tool.
- *Be flexible.* If possible, drop rigidity. Let the intention evolve, change, and flow. Be willing to accept a broader purpose.
- *Be.* Be present moment by moment in the here and now. Drop fixation on an intended, future outcome.
- *Hold.* Hold the intention in the background, or in the conscious foreground.

OPEN TO THE POSSIBILITIES

But when our hearts are open, Providence makes straight our path.
SARAH BAN BREATHNACH,[6] *Simple Abundance*

Opportunities are everywhere. But you must open your arms to embrace them by responding to your feelings and inner voice.

Simone Weil,[7] author of *Gravity and Grace,* reminds us, "Grace fills empty spaces, but it can only enter where there is a void to receive it, and it is grace itself which makes this void."

My Path—Listen to Inner Messages

On the way back from Africa, I planned to spend a few days in France. At the airport en route to Paris waiting to check my bags, I was overtaken with a strong feeling to go home. When it was my turn, I asked, "Rather than stopping over in Paris, can I go directly home with my tickets?" The answer was, "Yes. You can go today. There is room and there is no extra charge." Without an argument, I was going home.

When I arrived, Dick broke the news. My dear Uncle Wally had died at just the time I was standing in line. No one in the physical world knew where I was then. I did not have an itinerary or reservations in Paris. I would not have called home to check in. But I received the message. It came through my gut, then into my heart, and then into my head. My inner self told me "Go home, now." Luckily, I listened to this message. The result was more encouragement to embrace opportunities around me by following my heart, in harmony with my head and hands.

When I do not respond to these messages, I regret it later. In preparing to leave for a business trip, I heard my inner voice say, "Back up your laptop before you leave!" It had been weeks since I backed up my working files. I looked at my watch. Backing it up would take more time than I had if I were going to make the plane. I ignored the message, but got a tight feeling in my stomach. An hour later, the same message came. Again I ignored it and felt even more stressed out.

Later on the plane paging through a magazine, an article entitled "PC Security While Traveling" jumped out at me. Reading this article, the same message came from inside me, "Back up your laptop." I promised myself, "First thing upon return, I will do it." I was not thinking creatively, or I would have at least saved my most critical files for the project that was due the following week.

Disaster hit in the rental car lot. A car zoomed by and rolled over my briefcase crushing my laptop! Opportunities had come to alert me, and I deeply regretted not listening to the messages.

Opportunity as Grace

For me, grace is the unexpected gift, insight, or message from the Universe. The dictionary says grace is goodwill, moral strength, or unmerited divine assistance. Like a road sign, grace gives direction; like music, grace inspires; like a hug, grace encourages. Called different names, grace is one person's serendipity or another person's synchronicity, divine intervention, intuition, or random opportunity. Whatever the name, many people have found it to be real. Through grace, the Universe's infinite potential[8] is turned into possibility.

Where Is Grace?

Grace always surrounds us, yet we often do not perceive it. The messages might come from *outside*. A friend's mother died. When planning the memorial service, my friend could not decide what music would be appropriate. When she turned on the radio, her mother's favorite song was playing. A message had arrived when my friend needed it. Yet, she had to open her heart and ears to receive it.

Insights also come from *inside* as your wiser self brings answers that lie within. This part of you is connected with the flow of the Universe, the oneness of all, which some people call the God within. This connection with grace is my spirit companion, who is ready to be of assistance.

How Do You Open Yourself to Receive the Messages?

To receive grace, your must be aware. It comes at unexpected times in unexpected ways. Your perception must be peaked so that you perceive an ordinary moment as unique from other moments. This is why a person is more likely to embrace these insights or messages in times of crisis or great need.

In having the intention to open your heart and to look for messages, you are more likely to perceive them. But you cannot control it. In letting go of attachment to a specific outcome, you can most easily recognize the opportunities.

The heart is more open to the opportunities when you are present in the moment. Taking nature walks, listening to passionate music, being with children, and practicing meditation are activities that help you hear your inner voice.

Opportunity Is Everywhere—A Successful Entrepreneur's Story

A consummate entrepreneur,[9] Mike, who founded and led numerous profitable technology-based public companies that reaped hundreds of millions of dollars in return for investors, shared, "It is important to feel passionate about your endeavors. It is hard to be successful without feeling passionate about them."

Mike describes how he holds a broad intention, "I want to make things to solve the world's problems and to discover something new. It must be energizing and new from a learning aspect. I have to feel like I am making a difference. For me, it is never about making money. It is about making a difference. Money is just the enabler for doing the things that impact. If you invent things you make a huge difference."

Mike insists, "Opportunity is everywhere. You have to be open. Be open to people and things you meet around the world; take advantage of all experiences and learn from them."

Mike, like many Passionate Pursuers, envisions what he would like. "When Thomas Edison died, they turned the lights off around the world for some number of minutes because his achievements had such a great impact. Even though it's an extremely difficult goal to reach, wouldn't it be great if you could achieve something meaningful like that?"

Using the Connections Strategy is vital. Mike continues, "The people thing is a key piece. People I have worked with over the years provide learning and open my eyes to new ways to do things. Those people nurture you, educate you, fund you, and provide you support when you're down, encouragement, new ideas, and all that. I need to be in an entrepreneurial environment where boundaries are unlimited with a team of people around. People interaction is one of the most important textures of life." His creative effort and belief attracts results.

"It's the creative pull. It just consumes you. This explosion of creativity comes out, and you get to make things and they work and you change the world. It's overwhelming. It's so cool. You're being pulled. I am not forcing myself to work to four in the morning. I am working to four in the morning for the sheer joy of it.

"I have this inner sense that it will all work out. This is kind of like the *Shakespeare in Love* thing where the producer of the play says, 'Well I don't know how, but it will all just work out because it's just magic.' It always just works out.

"One can find a positive feedback loop. If you do something and it works, you feel even more confident about your ability to do it. Success builds on your success."

Mike has these practical pointers. "If you have a purpose, make sure to do the things in life that give you flexibility to pursue it. Manage finances extremely conservatively, keep financial obligations really low to maximize this flexibility, and keep consulting jobs on the side. Don't have kids when you're too young. Be willing to work hard. Have the right attitude. Take responsibility, but don't take things too seriously. Handle the basics for good mental health: Show up, don't sabotage yourself by being an alcoholic or a substance abuser, and get rid of your rough edges by dealing with emotional and psychological factors.

"Business leadership is all about putting people in positions where they explore their passions. This is essential in technology companies where a professional workforce is the key to success. Good employees can be passionate at all levels. People want to make a difference."

PRACTICAL POINTERS

- *Be aware.* Set the intention to see opportunities and hear guiding messages.
- *Be present.* Strive to hear your inner messages. Get quiet. Meditate. Go in nature. Be around people. Play with children. Engage intellectually and emotionally with fellow beings.
- *Move.* Pump oxygen to let your life force flow so that you will be more aware and open. The same technology entrepreneur said, "Keep exercising to be connected to life."
- *Affirm.* Say, "I am open to the opportunities that are everywhere and embrace the ones that are right for me."

THINK AND FEEL

Whatever the mind of man can conceive and believe, it can achieve.
NAPOLEON HILL, *Think and Grow Rich*[10]

Thinking and feeling passionately about the outcome will help you bring it into reality. James Allen,[11] in *As a Man Thinketh,* says, "He who cherishes a beautiful vision, a lofty ideal in his heart, will one day realize it." Optimally, the head and heart energy come together in harmony. Visualizing, believing, and talking are all parts of thinking, yet they become more potent when infused with passionate feelings about the outcome.

Visualize and Paint a Picture

Many have spoken and written about the power of imagination and visualization. Albert Einstein[12] said, "Imagination is more important than knowledge." To *imagine* is to form, believe, conjecture, and suppose a mental image of something not actually present to the senses. Imaging can stimulate physiological responses as intense as the real stimuli because your nervous system cannot distinguish between an imagined or real experience.

Create a vivid mental image of what you want. As Maxwell Maltz, the author of the bestseller *Psycho-Cybernetics,*[13] states, "Create a scene on the screen of the mind."

The picture is a vision and more. It invokes all the senses and stimulates the imagination. It inspires and uplifts. There are ways to increase the picture's clarity, while still allowing the vision to be broad. A broader intention allows for more possible ways to realize it.

In 1937, Napoleon Hill published his seminal inspirational work *Think and Grow Rich*[14] in which he explains that imagination is one of the 13 steps toward riches. "Man can create anything which he can imagine."

Maxwell Maltz in *Psycho-Cybernetics*[15] explains further, "A human being always acts and feels and performs in accordance with what he *imagines* to be *true* about himself and his environment. This is a basic and fundamental law of mind."

Richard Connolly, blacksmith (see Chapter 2), sees an image of the end product flash in his mind and then he lets his hands go to work. The masterpiece naturally unfolds. Mike, the technology entrepreneur, holds a vision of inventing something so significant that it would change the world in a positive way.

Visualize the outcome of your dreams. Use all your senses: Feel, smell, taste, hear, and see it. Engage your imagination.

My Path—Vision Changed the Course of My Life

My high school German teacher said something that changed the course of my life. Fraulein Tali said, "I see you as an engineer." A lightbulb went on inside, and I thought, "Yes, I can do this." Even though I excelled in math and science, the teachers of those subjects and my career counselor had never made that suggestion, but were directing me toward teaching. I then saw a mental vision of myself as an engineer. Unknowingly, I began the process to attract this desire. Five years later, my first job after college was being an engineer for Bell Laboratories, a world-class research and development company.

At Bell Labs, I attended a seminar that also affected my life. The leader asked all participants to define something we wanted. I blurted out, "I want a Porsche 911." He probed me, "Close your eyes and paint a picture. What color is it? Describe the interior. How does it feel to drive it?" I saw myself driving the midnight blue sports car down the highway with my hair blowing in the wind. Touching the smooth steering wheel and smelling the black leather upholstery, I felt free, energized, and alive. I let go of attachment to this desire and the time frame for its delivery.

Years later, I was driving Dick's midnight blue Porsche 911 across the country. I didn't realize it at first, but this was the car of my vision. By detaching from the outcome, the actual delivery was better than expected since I did not have to own or maintain it. Yet, the experience brought forth all the positive feelings of my image. It came years later, but my intention had been fulfilled.

Had I more actively pursued this car dream and sought to increase the power of my magnetic pull, I could have physically mobilized hands energy by visiting a car dealer. I could have sat inside a Porsche 911 to touch and smell it, taken one for a test drive to get the feel, or perhaps joined a Porsche Club to be around other enthusiasts. I could have stimulated head energy by visualizing myself driving one, looking at pictures, reading articles about these vehicles, talking to the dealer and owners, or drafting a personal financial plan on how to afford the car. I might have been saying positive affirmations about attaining a Porsche and thinking about ways to achieve my goal. I could have generated heart energy by becoming aware of the feelings that result from seeing, touching, talking about, or driving the car.

Perhaps it took over 20 years for me to have a Porsche because my energy level was low and my focus was directed toward other purposes. But I had clarity with an initial, vivid image and let go of attachment to receiving this car. The end result was still good.

Believe

Holding the intention and creating the vision is not enough. You must believe, with all your heart and all your soul, that it is real. When you truly believe, the mind does not know the difference between the imagined outcome and the actual. As you believe and put your passion behind it, tremendous energy is unleashed that attracts what you desire.

Believe that what you want will come. Have no doubts. You may not know when, where, how, or why, but you do know what you desire. Believe in the self, in the intention as a greater purpose, and in the process that pulls your desires toward you. In getting Radish funded with the first round of venture capital, we did not know when we would get funding or who would be involved or the terms of the deal, but we believed completely with no doubt that the money would come.

Belief is what Napoleon Hill refers to as faith.[16] "Faith is a state of mind which may be induced, or created, by affirmation or repeated instructions to the subconscious mind."

A colleague shared her husband's story about believing in the power of intention. George, an entrepreneur, set a goal of manifesting a million dollars. Actually, he joked about it. Whenever anyone asked what he needed, he would reply, "a million dollars." One day, his wife jokingly changed a one-dollar bill to read $1 million and put the intention out to the Universe with sincerity. Then they let go and detached from the outcome as George continued to work diligently on his venture. Later after the deal closed to sell his company, he realized that the sale had netted him $1 million. Now he is a true believer in the power of the pull.

Affirm

An affirmation is a positive assertion. It is a personal declaration, made in the present tense, that asserts the existence of your desired end point or optimal outcome. As you affirm, you so think and strengthen your belief. Florence Scovel Shinn,[17] wrote in *The Game of Life and How to Play It* "Continually affirming establishes the belief in the subconscious."

Affirmations are best if they are easy to understand, completely positive, believable, and invoke strong feelings. They should be stated in the present tense without time limits.

Author Louise L. Hay sold untold numbers of her classic books *Heal Your Body* and *Heal Your Life,*[18] which are built on the concept of using affirmations to realign your beliefs and energy field. Through affirmations, you use your head to further your belief in the outcome and to allow no room for doubt.

Create your own affirmations or try saying some of these sample affirmations daily to power the pull toward your passionate purpose:

- "I am proud of the fact that it is easy to visualize in living color and feel passionate about those things I want in life."
- "I easily direct my energies toward my intentions."
- "Just like a powerful magnet, I pull what I want toward me."

How to Use Affirmations

Here are some suggestions:

- *Create a list of affirmations that are right for you.* Some people put them on a piece of paper, in their Day-Timer or Palm Pilot, on index cards, and on sticky notes. Place the sticky notes in convenient, visible spots—on the bathroom mirror, PC monitor, phone, and refrigerator door. Put index cards and a sheet of additional affirmations in a file folder next to your meditation space.
- *Review and update your affirmations on a regular basis.* You should do this at least once each year as part of your annual planning process and whenever new goals or challenges face you.
- *Find a regular time at least once per day to state your affirmations silently to yourself.* To stimulate even more head and heart energy, visualize the desired outcome as you make the statement, and infuse it with good feelings.
- *Draw on these statements as positive self-talk throughout your day while driving, waiting in line, or dealing with a challenge.* My favorites include: "My self-talk is always very positive" and "I feel good, I feel great." Before an important phone call, presentation, or meeting, state an appropriate affirmation to yourself on the desired outcome.

PRACTICAL POINTERS

- *Stimulate.* Give yourself permission to reawaken and bring forth your creativity. Be around children and those who are naturally creative. Play.
- *Imagine.* Participate in visualization and imagination exercises.
- *Dream.* Take time to relax, let your mind wander, and daydream. Before falling to sleep, give yourself permission to remember your dreams. Keep a journal close by your bed and immediately record your dreams on waking.
- *Remove.* Permit yourself to be aware of and then to drop unnecessary, preconceived barriers hindering you from visualizing and believing.[19]
- *Believe.* Believe. Believe. Overcome doubt by building confidence and trust.
- *Affirm.* Strengthen your belief by positive thinking, feelings, and assertions. Create, update, and regularly say affirmations such as, "I am proud of the fact that I can visualize in living color those things that I want in life."

- Teach your children and other important people in your life how to use affirmations. When I tuck my daughter into bed, we say some affirmations for her as part of nighttime prayers.

TAKE ACTION

Whatever you vividly imagine, ardently desire, sincerely believe, and enthusiastically act upon, will inevitably happen.

MAXWELL MALTZ, MD, *Live and Be Free*[20]

Much of the Attraction Strategy is about thinking and feeling, but we cannot neglect the doing part of the pull. When you are doing activities, you create more and more energy in line with what you want. This is where action comes in. Attraction is more than engaging the head or thinking with talk and images. It is more than opening the heart to feel passionately. It is about physical deeds combined with this head and heart energy.

It is also helpful to take action to engage other people in your pursuit. They then direct their energy toward your intention. Hands energy comes through doing, acting, making, performing, working, and moving. Taking action varies based on the stage you are in. During the *Know and Nurture the Person* stage, you might go to the library to conduct research, read a book, go on a walk, or take a trip to a new place. The *Find Passionate Purpose* stage offers opportunities to explore how to bring your passion in harmony with the needs of the world. You might talk to people, experiment with ideas and try them out, and observe others. In the *Pursue Purpose* stage, once committed to a passionate purpose, you create and then execute the plan, piece by piece with persistence. Then in *Assess Progress,* you actively collect feedback. This requires doing and taking action.

That is why Lauren Ward Larsen, whose story is shared later in the chapter, gives speeches advocating blood donation. She is taking action for her cause.

Create a Physical Representation

The vision does not have to be imaginary and only in your head. You can create a physical representation of what you desire. Architects often erect a model of their newly designed building. Engineers build a prototype of the defined structure so as to better visualize the intended result. Graphic artists create thumbnail sketches of logos. Mathematicians generate formulas and equations. Computer scientists simulate the properties of a system. Entrepreneurs write business plans. Seamstresses piece together a sample garment. All these techniques and many others provide visualization.

Some people draw ideas on paper and others use a variety of media to create a model. The representation can be surrealistic or realistic; there are no rules. Anything that allows you to experience the desired end with all your senses is helpful. Create a road map or symbol of where you are on the journey (see Chapter 6). Construct a depiction of your goal.

My Path

One of the earliest engineering tasks at Radish was to build a system prototype. This slow, large product served as a rough example so that others in the marketplace could understand our concept by seeing and hearing via this new kind of communication. They then provided feedback and were inspired to support us.

Involve Proper People

If you can inspire people to take action—direct their head, heart, and hands energy—toward your purpose, you will increase the total energy that is focused on the intention. Howard Selby, entrepreneur and community leader mentioned earlier in this chapter, lets his intention percolate in the background while he interacts with people, learns from them, and inspires them to take on his goals.

People seek purpose, since it helps provide meaning in life. Yet many people without a clear intention of their own are looking for a cause to support. Provide them a means to jump onto your bandwagon. Sometimes it takes effort to involve people in a constructive way and you must let go of doing everything yourself. This is the role of business leadership—to put people in positions where they can align their passions with the organizational purpose. As a result, more energy—thinking, feeling, and doing— is directed to bring forth and attract the intended outcome.

PRACTICAL POINTERS

- *Try.* Undertake many different things that stimulate head, heart, and hands energy. Variety is the spice of life. Try lots of avenues until you determine what works best.
- *Experiment.* There is no right or wrong way to power the pull. Get creative.
- *Connect.* Reach out and ask for help. Get more people involved and increase the total energy.
- *Do.* Take action. Put in the effort.

ALLOW

Once you have undertaken the first steps of the Attraction Strategy—hold an intention, open to the opportunities, and think, feel, and act—then just relax and allow the energy to attract the outcome. In reality, you invoke the Allowing Strategy (see Chapter 10).

Trying to control only gets in the way, reduces intensity of energy, and slows down the process. By surrendering to the natural process, you let go of resistance. Allowing can be an additional lubricant reducing friction that is needlessly burning energy.

This does not mean you stop your effort or give up. You continue to consciously and unconsciously maintain integrity of effort—stoke head, heart, and hands energy. Think, feel, and act on your intention.

APPLY TO REAL PURSUITS

The Attraction Strategy has practical application to your pursuits. Here's how one courageous woman, who overcame a nearly fatal crisis, uses this approach.

A Living Example—Lauren Ward Larsen's Story

Lauren Ward Larsen didn't plan to become an advocate for blood donation. She was climbing the corporate ladder as a marketing executive in the publishing industry. But then catastrophe hit.

Everything was going along fine in her pregnancy a few weeks before the expected delivery date, or so she thought. Then suddenly she and the baby were in a serious toxic state known as preeclampsia, and the baby's heartbeat indicated that she was in distress. Something was terribly wrong. Racing Larsen into the operating room, the doctors worked as fast as possible to deliver her baby by cesarean section.

Just hours after the emergency surgery to save her baby's life, Larsen's own body shut down. Her blood pressure, which had shot up prior to the C-section, was now a critical 70/40, indicating an internal hemorrhage. But during a second surgery, her medical team was unable to determine why her blood serum continued to seep uncontrollably from her vessels and veins, a condition that carries an 80 percent fatality rate. Within days, her kidneys and liver went into acute failure and Larsen experienced a grand mal seizure. For six weeks in the Intensive Care Unit, she slipped in and out of consciousness.

Somehow, miraculously, Larsen received over 200 pints of blood components, all donated by complete strangers, and somehow, miraculously, she clung to life. Slowly she began to recover. She had a meaningful reason to live.

Now as a national blood donation advocate, Larsen travels the country speaking about the importance of saving lives by becoming a volunteer blood donor.

Lauren tells us, "I do believe in the power of intention. Know what you want. Allow for help from unknown places. We can't control everything, but we can influence it and we can respond differently. It is important to let go of attachment to the outcome. Then just see what happens. Be at peace however it turns out."

Lauren explains how she uses the Attraction Strategy, "To work with the intention, believe there exists help from some force. Know that you want energetic assistance. I write my goal down and put it on my meditation altar. Then I affirm, 'This or something better for the good of all involved.' It is a matter of sincerity and clarity."

She also took action—she got healthy, began training, and then ran the 26-mile New York City marathon to raise money, awareness, and blood for centers across the country. Using all her marketing experience and creativity, she continues to mail donation requests, speak, and fund-raise for this important cause. "Be clear on what you want and be willing to work at it. I have launched a campaign to give back. The goal is to raise $50,000 and 500 blood units." Larsen is also writing a book, *Wonderful Life,* about her story and the importance of blood donation.

The next year by involving more people, Larsen raised more funds through her enjoyment of running. Having learned to ask for more than monetary support from people, she relied this time on a team effort. Thirteen fellow board members from the Foundation for America's Blood Centers each ran two miles of a marathon distance.

In contemplating how she found her passionate purpose. Larsen muses, "Sometimes life taps us on the shoulder for a specific purpose. Philosophers have asked the question for years, 'Is it free will or is it destiny?' I think it's a little of both. Serendipity does exist in life. My purpose continued to unfold in ways I never imagined."

Postlude: The power of intention delivered. After speaking pro bono for two years whenever she received an invitation just because it was the right thing to do, a large pharmaceutical company offered her educational funding. Now the sponsor "gets goodwill, the blood centers get help for free, and I get to do something I love to do for a good cause—and am able to pay my bills."

Challenges

What if the Attraction Strategy does not deliver? From my personal experience, sometimes this is the case. Here are some possible reasons.

Blockages in Your Energy Field

Once I started using the Attraction Strategy, it almost always provided for me. Yet in one significant situation, it did not. I call this pursuit, Baby Plan II. Baby Plan I incorporated the Pursuit of Passionate Purpose strategies and resulted in the birth of our healthy, happy daughter. When Annie was close to two years old, my husband was finally willing to begin working on having a second biological child. Three years later after intensely pursuing this passionate purpose and experiencing close to every medical, psychological, and spiritual intervention on earth, I was still not pregnant.

Broadening the intention beyond having our own biological child was, in my opinion, the appropriate next step. This would allow the Universe to deliver through adoption, donor eggs, or other means. However, Baby Plan II did not, to my great sorrow, deliver a child. I learned that when your intention involves other people, it is essential to have a mutually shared intention, or the energy of each person can be blocked and canceled out. I also realized that by holding on to a certain outcome, I was not open to all the opportunities. In letting go of attachment to the outcome of a certain number of children, I finally evolved the intention into "having a healthy, happy family." Who knows? The birthing of this book is, in another sense, another child.

Not Being Open to or Recognizing the Opportunities

Your eyes may be closed when something quite different from your original intention is delivered. You may not see this as the intended gift. Consider the fable about the man who was stranded in a severe flood. He was not afraid because he believed that God would save him. In a little while, a person came by rowing a boat and asked him to jump in and go to safety. The man refused, saying that God would save him. In a few hours as the waters continued to rise, another boat came by to rescue him. Again, he declined the help saying that God would save him. Likewise, he denied help a third time. Standing at the pearly gates, the man asked St. Peter why God had not saved him. St. Peter said, "God sent three rescue teams and you turned them all away."

Breaking through Skepticism to Openness—Ida Halasz's Story

Halasz, financial and marketing consultant, shares her experiences with Attraction. "I was skeptical about the Attraction Strategy. I've never expected anyone or anything, like the 'Universe' to just provide for me. I've always believed that I should not rely on others. But my work was not bringing me the expected rewards—financially and otherwise—I had to do something. So I made a deliberate effort to follow the *Pursuit of Passionate Purpose* approach, especially the Attraction Strategy. I did what I call 'deep thinking' and realized I was very angry about promises that had influenced me to accept my current position. I also realized that I really didn't want to give up my investment in this work, but needed a new direction. I told myself to relax and not try to force anything to happen. I gave myself permission not to stay in my job and to explore other ways to use my experience. I heard myself saying to associates that I was moving on from anger to being open to new possibilities. Surprisingly, new opportunities did appear. Out of the blue, it seemed, within one week I had three job opportunities and a lucrative consulting assignment. I realize that it must be happening because I had opened myself up to new possibilities and allowed positive things to come to me. Right now, it's a bit scary, it's also exciting to know that the next phone call or e-mail might bring a wonderful new challenge."

Not Enough Intensity

There are times when you might be indifferent to the outcome, your persistence is weak, or perhaps your intensity of energy is actually negative. When the intensity is just not high enough, consider ways to strengthen head, heart, or hands energy.

Trying to Control the Outcome

If there is too much attachment to a specific outcome, control can hinder free energy flow. The antidote is to use the Allowing Strategy. If you let go of attachment to the exact outcome, you never know when or what will deliver. And there is the possibility that for unknown reasons, your intention is just not meant to be. It may be in conflict with other intentions. Perhaps you will discover the larger scheme or perhaps not. This is where you also need acceptance.

Focusing on What You Do Not Want

When you think of what you do *not* want, you create negative energy and attract the opposite of your intention. There is a subtle, yet significant difference. With negative energy, knowingly or unknowingly, you might be repelling instead of attracting the outcome. It is essential to focus your thinking, feeling, and doing on what you want, rather than on what you do *not* want.

Worrying or thinking of the worse possible outcome brings you exactly what you fear the most. This is why it is important to surround yourself with the positive outcome, and avoid the negative. Certain media and people tend to hype the negative, only pulling more of it into existence in the world. I choose not to read about or listen to bad news because I do not want to attract it into my life. Instead, I surround myself with good vibes and proper people who also focus on the positive outcome. You can choose to do the same.

Brian, the hiker and businessperson mentioned in Chapter 2, tends to be a worrywart, always thinking of the worst possible outcome and forecasting gloom and doom. It is no surprise that the outcomes he fears the most come into his life. A natural pessimist, he must exert tremendous effort to tune out the negative. Fortunately, he has great will power and has learned to intentionally focus on the positive outcomes he wants.

SUMMARY

- The Attraction Strategy enables you to attract what you want by holding a broad intention and opening to opportunities that are everywhere, while thinking, feeling passionately, and taking action to get it.
- Here are the tactics to use:
  —*Hold the intention or purpose.* Determine what you want to attract. Write it mentally in your mind and if appropriate for you, on paper.
  —*Open to the possibilities.* Open your heart, in addition to your head and hands, to guidance and grace. Tap your intuition.
  —*Think and feel passionately about getting it.* Paint a picture and vividly imagine the completed intention. Engage all the senses: Feel it, smell it, taste it, see it, and hear it. Believe that you will get it. Say affirming statements as if you already have it.
  —*Act to get it.* Take action. Create a physical representation. Connect with proper people and encourage them to direct their energy to attract what you want.
  —*Allow.* Let go of attachment to a specific outcome and allow what you want to come in its own time and way.

- Realize there may be challenges in attracting. Here are some suggestions to minimize the impact of these potential hindrances:
  —Remove blockages in the energy field by ensuring that all the affected parties mutually share the intention.
  —Be open and recognize the opportunities.
  —Intensify the energy.
  —Drop control or resistance and allow.
  —Focus on what you want to attract, rather than on the lack of it.

9

Persistence
Strategy

Premise: Mindfully continue with focused determination.

Path: Divide and conquer.

Outcome: Real rewards—tangible results, positive feedback, and a stronger self.

A big purpose, which can be overwhelming, is made up of many smaller purposes, intentions, and goals. The approach is to:

- Commit to a clear purpose.
- Divide the whole purpose into parts.
- Conquer the whole, piece by piece—persevere with unremitting will to accomplish each part.
- Seek feedback to assess progress, build confidence, and adjust the action plan.

Effective Passionate Pursuers use the Persistence Strategy to mindfully persevere with focused determination using a divide-and-conquer tactic.

For example, students who pursue a degree must complete several tasks: researching and selecting a school, applying, taking and passing courses and, if required, writing a thesis or dissertation. It takes disciplined work to finish each task, although this effort can become exhilarating when you get into the flow. The key is to accept that it is a process—set up a feedback loop and build confidence along the way.

178

WHAT YOU CAN GET FROM THIS CHAPTER

Persistence is a success strategy that most people find useful. Seekers can be persistent as they strive to find their passionate purpose. In-between'ers, especially those who are experienced Passionate Pursuers in transition, need to consistently give themselves permission to rest—this takes persistence. Passionate Pursuers must use perseverance throughout the pursuit to reach their goals. Once you determine your current level of persistence using the Persistence Inventory, consider practical suggestions for bolstering it.

USE THE PERSISTENCE STRATEGY

Persistence is the act of continuing steadily or firmly in some state, purpose, or course of action, especially despite opposition or obstacles. As Jacqueline Frischknecht, accelerated learning expert and author, puts it, "Determination, inventiveness, and stamina get me where I want to go." When you persist, you persevere and maintain your intention in spite of difficulties. Persistence requires strong willpower, unremitting determination, fortitude, and discipline. More than a single event, persistence is a process, requiring integrity of effort—a trait of Passionate Pursuers (see Chapter 3). For success in pursuits of passionate purpose and life, unrelenting effort is mandatory.

My Path—Perform with Persistence

Although my work conflicts continued and sleep at night was troubled, I persisted in living with the situation at Radish. The firm, however, made strategic changes. After making insufficient progress toward building a sustainable revenue stream, Radish embraced a revised business model.

But having a good plan was not enough. With our new business model in mind, we went to chip, PC, and modem manufacturers with the brainchild of embedding VoiceView into their products. After working diligently, we succeeded in holding meetings with the decision makers; they weren't interested in implementing the idea even though it could provide significant user value. In that competitive arena where every penny in hardware costs was tightly scrutinized, they did not want to add even 10 cents to their production costs. We received dozens of refusals from potential licensors of our technology.

How did we maintain our efforts despite this rejection? We used the Persistence Strategy. While staying focused on our bigger objective, we persevered in following ancient wisdom: We tackled one day at a time, moment by moment. We accomplished the steps to our goal by dividing them into manageable small tasks.

Discouraged yet determined to find a way, we pressed on. As luck and preparation would have it, we exhibited at the right trade show at the right time with the right product. The Universe delivered the opportunity: A Microsoft executive walked into our booth and said, "This is interesting technology. We have been working to develop something like this." Fast on our feet, we immediately responded, "Don't develop any more. Partner with us." That was the beginning of a risky, six-month courtship whereby Microsoft quizzed our engineers endlessly while investigating our technology. Were they trying to see if they could reverse-engineer our invention, or were they just determining the potential? Our patents protected our intellectual property, and Microsoft, the overpowering giant, eventually asked Radish, the small start-up, to dance. A partnership of sorts was born.

Now with Microsoft at our side, we went back to the same PC, modem, and chip manufacturers. No surprise—we received a welcoming reception. These firms now had a reason to add to their costs. Within a year or so, VoiceView was integrated into the Windows operating system and 90 percent of PCs, chips, and modems shipping worldwide. It became the de facto standard for voice/data integration. What a difference the right partner and persistence makes to the successful implementation of a plan.

Radish then focused on the continuing challenge: How to make money? We weren't making it from hardware—we were out of that business. We weren't making a lot of money from licensing the protocol. As a condition of Microsoft helping us proliferate VoiceView as an open standard, our licensing price had to be reasonable. That meant we had to make money from software applications and other novel advertising approaches. We persisted in searching for the "killer app."

Why Persistence?

"Lack of persistence is one of the major causes of failure. It is a weakness which may be overcome by effort" says Napoleon Hill,[1] author of *Think and Grow Rich*. And "Continue under all circumstances" is the advice Natalie Goldberg, author of *Writing Down the Bones* and Zen meditator,

After a six-month courtship, Radish's president signs the agreement with Microsoft as our protocol director looks on. With this endorsement, VoiceView was soon embedded in 90 percent of chips, modems, and PCs shipping worldwide and in the Windows operating system. It became the de facto standard for voice/data communications over a regular phone line. What a difference the right partner makes!

received from her teacher Katagiri Roshi.[2] (He was referring to meditation, but persistence is an essential success factor in all endeavors of life.)

Benefits

Persistence pays off and brings rewards. Abraham Lincoln ran for office many times before he won an election. Thomas Edison tried thousands of different experiments to determine the proper filament to light a glass bulb. Authors Jack Canfield and Mark Victor Hansen incurred over a hundred rejections before their best-selling *Chicken Soup for the Soul* was accepted for publication. While persistence alone does not guarantee achieving the intended results, I can guarantee that without continued, steadfast effort, success is much less likely.

When Is It Too Much?

How do you know if you are appropriately persistent? When should you back off or stop? How do you determine the boundary?

You know that you have crossed the line when you feel that something is not quite right. This requires being aware and tuned into your inner self. Or, you might get feedback from others that your persistence is too much.

When does persistence become pushiness? There is the same distinction between assertiveness and aggressiveness. Years ago, I was on the verge of hiring an additional product manager to complement my existing marketing team. One candidate interviewed well, was thorough, responsive, and persistent. But while I deliberated over several potential hires, his constant follow-up became overbearing. If this irritated me, even though I liked relentless drive, I wondered how others would react. I did not hire him because he had crossed from persistent to pushy.

Assess Your Persistence

When you have a purpose, do you persistently work toward it? The Persistence Inventory (Table 9.1) will provide a quick assessment of your level of persistence and some guidance on areas that might need attention.

The inventory also provides guidance on what areas might need more of your attention. Look at individual statements. If you scored 1 or 2 on any one, some consideration may be needed. Focus on strengthening these elements.

People who are overly persistent or pushy may find that they are not receiving the positive feedback and support they need from internal or

Table 9.1 Persistence Inventory

Identify a purpose you are pursuing: _____

Based on *your* perception of yourself pursuing *this purpose,* indicate how OFTEN each statement describes you. Using a 1–5 scale where 1 is rarely and 5 is most of the time, write the appropriate number of points in the corresponding column. Sum all the numbers to get your Persistence total points.

Consider now, the present—not yesterday or tomorrow. Don't overanalyze. Mark your initial reaction to the statement.

Purpose I am pursuing: _____ _____	*Rarely or Never*	*Seldom*	*Sometimes*	*Frequently*	*Most or All of Time*
Number of points per response in this column	1	2	3	4	5
1. This purpose is clearly defined.					
2. I am committed 100% to this purpose.					
3. This purpose is dividable into smaller parts, and I am working part by part.					
4. I easily focus my full attention on this purpose, or a subpiece of it.					
5. I work hard at this purpose.					
6. I am maintaining integrity of effort in the pursuit through a disciplined approach.					
7. I receive ample positive feedback for my efforts.					
8. I am passionate about this purpose.					
9. Pursuing this purpose brings me the rewards I need.					
10. I have the support I need for pursuing this purpose.					
Total points = _____					

Scoring

Points range from 10 to 50 and indicate your level of persistence. The higher the number, the higher your persistence level. What does the total score mean?

50–41   You are persistent in pursuing this purpose. Keep it up and continue to reap the real rewards of your efforts.

40–31   You have a solid foundation and many productive attributes. Some minor changes will help.

30–21   Your persistence needs strengthening. Consider where you need attention and take some action to bolster yourself.

Below 21   Oh dear! Consider what you can do to strengthen your persistence to a constructive level. Here is an immediate call to action. There is a lot of room for improvement.

external sources. They probably are not seeing the desired rewards either. Perhaps you have a good overall score as a result of high scores for many elements, but your score on item 7, 9, or 10 is lower than you like. Consider why. Experiment. Try easing up or backing off. It can also be helpful to ask others you trust for their opinions.

PERSISTENCE STRATEGY IN PRACTICE

> Divide et impera [Divide and rule]
>
> ANONYMOUS[3]

The more energy you focus toward a narrowly defined, clear purpose, the higher your persistence. Using the Persistence Strategy generates clarity, focus, and energy toward your purpose. Committing to a clear purpose provides clarity. Dividing the whole into parts supplies focus. Conquering the whole by thinking, feeling, and doing work on a piece generates energy. Positive feedback and support from others can bring even more energy.

Commit to a Clear Purpose

It is vital to define what you want, so that you can persistently pursue it. In the words of Lauren Ward Larsen, national blood donation advocate, "Be clear on what you want and be willing to work at it." It is not enough to just define it, you must really commit to this purpose with all of you—everything you have. This part of the process, defining what you want and committing to it, is explored in Chapter 4.

My Path

The "radishes," as we Radish employees sometimes called ourselves, committed fully to the new business model with all of our heart, hands, head, and soul.

Divide and Conquer

According to Nathan Thompson, entrepreneur, "Taking small steps to accomplish big things is rewarding." When Carlos Aguirre, opera performer, wanted to learn to sing Mozart's Requiem, he used the divide-and-conquer tactic. "Always move from the big picture to the small picture. Find joy in the moment. Pay attention to the details. I first found a section that I liked. Then within that section, I found a smaller piece I liked. And then within that smaller piece, I found an even smaller piece that I focused on and learned."

Divide your purpose into small segments to conquer a small part. If that is still too large, divide it again. Consider advice of author Jim Collins from Chapter 3 on managing huge projects, "Walk the 10 miles each day."

Dividing allows you to focus your attention and handle a slice of the purpose well. The smaller the portion, the more you can focus your efforts and direct your energy. Another benefit of dividing is that looking at fine details can build your interest and passion (see Chapter 4). As philosopher Dogan[4] said, "Caress the details of life."

When you pay attention, you are being mindful. When you continue paying attention regardless of distractions, obstacles, and challenges, you mindfully persevere. You try, try, and try some more and direct more and more energy to the end goal. You keep going and don't quit. The more you persevere, the more energy you accumulate until eventually you have the critical amount to break through and make progress.

Partitioning increases the likelihood that you will get a sense of competency from your efforts and will make progress toward the goal. And you can choose which section to tackle first. These three attributes— choice, competency, and progress—build intrinsic motivation,[5] which builds passion and more desire to continue.

To conquer each piece, determine a plan and take the appropriate action. Perform to plan. Conquering each piece of the puzzle takes some combination of your head, heart, and hands energy that is mindfully focused toward the intended objective.

My Path

We took the challenge of becoming the de facto standard for voice/data integration in stages so as not to be overwhelmed by the prospect of attracting these powerful technology companies to embrace our protocol. First we determined the firms to target, figured out how to open doors to their decision makers, and then contacted them one by one and convinced them to meet with us.

Systematically, we held meeting after meeting with the potential licensors. While steadily receiving rejections, we learned that we did not yet have a good enough reason for them to embed VoiceView on their platforms. Persevering, at each meeting we stressed different benefits or reasons for them to work with us. None of these overcame their cost objections. While hold-ing the intended outcome, we revisited our business model.

Develop a Feedback Loop

Mike, the successful technology entrepreneur,[6] told us, "One can find a positive feedback loop. If you do something and it works, you feel even more confident about your ability to do it. Success builds on your success." A feedback loop allows responses from some action to direct the next set of actions. Built from a behavioral[7] model similar to Pavlov's, a positive re-sponse encourages more of the same actions and builds energy. Negative feedback discourages actions and drains energy. It is necessary, however, to look for and listen to the feedback.

With pursuit of any passionate purpose, set up a feedback loop using the Persistence Strategy. Commit to a purpose; focus on a small subportion of that purpose; and direct your thinking, feeling, and doing energy to ac-complish that piece of the purpose. Persist until you get some positive re-action; then use that feedback to encourage you and generate more energy toward the goal. Direct that energy to continue working on the next piece of the purpose until you get some positive feedback, and so it goes.

The feedback can come from you internally through an increased sense of meaningfulness, choice, competency, and progress or just by pleasant feelings. The feedback may come from proper supportive people or from others in the web of life.

Shinzen Young explains how a feedback loop is developed in the prac-tice of mindfulness meditation, "When you become one-pointed on an ob-ject, you become fascinated with it. Fascination produces pleasure, which motivates you to become even more one-pointed, thus creating a positive feedback loop."

Otherwise, with long-term, huge projects, it is easy to get over-whelmed or lost within the project. If you try to do too much at one time, nothing gets done well. It is easy to feel incompetent. You feel defocused and scattered. It is difficult to see progress. As this continues, you begin to wonder if this effort is useless. A sense of hopelessness develops. You want to quit. A negative feedback loop or a *doom loop*[8] may develop.

When you get a rejection or negative feedback while on your pursuit, it can shake your clarity of purpose. With that confusion, you begin to doubt and lose some of your focus. This could lead to an internal conflict,

"Should I continue or not?" This inner struggle takes energy away from the intended outcome. You need to stop this course of action.

To reverse this doom loop, set up a positive feedback loop. Reaffirm commitment to your purpose (increase clarity), proactively refocus on some very small piece of the purpose (increase focus), and continue to direct your thinking, feeling, and doing toward that outcome (increase head, heart, and hands energy) until there is some positive feedback. This stops the doom loop and sets you back on a healthy course. If you try and try with full integrity of effort and cannot under any circumstances get any positive sign, move to the *Assess Progress* stage of the Pursuit of Passionate Purpose process and reevaluate.

My Path

In one sense, we had been in a doom loop. Microsoft's interest changed the direction, and potential VoiceView coalition members had the reason to license. We started receiving positive feedback, and an upward cycle prevailed.

No Such Thing as Can't—Mark Plaatjes's and Johnny Halberstadt's Story

> *You need a vision of where you want to go and you need to break it into smaller steps on how to get there.*
>
> JOHNNY HALBERSTADT, sub 4-minute mile running champion

From Mark Plaatjes's humble beginnings in South Africa as the ninth of ten children overfilling a small, crowded house, this runner learned early to take command. "At 5 years old, I decided I had had enough. I packed my backpack and walked miles over to my oldest brother's house. He was married, but they didn't have kids. I lived with them as their child. I wasn't happy with the situation and so I changed it. If your intention is clear, you will get what you want. Get clear on what your goal is and put that out to the Universe on how to get there. People and the Universe will help you. People will come out of the woodwork."

Now more than 20 years later as he approached this race's completion, his head, heart, and soul had taken over and were directing his body. After 26 grueling miles, the finish line of the World Championship marathon was finally in sight. The competitors had trained a lifetime for this day, this race, and this moment. Yet, only one runner would win.

"The person who wins is the one who wants it the most, the one with full self-confidence. The head is key. You must have self-confidence and know who you are." With his arms outstretched to embrace his achievement, Mark Plaatjes crossed the finish line first to become the 1994 World Marathon Champion.

Today, Plaatjes applies his winning strategies to help others as a world-renowned sports physical therapist and as an American entrepreneur in a series of retail running stores partnering with Johnny Halberstadt—another champion.

Halberstadt finished his first running race in South Africa third from last. In the next race he did better, finishing tenth from last. He continued to improve and started getting recognition, enjoying himself, and believing with confidence he would win. "Find something you're excited about and do what you love. There's no such thing as can't. If you want to do something passionately, you will find a way. Believe in yourself. It comes down to self-confidence, otherwise it is difficult to excel. Start from wherever you are. If you invest your heart and soul, things will come out right."

Halberstadt pursued his purpose of winning races by breaking big goals into pieces and unremittingly working at them with the right attitude. "If you want to climb Everest, you need a vision of where you want to go and you need to break it into smaller steps on how to get there. When you achieve a sub-goal, look up at Everest again and feel good

PRACTICAL POINTERS

- *Commit.* Pledge yourself to a clear purpose for which you have passion. Increase clarity.
- *Divide.* Choose to work on a small piece of your purpose. Build focus.
- *Conquer.* Take action and direct, with relentless determination, your head, heart, and hands energy toward your purpose.
- *Develop.* Establish ways to receive feedback. Open your ears and hear the response. Use this information to adjust as necessary and also to build your energy.
- *Allow.* Let go of attachment to a certain way to attain your goal. By reducing internal struggle, you increase the impact of your energy.

about the progress you have made, but continue working on the next increment of the journey. Once you got the process down, keep going."

Halberstadt went on to become a world-class, sub 4-minute mile runner. But many people have avocations and hobbies. Could he make a living from this passion? Halberstadt embraced a broader passionate purpose.

Through persistence in an area that had never been successfully conquered, he paved the way for athletes to earn a living from their sport. Immigrating to the United States, he found his fourth-fold in the intersection of his love for running, his MBA education, and the needs for quality running equipment. He designed and developed innovative footwear that he then sold through his retail running stores.

STRENGTHEN PERSISTENCE

Just as exercise strengthens your muscles, there are exercises to strengthen your persistence.

Passion Builds Persistence

If you find yourself lacking in persistence, this weakness may be remedied by building a stronger fire under your desires.

NAPOLEON HILL,[9] *Think and Grow Rich*

Passion is heart energy. So it makes sense that if you increase your passion, you will increase the total energy directed toward your purpose and thereby your persistence (see Chapter 4). But here's a hint: Mindfulness and development of one-pointedness generate interest and fascination, which feel good and stimulate passion.

If you try unsuccessfully to foster passion for a purpose and then lack both persistence and passion, reevaluate your pursuit. You may not have a purpose you really want to pursue. Move to the *Assess Progress* stage.

Practice Fosters Persistence

When you develop endurance, discipline, and perseverance—elements of persistence—in any part of your life, you can transfer that universal skill to other purposes. Brooks Preston, philanthropy consultant, follows this rule: "I connect with the endurance quality in running marathons, and then transfer that quality to work life."

Once you have learned how to successfully use the divide-and-conquer tactic to achieve results, it is easier to apply this approach in other areas. After you understand the importance of the positive feedback loop and you know how to build one, using this tactic becomes second nature. The experience in one part of work or life builds muscles, or the basic building blocks, for using persistence in other areas.

Whether you like it or not, life often offers opportunities to fortify your persistence, such as caring for an elderly family member, raising a child, or working on a complex work project. Other times, we create circumstances such as training for an athletic competition or working toward a challenging certification. When opportunities knock, use your perseverance skills. Just as exercise builds your muscles, using your persistence makes it stronger.

Meditation can strengthen your ability to focus and perceive more clearly, and thus improve your persistence. It also can release tremendous energy. Meditation also can strengthen your discipline, which is a required part of continuing, steadfastly toward a purpose. Experiment while meditating, and then put the resulting focus and discipline into use while pursuing your passionate purpose (see the Persistence Meditation in Appendix B).

If you practice persistence in less critical areas of your life, you may find it easier to persevere in your most critical pursuits of passionate purpose.

People Support Persistence

Phyllis Postlewait, financial consultant, offers this reassuring philosophy, "You will be afraid. But if you persevere and surround yourself with successful people, you will succeed." People help you persist. They provide suggestions on how to divide and conquer. They provide feedback on your progress and competency, which helps set up a positive feedback loop. They can take a load off your shoulders, so that it is easier to continue. They can be your support and encouragement. They feed and nourish the soul along the journey. People can help you focus your efforts. By questioning and probing, they help you clarify your purpose. They can be an additional energy source for the pursuit, as well as a builder of your energy. All this and more comes from our fellow beings.

When people are counting on you, you do not want to let them down. When people know of your commitment toward a purpose, you are encouraged to work hard so that you live true to your promises. People play many roles especially as a role model: "If you did it, I can too" (see

Chapter 11). In working toward a purpose together with a partner, you build and nurture relationships, thus bringing more meaning to the project.

Rewards along the Way

You can learn to delay gratification, but there is a strong need for ongoing rewards, both intrinsic and extrinsic, to fuel the continuation of the pursuit. Design them into the process, otherwise you will find yourself "running on empty."

What do you need to keep motivated and passionate? In addition to a sense of meaningfulness, choice, competency, and progress, I find that recognition, interaction with proper people, and breaks along the way help me keep up the pace. Sometimes it is a personal pause for a bike ride; other times it is a professional pat on the back.

The rewards may also include extraordinary results and financial compensation.

PRACTICAL POINTERS

- *Burn.* Identify a worthwhile purpose. Keep your fire, passion, burning for your purpose to strengthen your persistence.
- *Use.* Practice persistence in other areas of life, and then transfer this endurance to your pursuits. Try the Persistence Meditation as one technique.
- *Connect.* Surround yourself with the proper people, who can encourage your pursuits.
- *Reward.* Make sure that you build in intrinsic and extrinsic rewards.

APPLY TO REAL PURSUITS

What helps keep you going when you feel too tired to continue? Perhaps the positive feedback from persistently working to conquer one small slice of your dream will rekindle your energy.

Here's an example of how one accomplished businessman persists in directing his unwavering passion to complete worthwhile purposes.

Persistence in Achieving Goals—Nathan Thompson's Story

"Be careful in setting goals," concludes Nathan Thompson, data storage entrepreneur, in analyzing his experiences in life and in building a $60 million plus company, Spectralogic, Inc. "Have an appropriate overall goal. If you set ridiculous goals, you will be unhappy. If you do not set good goals, you won't achieve anything. Take many ballerinas, for example, they can't lose enough weight. And so they live in a state of unhappiness, because they do not accept their own limitations. While understanding what your limits are, define what you want in life. If it is impossible to make this goal, then set another more appropriate one."

After growing up poor in Kansas, Thompson was only 19 and a full-time engineering student at the university when he started his data storage business. "I had no other means of support." Now over 20 years later, he still finds running the company a fun challenge. "I get to take on new tasks as we grow. I love setting and accomplishing goals."

Thompson gets motivated through planning. "There is no life other than this one. This is not a dress rehearsal. Life is a series of steps, or work actions, to get to where you want to go. Failure left a bitter taste behind, and so I learned to fear and hate failures. To get beyond failure, I needed to motivate myself. If I wrote down goals and steps to the goals, this would motivate me and provide focus. Taking small steps to a big goal is rewarding. I like crossing things off."

"I start by setting the goal. First, on paper and then each year at Christmas time, I put the goals in my Palm Pilot. If I can determine great goals, they will take care of themselves. Then over time, I review them."

Thompson uses the divide-and-conquer tactic to accomplish personal as well as professional goals. "My goal was to go from 218 to 195 pounds. I visualized the process of making the goal. Then I figured what is my reward? A Jaguar was a good reward. Then I determined how to get to the goal by breaking it into little steps: Track calories with 2,000 calories per day as the goal and burn so many calories per week. This led to another goal with an athletic component of completing a triathlon."

Thompson shares four practical pointers to success:

1. Master yourself. Decide how to allocate your time, energy, and personal resources. To accomplish great goals, you need to delay gratification and get gratification out of things that seem like work. Fundamentally, the most important positive force is internal. It's an

issue of self-esteem and recognition. There are things you have to overcome within yourself.

2. Next, have a crystal clear vision of what you want out of life and this day. Without this clear picture, you waste a lot of energy.

3. Third, develop practical skills. If you want to be an engineer, develop math skills. If you want to be in a sales position, develop people skills.

4. Fourth, get negative people out of your life.

Nathan Thompson sums it up, "The journey becomes the destination. Anything worth doing is worth doing passionately."

SUMMARY

• Use the Persistence Strategy to mindfully persevere with focused determination using a divide-and-conquer tactic.

• Persistence is an essential element of successful pursuits of passionate purpose and includes the following steps:

—Commit to a clear purpose.

—Divide the whole purpose into parts.

—Conquer the whole, piece by piece—persevere with unremitting will to accomplish each part.

—Seek feedback to assess progress, build confidence, and adjust the action plan.

• Persistence when taken over the edge, to its extreme, becomes pushiness, which can hinder rather than help the pursuit. It is a form of control and resistance.

• The Persistence Inventory helps you determine your strengths and areas that need further development.

• The more energy you focus toward a narrowly defined, clear purpose, the higher your persistence. Using the Persistence Strategy generates clarity, focus, and energy toward your purpose.

• The following actions can strengthen persistence:

—Building passion and aligning it with a worthwhile purpose.

—Practicing will power and discipline.

—Being with proper people.

—Providing intrinsic and extrinsic rewards, such as the response received in a feedback loop.

10
Allowing Strategy

Premise: Resistance escalates pain into greater suffering.

Path: Be clear on *what* you want and allow *how* you get it to unfold.

Outcome: Freedom from suffering and deeper satisfaction.

Allowing is also called surrender, nonresistance, lack of control, acceptance, or equanimity. Use the Allowing Strategy to be clear on *what* you want and allow *how* you get it to unfold. Effective Passionate Pursuers are flexible, open to possibilities, and receptive to options along the way, yet hold firm to the broad intention and pursue it persistently. The Allowing Strategy is about surrendering, with equanimity, to the natural flow instead of struggling and resisting. It is not about giving up your purpose, but in accepting alternative ways to get what you really want. When you drop resistance and allow, you experience less suffering and deeper satisfaction. As a result, you may pursue your passionate purpose with more ease.

WHAT YOU CAN GET FROM THIS CHAPTER

This strategy is valuable to people of all profiles. Passionate Pursuers may find opportunities during the *Pursue Purpose* stage to surrender to the unfolding process and allow, rather than control and push, how they pursue their purpose. They may be surprised at the ease at which novel options appear. In using this strategy, Seekers and In-between'ers give themselves permission to be where they are in the process. By reducing resistance, they do not lose their energy with friction or internal struggles. Instead, they can use it more effectively to *Know and Nurture the Person* and *Find Passionate Purpose*.

USE THE ALLOWING STRATEGY

When I let go of what I am, I become what I might be. When I let go of what I have, I receive what I need.

JOHN HEIDER, *The Tao of Leadership*
(based on Lao Tzu's *Tao Te Ching*)[1]

There are many names for the concept of allowing.[2] This strategy encourages you to surrender to the process, instead of trying to control it. In allowing, you move your resistance closer to zero. Jon Kabat-Zinn[3] explains, "Letting go is a conscious decision to release with full acceptance into the stream of present moments as they are unfolding."

The Allowing Strategy is consistent with holding a clear intention and pursuing it persistently with all of you. Yet, you are flexible and receptive to options in the implementation of your plan. You may have to adjust your plans as conditions dictate. Stop trying to control uncontrollable elements in your journey to reach the purpose. You may be surprised at what your creativity and serendipity delivers.

My Path—Breaking Through

While holding firmly its head purpose of building financial success through innovation and by letting go of its initial business model to allow the emergence of a new approach and supporters, Radish broke through and was on its way to greatness. Bill Gates, in a trade show keynote address to thousands of people, announced and gave a live demonstration of VoiceView capabilities. The audience sat in total silence for a few seconds. Then a loud vocal expression of awe came pouring forth as they appreciated this slick capability that would soon ship as a standard part of the Windows operating system and off-the-shelf modems, PCs, and chip sets. Soon thereafter, Radish was featured as one of *Fortune*[4] magazine's hottest technology companies to watch. VoiceView and the coalition supporting it, which included Intel, Rockwell, and many other major firms, were covered in the *Wall Street Journal*,[5] *PC Week*,[6] and most every major business and information technology publication. VoiceView was on its way to being recognized as the worldwide de facto standard for voice/data integration over a normal telephone line.

During the months preparing for this public announcement of the coalition of support, Radish continued to work hard pursuing the killer software application that would provide our ongoing revenue stream. Original equipment manufacturers, who licensed our technology, brought the answer. VoiceView was ideal for solving their critical problem—PC technical support. As Radish focused resources on developing this application and pursued an e-commerce business model, it let go of many other potential applications. Radish now had the winning formula.

Personal Breakthrough

I had come home from Africa with renewed energy, integrated self, and high hopes. They were all soon depleted as I resumed work at Radish. Even my daily meditation practice was not enough to sustain me. I was swept along with implementing and then announcing the exciting new business model in a workplace that conflicted with my core values and made it impossible for me to contribute and be recognized to my fullest. I had tried to change the situation to no avail. I had tried unsuccessfully to live with it. My own resistance and lack of equanimity converted my tremendous pain from the situation into unbearable personal suffering. There was only one option for me now.

The trade show with Bill Gates's presentation was over. I knew I had completed my last official role representing Radish to the world. One would have thought that my heart would not have been into it, but rather I was just as totally dedicated to the cause as always. Knowing this was my last formal chance to make Radish shine, I worked my hardest to the very end to make that happen. Now I was drained, especially thinking of what lay ahead. How could I move on?

In returning from the show confident that Radish would now survive, my pivotal point arrived. I was waiting at the airport for my delayed flight, when I met, by chance, an experienced organization development colleague. This gift of grace from the Universe helped me. Quickly discerning my need, she led me through a "destiny visualization." In my imagination, I opened a book. The page I randomly selected had a one-word message for me about the next step in my life's journey: BABY. My biological child, not Radish, was calling. This message helped me reconnect to my bigger purpose in life encompassing more than building a worthwhile company. It helped me shift my attention between the interdependent poles of work and family. I let go of the narrower Radish purpose and embraced a broader intention. It was time for me to move on from Radish, so that I could, if it was not too late, have a real baby. I somehow felt better, as if there was a divine purpose in my leaving the company.

So on that plane ride, I wrote my resignation letter and committed to the most difficult decision in my life. The words flowed onto the paper as did my sorrow. "I am writing to let you know of my decision to leave Radish. I can no longer contribute to my fullest in this environment. I cannot live true to my own highest convictions. . . ." In arriving home that night to Dick's comforting embrace, I knew I made the right decision.

With a broken heart and lump in my throat, I came in the next day to resign from my board and management positions. What a sad day! I did what I had to do. Like the mother in the biblical story of King Solomon who gave her baby to the false mother to save the child's life, I gave my first baby, Radish, to stepparents who I knew would keep her alive. Dick remained.

A few days later at my going-away party, cold rain and sleet incessantly fell outside. It was as if the entire world was crying with me. I sang this song:

> Take good care of my baby.
> Tell her that I love her so.
> And if you really love her,
> Then help her grow and prosper.
> Baby . . .

ALLOWING IS NOT GIVING UP

Allowing does not mean giving up on your broader purpose and intentions. Stephanie Nestlerode, management consultant, stresses that attitude, "I don't let go of purpose. I let go of attachment to the outcome or knowing how the path will unfold." It is not about being indecisive, and just taking anything that comes your way. It does not mean compromising on standards of ethics, integrity, quality, and values. It may mean letting go of a narrowly defined outcome and being less rigid.

To allow the natural process in the pursuit, there are times when it appears necessary to change, reframe, broaden, or evolve a passionate purpose In leaving Radish, I had to drop attachment to my role in Radish's success. I was still, along with others in the firm, committed to the broader head purpose of building a financially successful company, but in resigning I detached from the narrower outcome of being involved on a day-to-day basis.

I evolved to the next stage of my bigger purpose and began to "build a happy, healthy family, while contributing through meaningful work."

Sometimes with allowing you are not letting go of your purpose, but rather letting go of attachment to a certain outcome. Broaden your vision—consider what other outcomes look and feel like. Consider Deb,[7] who after extensive medical intervention delivered a wonderful baby boy. But in striving for a second biological child, she was not as fortunate. Eventually she broadened her vision and let go of the attachment that she had to have another biological child. "I let go of needing to be pregnant. There was another path. We adopted a daughter from China. She was destined to be our daughter."

What Are the Rewards from Allowing?

Allowing, or nonresistance, frees energy so that you are open to the possibilities that abound. Then you are able to recognize and embrace something else, the something that may be right for you. Florence Scovel Shinn[8] in *The Game of Life* shares the story of a woman who sought a good relationship. The woman determined that a certain man was the one for her, and she was obsessed with snatching him. Things were just not working out, and eventually she began to let go. As she did, she opened to other opportunities and the man of her dreams found her.

In reducing resistance and allowing, you become more flexible and pliable, like the wind or water, and ultimately are stronger. Consider the classic Tao example of water and rocks.[9] Water is fluid and yielding. Rocks are hard and rigid. Yet, in the long run, water—which is soft—wears away rock.

Freedom from Suffering

The real reward from allowing at the appropriate times is freedom from suffering and deeper satisfaction from life. As mentioned, all of life and behavior consists of polarities such as pain and pleasure. Shinzen Young[10] offers great insight into a way to resolve situations that are not working or have pain. He has a simple formula, representing what is behind these difficult circumstances:

$$\text{Pain} \times \text{Resistance} = \text{Suffering}$$

Difficulties in your pursuit of passionate purpose can produce pain. Your resistance or efforts to control the situation will multiply that pain.

The result is suffering. By bringing the resistance to zero or allowing, you can bring the suffering to zero.

The values clash at Radish caused me pain. By insisting that the original Radish values be used in the way I wanted, I created great resistance. Unknown to me at the time, this resistance converted my pain into such suffering that it was impossible for me to stay and live with the situation. Had I been able to reduce my resistance by allowing the values to evolve as they were being lived out, perhaps I could have stayed in the firm despite the pain. Because I could not or would not compromise on the values nor on my desire to control them, the only way to alleviate the suffering was to leave. I do not regret standing firm on my values.

Deeper Satisfaction

Consider situations that are pleasurable. Young's formula, representing what is behind these joyful circumstances, is:

$$\text{Pleasure} \times \text{Equanimity} = \text{Satisfaction}$$

Equanimity, or nonresistance, goes down as the level of grasping, craving, or resistance goes up. So another way to view this is:

$$\frac{\text{Pleasure}}{\text{Resistance}} = \text{Satisfaction}$$

As you bring your resistance down by allowing, your level of satisfaction increases. So allowing can reduce suffering and bring greater satisfaction in life.

What Happens When You Don't?

When it is necessary and you don't allow, or let go of control, there can be serious consequences. Karen Bernardi, realtor, realized, "Pain came from not letting go. When I finally let go, there was no suffering in it." Here are some of the prices you may pay for inappropriately resisting:

- Through the continued resistance, pain is converted to greater and greater suffering.
- Without progress, you are stuck. There is the risk of stagnation because the new has no space to enter.

- You and the situation may get more and more unhealthy.
- You limit your opportunities.
- A downward doom loop can develop that eats away at your confidence, self-esteem, and optimism. Cynicism can prevail.
- There is no enjoyment in the process and in life.
- Life begins to lack meaning.

Why Is It So Difficult to Do?

If you are like most people in this study and in my workshops, allowing or letting go of control during your pursuits is difficult. People have interest in exploring how to allow more effectively. I have found out the hard way that the ability to surrender is part of my lifelong lessons to be learned and relearned. Ellie Sciarra, tap dancer, puts it this way: "Letting go will be a lifelong goal. It is the hardest thing."

Allowing requires trust. Trust in what you ask. Trust in something beyond yourself. Some of us have learned from earlier life circumstances to not trust. As Howard Selby, community leader, shared, "There is a preconditioning to hold on." Trusting, however, becomes easier as you strengthen your heart energy. In this society, our hearts are easily closed down and we become overly dependent on our heads. And the rational, logical head can twist things and bias the analysis.

Often, there is an unknown in allowing. The status quo, no matter how painful, is a known and the consequence of surrendering is a mystery. People often choose a known over an unknown, even if the unknown has great upside potential. Consider the story of the Cling-Ons.[11] These little creatures lived under the water in a fast-moving stream. They had determined that to avoid being carried away they had to hold onto rocks at the bottom of the waterway. This purpose, to hold on, grew more and more difficult over time. Finally, one Cling-On broadened his purpose of life to be survival, not just holding onto the rocks, and embraced the possibility of another way of claiming it. Discerning that death would be better than this kind of continued existence, he chose to let go. He did not die, but instead found enjoyment in moving downstream with the current. "Wow, this is great. Going with the flow is an infinitely better way to survive than fighting to hold on. How can I help the other Cling-Ons learn this?"

Perhaps you need to consider whether you are a Cling-On with too narrow a passionate purpose. Are you able to broaden your purpose so that you can allow other ways to achieve it? Jeanne Teleia, dolphin-therapy facilitator, shares, "It is not about letting go. It's about flowing with the river."

The Strategy Paradox

Chapter 9 stresses how the Persistence Strategy—mindfully persevering while dividing and conquering—is essential to getting to what you want. Yet, there is a time for allowing. Are these in conflict with each other? This seems like a paradox.

This apparent paradox may really be a polarity. You can persistently allow. You can persistently pursue while allowing the process to naturally unfold. Instead of choosing one over another, use the Polarity Strategy to embrace both poles and thereby find strength in the dynamic movement between them (see Chapter 7).

STRENGTHEN ALLOWING ABILITIES

It helps to realize that allowing is just part of the cycle of life. It is part of the process in pursuing any purpose. People in my study have determined that the following approaches do *not* help:

- Use only your head and planning skills.
- Listen only to others, and not to your inner self.
- Try to control things.
- Stay angry, have insecurities, and be biased by preconditioning.

There are many methods to strengthen allowing.

Meditate

Carol Grever, author, describes the process: "Meditation helps in letting go. Let go with the breath. Be in the present moment. Stop the old tapes. Stay focused on your vision and you will move toward the dominant thought." Use meditation or some form of contemplation to focus on the here and now. Be in this moment while letting go of attachment to a certain outcome.

Recall that the two basic premises of meditation are being mindful and then accepting of what is. Using Shinzen Young's Core Practice (in Appendix B), will strengthen your ability to allow. The more you meditate, the easier it will be to allow with noninterference in your pursuits. When faced with a challenging situation that requires surrender or nonresistance, try this Allowing Moment by following these steps in quick real time:

- Pause for a moment and set the intention to allow. Say internally to yourself, "When appropriate, I easily allow and go with the flow."
- Focus for an instant on some small part of your stream of body sensations, mental images, and internal talk—feel the sensations in the bottom of your feet as they touch your shoes, see a mental image of yourself, or become aware of your inner voice saying "allow, allow."
- Exhale and release your breath as a real-time instant of allowing.

"Don't kid yourself that it will be easy," said Carol Grever. I found this to be true. Even after more than 25 years of practicing equanimity during my daily meditations, transferring this skill to everyday life took intentional effort for me.

Do It

According to Martha Arnett, retired university secretary, "Letting go is maturity. The more you do it, the easier it is to do." One way to get better at allowing is to experience doing it, even with unrelated matters. Arnett suggests that we learn how to do this by cleaning out. "When you clean up your house and get rid of things, you practice letting go. What is this focus on collecting things? We can't be our stuff, we must be ourselves." In this activity of shedding the old, there is an opening of space for the new. Try doing it on small things, so that when larger opportunities come forward you have strengthened this nonresistance muscle.

Honor your past experiences. It is easier to allow, when you realize that you have done it before. You have let go many, many times in your life. Consider your own breathing. With each breath, there is an allowing. As you breathe out, you are releasing the in-breath and letting your lungs contract. As you breathe in, you are allowing your lungs to expand. Moment by moment, you are surrendering to the natural flow.

Ask for Help

You are not alone. Help comes from many places to assist you in allowing. The key is to be open and to ask for what you need. This is an individual process that may include internal talk or prayer. Mariella Mathia, counselor and trainer, tells us, "Each time when I had come to the end of my rope, when I surrendered to the fact that my dream and vision wouldn't work out, a miracle happened and I received unusually and amazingly generous help and support from outside sources." For some people, the help may come from the inner self, for others from proper people, and still others find support through spiritual sources.

Take Leslie Gura, finance director at a hospital, who was trying to determine what she wanted next in her career. She realized that she needed to allow. "It helped to use a coach to determine next steps. And I was influenced by spiritual forces."

Affirm

Create internal affirming talk that stimulates positive head and heart energy toward allowing. Try some of the following Allowing Affirmations,[12] or make up your own:

- I easily, when appropriate, allow and go with the flow.
- I let go of attachment to a certain outcome.
- I release all tension. I release all fear. I release all anger. I release all guilt. I release all sadness. I release old limitations.
- I let go of any unhealthy patterns in my life or consciousness.
- I allow and am at peace with the process of life.

PRACTICAL POINTERS

- *Broaden.* While following your plan, allow the path toward your purpose to unfold. Don't be vested in the exact outcome, but committed to a broader intention.
- *Be present.* Live in the moment and use meditation to learn noninterference.
- *Affirm.* Create affirming internal talk to stimulate you to allow.
- *Honor.* Realize that you allow in every breath you take. Look for other experiences in your life.
- *Trust.* Have faith that the Universe, God, or your spiritual protectors, whatever wording works for you, will not leave you now.
- *Accept.* Be open to serendipity and help from others.

APPLY TO REAL PURSUITS

Think of the situations in your past where you have allowed. Think of the consequences when you have been allowing. Where might you currently need to surrender? Consider this nonprofit executive's story.

When Passion Is Not There—Leslie Durgin's Story

Leslie Durgin, social services administrator and nonprofit executive, has experienced the ecstasy of pursuing and attaining worthwhile objectives. As the Mayor of Boulder, Colorado, she exercised political courage by working with others to challenge an amendment to the state constitution that would limit the rights of certain segments of the population. The U.S. Supreme Court ultimately ruled the amendment unconstitutional. "It was magic. I was standing on the steps of the Supreme Court with a group of honorable and respected colleagues. There was a sense of doing the right thing. I love bringing ideas and people together to make others' lives better."

She has intensely pursued that purpose as a senior state government administrator, an elected official, and as a profit, nonprofit, and educational institution executive. All these roles had certain elements in common. Durgin comments, "It was intellectually stimulating and I was learning and using my skills, personal relationships, and passion to identify and address real issues. Passion is fundamental. It is first and foremost. . . . When passion is not there, I can't fake it. You can do it without passion, but then you are missing the key piece of what makes life interesting and fun."

Even with this wisdom, Durgin found herself in a difficult leadership situation without that sparkle as a result of not allowing her inner voice to guide her path. "In my current job, I'm unhappy. I lie awake at night. I am not using my talents. With this job, I called and wanted to resign. They said no. I listened to others and not myself. I got caught up with what others say."

It is helpful to know when it is the right time to move on. "The rule of thumb is to do an up-front assessment. I need to give myself enough quiet time to listen to my heart, rather than my head. I must listen to my own voice and instinct and not get caught up with what others say. I listen while I'm gardening. There has to be passion. I think I can fake it and in my head I do a spin."

It is a challenge to allow the heart its voice. "I make mistakes in trying to use my head to overcome my heart. I reframe artificially to create a heartfelt concern. I need to know when to turn off my head."

Durgin has this advice for those seeking passionate purpose: "When you are first starting out, try many things and sort out what is passionate and what is not. There is a role of volunteering to help you find your purpose and fill your life. Then get clear on what your purpose is. Make sure your decisions fit with what is important to you, your purpose."

Durgin finally surrendered to the fact that this position was not right for her: "I get clear with myself on what is and what is not working. Then I get clear with others. I went to the Board and said this isn't working. Let's do a transition and I will finish up."

SUMMARY

- The Allowing Strategy involves being clear on *what* you want and allowing *how* you get it to unfold.

- Most people are interested in learning how to more effectively allow, surrender, and let go of resistance because there are many rewards to doing so and it is often difficult to do.

- The real reward from letting go is freedom from suffering and deeper satisfaction from life. Use Shinzen Young's formula, representing what is behind these difficult circumstances:

$$\text{Pain} \times \text{Resistance} = \text{Suffering}$$

- As you reduce your resistance to zero, your suffering will likewise go to zero.

- Allowing requires trust. There are many unknowns.

- There can be major consequences if you do not allow when it is needed. These include tremendous suffering, stagnation, lack of enjoyment, and lack of meaning.

- Allowing is the opposite of resistance, it is not the opposite of persistence. You can persistently allow. You can be allowing while you persist in your pursuit.

- There are ways to strengthen your allowing capabilities. These include:
  —Meditating.
  —Doing.
  —Asking for help.
  —Affirming.

11

Connections Strategy

Premise: We are part of an interconnected web of life.

Path: Build relationships with self, proper people, other beings, and spiritual sources.

Outcome: Meaning in life, as well as support along life's journey.

Make proper connections to the web of life. Participants in my study agree that proper people are the greatest energizer for their pursuits, while other people are the biggest hindrance. The most effective Passionate Pursuers realize that it is vital to build relationships with and bring along on life's journey the *proper* people and support network and lessen the impact of improper ones.

Many of the participants include the following in their networks:

- Self.
- Proper people.
- Animals, plants, and other living things.
- Spiritual sources.
- Environment.

WHAT YOU CAN GET FROM THIS CHAPTER

People of all profiles benefit from connections. This chapter helps you determine who is or should be part of your support network and for whom do you provide this support. Support serves as an energizer and is a key element in pursuing, seeking, or resting between purposes. The support received from others is really just another way for the sacred voice of the Universe to speak, be heard, and affect our lives. As interconnected beings, we indirectly or directly, help each other when we find and pursue our purpose.

Some of us are gregarious and social with far-spanning networks, others introverted and quiet with narrower reach. Both are fine. There are different methods to intentionally build a network while remaining open to new opportunities.

My Path—The Source of Wisdom

As I got to know myself better and allowed for exploration, a remarkable thing happened. I connected with my inner self. My heart and hands began to speak balancing my dominating head. Here was a vital resource that I had previously neglected. I discovered that an infinite wisdom was within me. I also determined that bringing the proper people on my life's journey, and leaving the improper ones behind, provides real rewards of life—meaning, extraordinary results, and enjoyment. Now let us explore some of the elements of people's networks.

SELF

Listen to yourself. Many of us recognize this as intuition, instinct, or sixth sense. Passionate Pursuers have the ability to connect with this inner voice. Virginia Corsi, management consultant, reminds us, "Trust your instinct, follow your heart, and give back. If you help others, you will be helped." Messages from the wise self may be communicated through head, heart, or hands energy, as well as through intuition. This perception capability is defined as direct knowing independent of rational thought and inference. Your wiser inner self communicates through insights or a sudden flash or idea. You might even have a visceral or gut reaction and feel pain or pleasure.

Your inner self, or spirit companion as I personally call this part of me, is always there as a source of wisdom and connection to the flow of the Universe. How do you tap into your intuition? Some people have learned to listen to their heart, trust their gut, *and* understand the logic of their head. Others need help. Use any of the exploration techniques mentioned in Chapter 3. Only you can determine what works best for you.

PROPER PEOPLE

The most important thing in life is relationship. Make them as harmonious as possible.

MARTHA ARNETT, retired university secretary

Interviewees in my study repeatedly cited the support of others as a positive force encouraging the pursuit of passionate purpose. These people play various roles and may not even know the impact they make on others. People also recommend that the impact of those who drain energy needs to be mitigated.

Author Jim Collins said, "The right people help along the way. This inner circle of people with integrity won't let you down. If you were on a boat in a stormy ocean, you could rely on them." Not surprisingly, "having the right people on the bus" is also mentioned in *Good to Great*[1] as one of the determining factors distinguishing great organizations from those that are merely good, and as the closest link between a great company and a great life. People genuinely want to help, although some may not be as tactful and others not as forthright as you would like.

Supporters

Marsha Semmel, museum director, recognizes the value of supporters, "I used to think it took single-minded dedication and that I could do it alone. From experience I learned to put the right people in the right place at the right time." Many people with different roles can help in your pursuits, if you let them. Build a support system of those you can trust:

- *Players* take a load off you and do real work. They get as deeply involved as you allow. They provide new perspectives and ideas, too. At Radish, they were our initial consultants, employees, executive team, and board of directors.
- *Investors* believe in you and provide funding. Many passionate purposes require money and additional resources. At Radish, they were initially our friends and family and later the venture capitalists.
- *Role models* have successfully done it before. You can say, "If they did it, so can I." They are living proof that it is possible to climb the mountain, run the four-minute mile, or get the degree while working two jobs and raising kids. Marie Curie, the Wright Brothers, and

Connections with the proper people are part of the winning formula. The Radish family, shown here at our holiday party, grew and celebrated along the way.

Thomas Edison are often considered role models. They persevered to make a difference. Find the role models who are relevant to your passionate purpose. Consider the advice of artist Alyson Mulvany, "Keep inspiring people in mind." At Radish, successful technology entrepreneurs were our role models.

- *Advisors, teachers, and coaches* provide advice and are your cheerleaders. Just as an athletic coach can take the team to new levels of performance, these mentors guide you through rough times. Usually they have done it themselves, but they move beyond being a role model to actively show you the way. You can find individuals for this role. Carlos Aguirre, opera singer, shares, "To go deep into your passion, learn from everyone—your teachers, students, everyone." At Radish, we were fortunate to have friends who were experienced entrepreneurs, and graciously provided advice and contacts.

- *Confidants* are your most intimate partners in life. With them, you can anguish about your problems and laugh at your foibles. They provide frank feedback. At Radish, Dick and I had each other. Additionally, I had close friends and my women's support group.

- *Purpose partners* have their own mission, but combine efforts and align with your mission to bring about a greater impact. At Radish, our business partners played a big role in our success.
- *Support team members* provide additional help to get you where you need to go, sometimes for pay and sometimes pro bono. At Radish, we had legal counsel, patent attorneys, graphics designers, accountants, and bankers among others.

Consider your web. Sometimes Passionate Pursuers try to do too much alone and don't ask for enough help. When you promote in the *Pursue Purpose* stage, you build your web and allow others to embrace your passionate purpose as their own. As they become champions of your purpose, and Passionate Pursuers in their own right, they find worthwhile work and connections. This brings them a *raison d'être* and real rewards to their life.

Nonsupporters

There are also people who can have a negative influence, if you allow them. Intentionally or not, they are a discouraging force. Some resisters see your passionate purpose as a threat. Others mean well but are unconstructive. Still others are naysayers with pessimistic perspectives. They are energy zappers. Nonsupporters might be family members, coworkers, or even supervisors that you cannot easily avoid. Learn from them, and as appropriate, incorporate their wisdom, yet lessen their impact.

Dealing with People

Since people can have such a big impact on you and your pursuit, it is wise to assess their effect and take appropriate actions. Proper and improper people can be viewed as a polarity to manage (see Chapter 7). Seek to minimize the negative results (or downside) of the improper people and maximize the positive results (upside) of the proper people. This polarity may alternatively be stated as engagement and avoidance of certain people.

Tune into your physical sensations, or hands, when you are around a particular person or group by doing a quick body scan. While holding a mental image of a person, tune in to your body sensations. Ask yourself, "How does this person make me feel?" Do not think about it. Just listen for your instant, gut response—good, neutral, or bad. If you feel good or neutral, then these people are not having a negative impact. If you feel bad this is a Red Flag indicating you should try to mitigate their impact and take action steps to experience the upside of and engage with proper people.

Vigorously seek people who make you feel good and energized, get in a different setting, and say positive affirmations. Avoid the negative ones, if doable, and reduce their ability to influence you. Try the "Lessening the Impact" Meditation in Appendix B to mitigate their effect. Caregivers can use this technique when around the sick and needy, so they can give positive energy without absorbing the negative forces coming from those needing care.

Surround Yourself with Supportive People— Josephine Heath's Story

"Surround yourself with supportive people," says Josephine Heath, currently president of a community foundation. She previously had a political career that included serving as county commissioner and then running for U.S. Senate. "From early on, I had a strong sense of justice. If someone was picked on in the playground, I would feel bad and try to change the situation. As a young girl, I lived next to the fields and worked alongside the migrant workers. They worked so hard, much longer than I. But I had the ability to visualize a better future and see the possibilities. This is why later as a county commissioner, I worked so hard to build the first housing of its kind in the nation for migrant workers.

"I have more ideas than can be implemented. This is a 'glorious burden.' Thinking 'how can you do it?' and creating a road map builds excitement. Use this plan to educate people so they get behind your idea and collaborate. My plans are not necessarily written; some are in the head. Written plans would be helpful for communication.

"I must feel that the idea will not harm someone or if the risk is great, that I can assume the risk. . . . There is a responsibility that comes along with passion, that you don't harm someone else. . . . You must be especially careful not to harm children. . . .

"It helps to realize that we may or may not change this, but we will open the door a little bit. There is a responsibility to let people see that change does not happen overnight. You are a part of a whole set of nameless, faceless people who came before you and paved the way."

Heath has advice on proper and improper people. "Use people as the screen for ideas. My staff, husband, and others see me coming and say, 'No, not again!' Recognize who you can trust and try your idea out on them. Realize that there are naysayers, but don't be easily discouraged by them. Sometimes you need to ignore naysayers realizing that people have their own agendas. If you are traveling with those who don't like your idea, try to change it, see if you can live with it, or evaluate and move on. Determine when to hold 'em and when to fold 'em as you might need to get out of this group."

Passionate Pursuers nurture their supportive network. "Success has a successor. A major part of any project is to inspire people. It is not really successful until you've done this."

Heath's advice is to determine each day how to act on those things about which you feel strongly. "It is okay to feel passionate and to act on it. There is always some way to act on your passion. Passion can happen in small pieces. It doesn't have to be the big dream. Reward yourself for little dreams. Find the way to act in every day; perhaps it is writing a letter, welcoming someone, or telling a coworker she is doing a good job."

PRACTICAL POINTERS

- *Review.* Take a look at the significant people in your life. Who plays what roles? Are you missing certain kinds of support? Who would you be better off without?
- *Adjust.* Make some decisions on who should be part of your project. Sometimes people really want to move on, but need your permission to let go.
- *Meditate.* Use the meditative techniques described in this book to assess and mitigate the impact of certain people.
- *Ask.* The Bible[2] says, "Ask and ye shall receive." People want to be wanted. They like to help. Some are standing on the sidelines wishing they could be involved. Perhaps your passionate purpose can bring meaning to their lives, and it may even become their reason for being.
- *Appreciate.* Be sure to take time to thank the people around you. A little appreciation goes a long way. Let your supporters know you value them.
- *Help others.* It never seems to fail—when you help others, others will help you. You learn a lot in the process, especially about how to involve others in your quest.

OTHER LIVING BEINGS

Connections extend beyond people to animals and plants that energize some people's pursuits. People live longer when they have a living connection, even a plant, that needs their care.

Seeing Eyes—Morris Frank and Buddy's Story

Morris Frank[3] had no idea that a German shepherd would transform his life and the lives of thousands of other disabled people. But indeed Buddy was the vital support element to freedom and self-sufficiency.

After being totally blinded in 1927 at the age of 16, Frank instantly lost his independence. With a few notable exceptions such as Helen Keller, blind people were not accepted in a sighted society and were often relegated to doing menial work such as making brooms or, worse, spending their lives in an institution.

Fortunately, Frank, then 20, discovered a new aid introduced in Europe, a dog guide. He instantly knew his calling—to train to work with such a dog and bring the concept back to the United States to help other blind people.

Letting nothing stop him, Frank passionately pursued this purpose and established the most important relationship in his life. Buddy, taking on the role of Frank's eyes, was a special being with a strong commitment to serve. Once when Frank nearly refused to follow Buddy's lead to stop, Buddy saved Frank's life by physically blocking him from walking into an open elevator shaft.

In 1929, Morris Frank and Dorothy Harrison Eustis, who provided the $10,000 seed funding, started *The Seeing Eye,* an organization that trains dogs and blind people to work together. Much work was needed to build acceptance for dogs from banned areas. Frank traveled, gave speeches, showed how he could go anywhere and cross any street with Buddy's guidance, educated the public to allow guide dogs into public facilities, and raised funds. With the partnership of Buddy and many others—dogs and humans alike—The Seeing Eye has provided independence and dignity to blind people across the country and around the world.

SPIRITUAL SOURCES

Spiritual connections positively influence some people's pursuits. Depending on the individual, this spiritual source, guardian, or companion might be called God, angel, Universe, Presence, serendipity, dreams, visualizations, nature, or even the wiser self.[4] These forces may or may not be real for you. If they are, recognize and embrace them. Many people such as Stephanie Nestlerode, management consultant, find, "Spiritual energies are available to guide me." Likewise Martha Arnett advises, "I feel protected by an angel. If you don't, ask for one."

Connection to God and People—Don Vanlandingham's Story

"Life has brought challenges" to Don Vanlandingham, retired chairman and CEO of Ball Aerospace and Technologies Corp. and his family "We lost a grandson to sudden infant death syndrome. Another 3-year-old grandchild developed childhood leukemia. That was hard."

Growing up in a lower middle class, yet stable, Christian home in Oklahoma with loving parents who set high expectations, Vanlandingham acquired high self-esteem and a strong work ethic. "My mom said, 'You can do anything.' My dad showed me how to balance work and family."

For Vanlandingham, belief in God is the essential element of a meaningful life. "I believe that without a belief in God and Jesus Christ life cannot have a purpose. The grand purpose in my life is to achieve eternal life through faith. . . .

"Early on there was a decision point to believe or not. I chose to believe. Starting in ninth grade, I also chose to pursue a career in electrical engineering."

Over the next 35 years, Vanlandingham steadily moved from junior engineer to project manager and on to president and ultimately chairman of Ball Aerospace, a fast-growing, $500-million company providing leading space technology. "I don't wear my belief in God on my sleeve, but it shows through in my integrity and management style—and if people ask me, I'll talk. . . . My path to success was to live my values and beliefs, get the best education I could, and apply myself diligently in my work and to my family."

The corporate culture makes a difference. "Working on things that would go into space was exciting. It just felt right. Then I realized that our unique culture revolved around the people, outstanding and very smart people who do things that never have been done before.

"Ball Aerospace combines meaningful work with passionate people. A lot of people would work if you didn't pay them. We value integrity and professional freedom. It helps to have an open door policy. Even with a title, you need to earn people's respect. When there is a problem, management listens and tries to take action. We work at building trust and good communication through quarterly state-of-the-company speeches, one-on-one communication, and breakfast discussions every two weeks with twenty people at all levels."

Vanlandingham managed the polarities of life. "I worked hard at keeping a proper balance in work and family life. The tensions came from family versus career. I did not always succeed in making the best choices, but simply did the best I could. I was willing to back off some on my career after I saw others with problems, who had lost their family along the way.

"With my retirement, I am spending time guiding and loving my grandkids, helping in the entrepreneurial world and with church activities, and playing. It has been a great life."

ENVIRONMENT

Defined in different ways by various people, the right environment might mean: Surrounding yourself by success, putting yourself in situations that can provide necessary resources and diversity, or a space that frees your energy.[5] People recognize these factors as positive forces.

For some people like me, not watching TV creates an energizing environment because I can limit negative media inputs and focus instead on goodness. For others, watching TV has a positive effect. Others in my study need to be close to nature, immersed with passionate music, near flowing water, surrounded by soothing color, or in a space free of clutter that allows *chi* or energy to move. Only you can choose what is right for you. What do you need in your environment to energize you?

PRACTICAL POINTERS

- *Identify.* Ask yourself who is part of your support network?
- *Question.* Who or what, if anything, is missing?
- *Connect.* Build a supportive environment with connections to self, proper people, animals and plants, and Spirit.

SUMMARY

- Make proper connections. Use the Connections Strategy to build relationships with the self, proper people, animals, plants, and spiritual sources. Effective Passionate Pursuers bring the proper people and web of life along and lessen the impact of improper ones.
- A support network might include these elements:
  —Self.
  —Proper people.
  —Animals, plants, and other living things.
  —Spiritual sources.
  —Environment.
- Determine who or what you need in your support network and build those connections. Bring the proper connections along.
- Reduce the influence of those who drain energy, the improper connections. Learn from them, and as appropriate, incorporate their wisdom, and lessen their impact.

12

Pack
Strategy

Premise: Certain things help and hinder in life and in pursuits.
Path: Bring energizers along and remove hindrances.
Outcome: Movement in the pursuit of passionate purpose.

Have you ever gone on a journey without a suitcase or backpack? It is just as important to pack essentials when embarking on a path of passionate purpose. It is helpful to pack energizers, positive forces, that encourage you along the way. Instead, people often pack hindrances, negative forces, that discourage them.

WHAT YOU CAN GET FROM THIS CHAPTER

Passionate Pursuers, who know how to pack appropriately for the journey, may reaffirm what they are already doing and discover ways to be even more effective. Seekers and In-between'ers, in using this strategy, may become aware of their energizers and establish how to rise above hindrances.

My Path—Leaving Hindrances Behind

After leaving Radish and being an In-between'er for a while, I pursued a new passionate purpose, the Baby Plan. The right doctors and medical technology, other supportive people, and my own passion for having a family energized me.

But I had not really let go of the resentment that was holding me back from healing from the experience at Radish. I had left the company nearly two years earlier, but as a founder and major shareholder, my stock was subject to considerable restrictions with each round of funding. The new investors were constraining the founders even more with the latest round of funding.

This made me very angry. Dick and I held less stock than many of the investors who would not be subject to these terms. Why weren't other top executives of the firm also being asked to sign these confining documents?

Initially, I agreed to sign the documents if other key leaders would also be subject to these terms. This seemed just to me, especially since I wanted revenge for the pain and suffering they had "caused" me by taking my first baby, Radish, away from me. Dick didn't agree with my rationale.

Nearly seven and a half months pregnant, I had just left the hospital from a scary episode of preterm contractions. If I was not careful, Annie, our real baby and dream come true, would be born too early and perhaps not survive.

Yet, my anger and the stress of this situation were triggering intense contractions again. I could feel Annie churning inside me. "This just isn't worth it. I am hurting my real baby and me," I concluded. My top priority, Annie, was sending me a message. To get clear on a decision to let go, I did a visualization. While I don't remember the exact image, the survival message from my heart was clear: "Let go of this resentment. Let go of it NOW!"

I immediately knew what I had to do. I signed the documents, ran outside and put them in the mailbox, and spontaneously broke into sobs. As the tears streamed down my cheeks, the toxins that I had been carrying from feelings of grief and betrayal were washed out of my system. The emotional release of letting go of this revenge was substantial. I felt drained, but ready to move on after overcoming this significant hindrance.

Annie calmed down, the contractions subsided, and I delivered a healthy, full-term baby. My real baby was born and no one would take her away from me.

I lightened my pack by shedding resentment and bringing along love and other energizers. What about you and your pursuits in life? What is best for you to take and what should you leave behind.

ENERGIZERS

Positive forces, or energizers, lighten your load and encourage your movement toward your goals. Anny Lee, facilitator of healing arts, explains, "Forces are just energy. There is nothing as good or bad energy; it is just

Breaks along the way, help you enjoy the process. My daughter Annie and I hang out in the hammock in our secret garden, as my life's pursuit progressed from Business Plan to Baby Plan to Family Plan.

your perception. Regardless of what it feels like, I know I am moving forward." What are the most important energizers helping people in their pursuits of passionate purpose?[1] The two most frequently mentioned are:

1. *Internal factors* revolving around the self such as values, gifts, and traits as well as use of the Pursuit of Passionate Purpose process and strategies.
2. *External factors* such as connections to the proper people, spiritual forces, and environment as well as the purpose itself.

Internal Factors

Self

Explored in Chapter 11 as a success strategy in itself, connection to and support from your inner self is the most important encouraging force. Tremendous wisdom to energize and guide your pursuits comes through your inner voice. You only need to turn on your listening ears. People in my study also mentioned certain traits that supported their efforts. Consider Mike, the successful technology entrepreneur, "I have confidence that I will be successful when I have found a meaningful opportunity and matched it with my abilities. Then I've minimized self-doubt." It is helpful to bring the following traits along in your pack: confidence and self-esteem, curiosity, energy, optimism, integrity of effort, passion, regeneration, and wholeness (see Chapter 3).

Purpose

A clearly defined purpose and a vision of its successful outcome are positive forces. Knowing what you want to bring about as the desired state and having a "why" for the journey brings more passion, which results in more energy. Diana Sherry, adult literacy champion, voiced that effect, "A positive force was knowing that there is a great opportunity to make an impact." Also, consider the wisdom from *The Way of the Peaceful Warrior*,[2] "There are no accidents. Everything is a lesson. Everything has a purpose, a purpose, a *purpose*."

Enjoy the Process of Getting Where You Want to Go

The energy comes from learning, movement, change itself, and sense of curiosity that are nurtured along the way.

Intrinsic Rewards

These internal rewards,[3] which include a sense of meaningfulness, choice, competency, and progress, can stimulate motivation that serves as an energizer. For example, when you use the Persistence Strategy, you can create a positive feedback loop from setting a small goal, persistently working toward it, and then celebrating and feeling good when you reach it. This brings a sense of progress, as well as higher confidence and satisfaction levels. Thereby, you may seek more endeavors.

External Factors

People and the Web of Life

In my study, participants repeatedly cited the support of people as an encouraging force. They mentioned parents, other family members, supervisors, coworkers, teachers, friends, spouses, mentors, coaches, others who help in some way, and even the public. These people provide support, encouragement, and external validation—whatever the Pursuer needs. Jeanne Teleia, program director for dolphin-assisted therapy, recognizes the value of these contributions: "Often people who come and go in your life can make a significant impact in encouraging you on your path." Sometimes these people may not even realize the impact they have on others. The crucial need to make connections is discussed in detail in Chapter 11.

The Right Environment

The right environment is an encouraging factor. "Surround yourself by success and the sky is the limit," says Johnny Halberstadt, runner, footwear inventor, and entrepreneur.

Recognition

When you make progress implementing and promoting your plan, people may notice and give feedback. Recognition is a big energizer for some people.

Adversity

Difficulty is also meaningful, and even useful, in the pursuit of passionate purpose. People with the proper attitude appreciate that hard times, far from being a hindrance, can propel you forward.

Pack Energizers for Your Journey

Now you know what energizes others. What are your energizers? What are you doing to strengthen their impact in your life?

PRACTICAL POINTERS

- *Be aware.* The first step toward increasing the strength of your positive forces is being aware of what energizes you. Notice what makes you feel alive, engaged, and energized.
- *Build.* Another step is to intentionally nurture and build the positive forces. Seek to build up your self, support system, spirituality, and other energizers.
- *Remember.* A critical step is remembering to take the energizers with you. Often we learn a lesson, then forget it, and later must re-learn it. Your support team is helpful because it can strengthen the collective memory and remind you what to bring along.

Realize that you can modify your pack along the journey. You may change its contents just once or for portions of the trip because you change during the trek. You may have packed self-doubt initially, but through the positive feedback loop from one part of the excursion, you build confidence. Maybe you throw out the doubt and proceed with assurance.

HINDRANCES

We all face challenges. It is what we do with those challenges that make us the people we are.

EILEEN JOSEPH, philanthropic consultant

Negative forces holding us back can be even stronger than energizers. The solution is to identify and unpack them by rising above the hindrances. People identified restraining forces hindering their pursuit of passionate purpose.[4] Not surprisingly, many are consistent with Buddhist hindrances to enlightenment.[5] Many obstacles are the mirror image, or the polar opposites, of energizers. The following obstacles are listed in the order they were most frequently mentioned:

- *Internal factors* such as self-doubt, fear, resentment, impatience, and resistance.
- *External factors* such as unsupportive people, societal pressures, and adversity.

Rising above the Hindrances

What can be done to lighten the pack? One tactic is to remove the hindrances. Another is to turn them into energizers or helpers. Specific antidotes follow for individual hindrances, yet the overall approach is the same for all:

- *Face and name.* Become aware of the discouraging forces that burden you. Identify and name them so it is easier for you to overcome them. The way to work with obstacles is to admit them, not repress them.
- *Cultivate.* Choose the strongest hindrance and cultivate the opposite quality. Intentionally nurture and build the opposing positive force.

- *Modify*. Determine an antidote to dissolve this force or transform it into an energizer.

The recommended actions all revolve around connections to the proper people and web of life. The most important person is you. Your thinking, feeling, and doing can transform your life.

Internal Factors

"There is a tension between accomplishment and smelling the roses," as Pete Palmer, geologist, points out. Most internal obstacles boil down to tension between different parts of self, head and heart, work and personal aspects of life, and other polarities. Liz Valles, financial controller and musician, supported this observation, "A discouraging factor comes from the personal conflict of not listening to my heart."

Self-Doubt and Judgment

Self-doubt is often experienced as an internal, negative nagging voice difficult to quiet. Judgment is the inner "critic" evaluating and expressing disapproving opinions about your self. The amount of self-doubt and judgment is high when a person's level of self-esteem and confidence is low. However, even those with relatively high self-esteem and confidence can benefit from tools that quiet nasty self-talk. Some very successful people, as measured

PRACTICAL POINTERS

- *Affirm*. Discipline yourself to reject the negative voice and instead fill your mind with positive thoughts.
- *Feel*. Visualize a positive outcome.
- *Recall*. Remember positive experiences to counterbalance the negative ones.
- *Refocus*. Let go of controlling the situation. Focus intently on something else.
- *Find support*. Be with people who encourage you.
- *Forgive*. Pardon yourself for not being perfect.
- *Use the positive feedback loop*. Establish a small goal, work on it, achieve it, and let the resulting feedback encourage you.

outwardly by traditional societal standards of accomplishment, have said that self-doubt and critical judgment are discouraging factors for them.

For many of us, our internal critic speaks all too loudly and is a difficult gremlin to quiet. Linda Shoemaker, former attorney and community leader, along with many others in this study, has experienced this, "A little voice in my own head said you won't be able to do it and won't be successful."

Fear

Both the known and the unknown can trigger fear—the strong, unpleasant emotion associated with anxiety and fright. Its voice can sometimes be labeled "the coward" or "the victim." Fear is an obstacle for many people.

While attempting to kayak in turbulent whitewater that was much more than I could handle, I experienced rational fear that was part of an innate survival instinct. After unsuccessfully trying for years to improve my kayaking skills to reduce my fear, I finally chose another form of recreation. During my PhD program, I experienced irrational fear. For over three months, I feverishly studied for my comprehensive exams by day and woke in a sweat in the middle of the night with nightmares. I responded by studying harder. Perseverance won out—I passed the exams and completed the degree.

There are at least two kinds of fear: Irrational fright that you make up in your head and rational panic that comes from true danger. Both feel real. There is a time and a place for working through fear with persistence and another for getting out of the situation. Wisdom is knowing when to appropriately use each one of these. Strive to resolve irrational fears.

If fear is one of your negative forces, you are not alone. Many people experience various kinds of fear. Deborah Myers, in turning her passion for writing into her career, shared, "I had to overcome the fear that I wouldn't make it."

PRACTICAL POINTERS

- *Act*. Take positive action and keep working at it.
- *Surround*. Encircle yourself with supportive people.
- *Just do it.*
- *Use good judgment*. When there is real danger, your best recourse may be to move on.

The Obsessive Mind

The obsessive thinker is difficult to turn off. Thinking about something over and over again is a hindrance. While it is important to plan, analyze, rehearse, review, and remember, it becomes a burden if you are constantly reliving the same situation.

During my last few hours in the office before a much-needed vacation, I had the final confrontation at Radish. Unable to resolve the issue before the trip, I carried it with me. During the day, my mind ran rampant on repeat cycle. At night, I woke up with images and talk playing in my head over and over again. There was a dull fog over everything, even the most pleasant and beautiful moments. I had to stop it or I would go nuts. Finally, recognizing this as the pivotal point, I wrote down all my thoughts and made the decision to resign from Radish after the upcoming trade show, where Bill Gates would demonstrate VoiceView to the world. I then made a forceful decision to quit thinking about the issue until after vacation. My mind quieted.

PRACTICAL POINTERS

- *Don't delay.* Deal with issues immediately, so they cannot fester. Waiting only makes things worse.
- *Write it down.* The mind repeats so it will not forget; thus you will eliminate the worry that you won't remember.
- *Decide.* If possible, determine a course of action.
- *Meditate.* Whenever you perceive the internal talk or images, mentally note "talk" or "image" and refuse to get caught in the content. Recognize that the talk is there and then let go of it. Go back to body sensations. This takes discipline. The mindfulness part of meditation recognizes the talk and then the equanimity part of meditation accepts it and lets it go.
- *Be in the now.* Be present in this moment. Worrying is not being present. It is about the past and the future, not the present.
- *Use rational thinking.* Ask yourself and answer "What is the worst thing that can happen?" Then you know that you will survive and that this is not the end of the world.

Emotional or Mental Challenges

Challenges from depression, emotional instability, mental illness, and strong mood swings can be hindrances. Some of the most brilliant, creative people in the world have carried these burdens. Vincent Van Gogh, who suffered from severe depression, died thinking he was a total failure. Now when one of his paintings sells for millions of dollars, we appreciate his genius and ability to continue to pursue his passionate purpose.

Many do not overcome these types of challenges, and yet still others find a way to pursue their dreams. At age 60, Dawn,[6] the retired teacher profiled in Chapter 2, shared, "I was depressed, overwhelmed, and lacking confidence. It was only after therapy and medication that I have come to a better place."

PRACTICAL POINTERS

- *Seek professional help.* Depression and other mental disturbances, are real illnesses that might be helped with therapy and medication. Give it a try.
- *Be kind.* Forgive yourself. No one is perfect. We each have our own challenges to overcome.
- *Be patient.* Take it one day at a time.

Anger and Resentment

Holding on to ill will, wrath, or displeasure can cause great resentment. The one who suffers is the "grudge carrier" who lugs the bitterness, not the person who caused it. From carrying hard feelings about Radish, I know this well.

The Jews in celebrating Rosh Hashanah, the high holy day, end the year with a review and atonement for sins. This includes assessing and then freeing any resentment through forgiveness. With all these burdens lifted, one can begin anew on a solid ground of goodness.

PRACTICAL POINTERS

- *Forgive yourself and others.* Move on with renewed joy in life.
- *Give your all.* Try your best. Accept that your best is good enough.
- *Focus on your progress, not perfection.*

We are often hardest on ourselves. Ask, "Can I forgive myself for any mistakes I have made?" Perhaps it is time to free yourself from resentment.

Impatience

Pursuing passionate purpose takes patience—the capacity to calmly bear pain and steadfastly continue despite difficulty, adversity, strain, or opposition. Yet, the tension between patience and the eagerness or restlessness found in impatience propels you to move forward. Too much patience results in little progress; too much impatience produces hasty, impetuous actions. Impatience is a form of desire.

Patience Pays Off—Joseph Rush's Story.   Growing up in a large, poor farming family in Texas, Joseph Rush wanted to be a scientist. Finally, after years of waiting, he and his wife Juanita scraped together enough money so that he could go to college for one year while she worked. Then the Great Depression hit and his family lost their farm. He had to support his parents and younger siblings through a job as a radio operator for the local sheriff's office. For seven years, Joe held this job to support his family hoping that he could return to college someday.

When the economy recovered, Joe was able to go back to school. Persisting through a long struggle, he finally completed his PhD in physics and became an atomic research scientist for the federal government. Somehow he found the patience, more than he ever dreamed would be required, to persevere.

PRACTICAL POINTERS

- *Believe*. Hold the vision, let go of the outcome and the timetable. Trust that somehow "the invisible hands will come."[7]
- *Visualize and imagine, fantasize and dream*. Savor the moments, even if not yet in reality, when you are with your passion. Feel it and the end goal. Let your passion percolate inside you.
- *Learn*. Take the perspective "What can I learn from this?" Try to find something positive out of the situation.
- *Prepare*. Even if you cannot pursue your dream, determine what you can do to prepare and begin. Read about it and keep your

(continued)

interests up by continuing to learn and grow. Write a journal with
your thoughts, ideas, and plans.

- *Help pursue others' dreams.* Live vicariously through someone else
  for this moment. By giving support to others you can help yourself. Later that support may even come back to you.
- *Persevere* even when movement is slower than you would like. As
  Natalie Goldberg,[8] author of *Writing Down the Bones,* says in her
  workshops, "Continue under all circumstances."

Desire

Desire is the conscious longing or craving for a certain outcome. The craver
and yearner may seek the promise of enjoyment or satisfaction so much
that it takes them off track from really working hard at the pursuit. Karen
Bernardi, realtor, wisely perceives, "The pleasures of life, which are hard
to push away, can hold me back from pursuing my passionate purpose."

I realized that the desire to finish this writing project was blocking my
ability to enjoy the process. Of course, it was also blocking me from completing the project because I needed to be present in the moment to bring
my creativity to its development. I found that if I embedded more opportunities for play along with the work projects, my desire for completion was
manageable. Using Polarity Strategy terms, allowing ongoing movement

PRACTICAL POINTERS

- *Focus on the here and now.* Put attention on your breath as one
  means of being present. Or feel your feet firmly on the ground. Put
  your awareness on something tangible in this moment. If your mind
  wanders away again, gently bring it back to this concrete object.
- *Seek meaning.* Meaningfulness brings more passion. Passion brings
  more enjoyment of the process and fuels the pursuit.
- *Balance polarities.* If you have been overly focused on one pole to
  the neglect of the other pole, attend to the opposite pole. Perhaps
  you need to play along the way. Instead of only having fun after
  getting to your goal, reward yourself and find pleasures along the
  way. Make the pursuit enjoyable in its own right.

between work and play polarities, reduced the pent-up need to attend to the play pole and the overwhelming desire to complete the work project.

When you get so focused on attaining the outcome that you are fixated on the pleasures of accomplishment, desire becomes a hindrance. Having a purpose can be helpful, but having a narrow preference on the exact outcome and how it will come about can lead to difficulties. The successful pursuit of passionate purpose requires living in the present and enjoying the process.

Need to Control

Some people noted that their need to control stood in the way. By restraining, managing, and ruling, they try to have power or influence over the outcome. The controller is also depicted as the commander, resister, or sometimes the perfectionist. Liz Valles, financial controller and musician, described this well, "My wanting to control everything was a constraining factor."

When out of balance, overcontrol can lead to the disenchantment and disempowerment of others. Recall my Radish example from Chapter 6, where my micromanagement caused my staff to feel discounted. The answer may not be from either having it or not, but from appropriately balancing the polarity of control and going with the flow. Too much control forestalls spontaneity and creativity, and does not allow the possibilities to come to you.

PRACTICAL POINTERS

- *Balance.* Set the intention to balance control with letting go. Try the Polarity Strategy concepts in Chapter 7 to create a balance.
- *Experiment.* Try letting go of control when there is not much at risk. See what the end result is. Did you or the project die or something worse? Or, did you perhaps find some unexpected reward?
- *Look.* Observe how to balance control with letting go.

Lack of Energy

The sloth lacks energy and is unwilling or unable to work hard. Many of us experience this at times, even the most productive. Margaret Hansson, successful serial entrepreneur, recognizes this part of herself as a potential hindrance, "I have a lazy streak."

PRACTICAL POINTERS

- *Pamper yourself.* Rest, meditate, and take a break. Have you been pushing too hard? Maybe you are just worn out. If appropriate, forgive yourself for being a mere mortal. Realize that downtime is an important part of the cycle of life; it is natural. Just as the year has seasons with a time for bountiful harvest, the year also has winter, when the earth rests.
- *Go with the flow* on whatever sparks your interest. While this may not be the priority project you had intended, feel good that there is some energy somewhere and something is getting done. Put any energy you muster into discerning what burden needs to be lifted and then resolving that load.
- *Surround yourself* with people who understand, provide support, and have dealt with these cycles of life.
- *Get help.* If laziness continues a long time, get a health checkup. Sometimes professional help is needed.
- *Think.* How have you successfully handled laziness in the past? What tactics work for you? The past can provide proof that you survived before and so you will again.
- *Change.* Are you on passionate purpose? Modify something, experiment, and see the results. Perhaps your energy is lacking because it is time to assess progress and alter the course.
- *Kick.* Sometimes you may just need a kick in the pants to get moving again.

External Factors

External obstacles come from the web of life—people, societal pressures, life circumstances, and more.

People

While supportive people are often an energizer, unsupportive people are frequently a hindrance. It can be hard to identify in advance those who will be positive forces and those who will not. People may not even realize their negative impact on you. See Chapter 11 for ways to lessen this

- *Realize.* Become aware when people are having a negative impact on you and then take appropriate action.
- *Avoid.* Cut unsupportive people out of your circle. "I have learned to quickly get people who are not positive out of my life." advises Jeanne Teleia,[9] program director, dolphin-assisted therapy.
- *Tune out.* Just accept who they are, but do not react or let their actions affect you. Lessen their impact.

impact. Bob[10] (see Chapter 2) felt subtle pressure from his family to become an engineer instead of a teacher.

Societal Pressures

Society, in subtle and more overt ways, may discourage your pursuit. Some people are more susceptible to external forces than others who somehow rise above them. If you find societal pressures are a hindrance, you are not alone. Stephanie Nestlerode management consultant, reports, "Pushes from society were discouraging factors." Marsha Semmel, museum director explains, "How girls and women are treated in society is a negative factor."

Society, this undefined yet so strong influence, can affect everything you say and do—what you eat, who you date or marry, what you wear, when you sleep, how you make a living, and more. Pressure to perform a certain way or to keep up with one's peers is part of the capital machine driving our economy. In certain cultures, the price for breaking the code is high, including death. A form of socialization that many people are working to change has been the pressure on girls to hide their prowess in math, science, and school academics in general, so they don't outperform boys. To project an image of financial success, a person may stay in a high-paid, yet unfulfilling job.

Many people never find their calling, pursue their passionate purpose, and live their dream because outside pressures, whether spoken or not, constrain them. How do we free ourselves from experiencing them as an obstacle?

PRACTICAL POINTERS

- *Discern*. Determine your own values so you can use them for ethical evaluation. Decide what it means to live true to your own highest convictions.
- *Pause*. Take time to analyze and feel, using both your head and heart, so that you distinguish what is right or wrong, important or trivial, for you.
- *Plan*. Realize the consequences of certain actions and consider whether there are ways to minimize any negative impact. Don't be blindsided or naive. Keep your walking papers in order and have some options if you need to fight.
- *Stop and think*. Choose the materials that you and your family read. Block ads. Turn off your TV and radio, or learn to shut off your senses when the advertisements run. In preferring to get my news from print media, I have more control over the ads I see. Become aware of the manipulative messages conveyed in so much of the media.
- *Find*. Surround yourself with people who encourage you to be you and who are not so strongly influenced by outside pressures. Find people who align with your values and beliefs.
- *Choose*. Decide what battles are worth fighting.

Adversity

Financial realities of human existence, lack of time, skills, contacts, information, or knowledge, and other challenges in life hold us back from pursuing passionate purpose. These factors are real and serious. Stephanie Nestlerode, management consultant, shares, "It is a challenge to find time in the midst of chaos for my daily practice." She is not alone. "As a single mom with three kids and no child support, it is difficult to walk away." securities broker Karen Ashworth laments.

Consider the advice from André Pettigrew (see Chapter 7), "There are barriers such as racism and lack of economic means. Accept that's how it is. Try to not see them as limitations. Flip the glass into being half full, not half empty. Look at these as character-building experiences. You can turn barriers into positive forces with the right attitude. Show up—be there and be prepared."

PRACTICAL POINTERS

- *Change your attitude*. Hindrances are your gift. Adversity is a positive force. Recall the stories of the Passionate Pursuers who turned the worst of times into the best of times through their life spirit and drive. Have hope. If they did, you can, too.
- *Persist*. Keep working at small pieces of your purpose until you make some progress. Let this positive feedback encourage you.
- *Recognize*. Look for small victories every day as a way to encourage and give hope.

APPLY TO REAL PURSUITS

What do you pack for your pursuits and what do you leave behind? Consider how this dancer uses her support network, passion, and attitude to overcome and unpack discouraging forces.

Taps Are Talking—Ellie Sciarra's Story

Ellie Sciarra started dancing when she was four and this led to a life full of performing, teaching, and producing meaningful shows from New York to Europe to Boulder. "Tap dancing is my passion. It's a celebration of life that brings people together to create community. And, it brings me back to myself to experience absolute pleasure and joy. My mother was my support. She bought me my first tap shoes and took me to lessons. My friends, partner, and students are also encouraging forces.

"I thank my students for showing up and experiencing life together. Magic happens in the classroom—it is a 'heart' place. It provides a metaphor for learning to dance in all parts of life. After a New York student called to thank me, it became so clear that this is my gift. I realized that you don't know how you're going to impact someone."

Sciarra recognizes discouraging forces and how to overcome them: "The Arts do not get a lot of support and yet our souls need it desperately. My own internal voice with its self-doubt and questioning is another negative force. Yet, studying about other women and what they have to say is an inspiration. . . . I ask for help at a spiritual level knowing there are unseen positive forces."

Sciarra, who has now started a nonprofit organization to support tap dance education, has advice to others pursuing passionate purpose. "Applaud yourself and go for it. Be grateful to have known your gift. Trust your heart, for it always tells the truth."

SUMMARY

- Passionate Pursuers know how to pack for the journey. They pack many energizers and few hindrances. The success strategy is to ensure that you take a light bag of essentials.
- There are forces that encourage or hinder pursuits of passionate purpose.
- When pursuing a passionate purpose, pack energizers (positive forces) and leave behind hindrances (negative forces).
- During different parts of the journey, or stages in the pursuit of passionate purpose process, reassess and repack your bag. There may be changes in the energizers or hindrances along the way.

PART FOUR

CLOSING: PRACTICAL PRESCRIPTION

Premise: There are ways to apply the Pursuit of Passionate Purpose formula to work and life situations.

Path: Put the process and success strategies to work.

Outcome: Real rewards of life.

13 Put Passionate Purpose to Work

Premise: A proven process and guiding success strategies exist.

Path: Apply the formula to your pursuits.

Outcome: The real reward of a more meaningful, satisfying life.

You are now prepared to put the process and success strategies to work in your own life. Whether you take that action is up to you. This book provides a guide to the Pursuit of Passionate Purpose approach and how to use it to get all that you want in life.

There are specific examples for using the formula in aspects of life such as personal development, work, love and relationships, and service. The stories of people on their paths give hope that the pursuit of passionate purpose is possible and brings real rewards. These people, who have encountered and overcome obstacles along the way, are the inspiration that a passionate life is one worth living.

Path to Real Rewards—Linda Shoemaker's Story

Linda Shoemaker has come a long way from the days when she slept in a sleeping bag on the floor of her office because she couldn't afford to pay rent for an apartment. In the pursuit of her passionate purpose, Shoemaker cut corners to go back to school while keeping alive her fledgling mountain newspaper, the *Weekly Newspaper*. "Luckily the office building had a shower," she recalls.

She is a good example of following the Pursuit of Passionate Purpose approach. During the *Know and Nurture the Person* stage, Shoemaker traveled as a youngster all over the country with her family and attended 10 different schools. As the editor of her high school newspaper, she discovered an interest in writing. By being part of a model legislature, she also found her fascination with law. Although she was one of a handful of women accepted into law school, counselors discouraged her from pursuing a legal career so Linda completed an undergraduate degree in journalism. In the *Find Passionate Purpose* stage, she aligned her passion with running a small business and publishing a local newspaper. Then the real work began and for the next 10 years she did whatever it took to *Pursue Purpose.* Eventually when it came time to *Assess Progress,* she decided to make some midcourse corrections.

After building the newspaper, Shoemaker returned with even more self-confidence and enthusiasm to the *Know and Nurture the Person* stage—she reconnected to her passion with law. In the *Find Passionate Purpose* stage, she committed to succeed as a lawyer. During the *Pursue Purpose* stage, continuing to use the Persistence Strategy, Shoemaker overcame adversity to graduate first in her law school class while still running the weekly newspaper business. She became a business attorney for a prestigious law firm, and later became a partner of another firm. She also spent considerable time sponsoring and mentoring young female attorneys, paralegals, and law students.

That's when life brought Shoemaker another opportunity to *Assess Progress.* At the age of 36, she had her first and only child. As the mother of a toddler, Shoemaker was juggling personal and professional priorities. Then the pivotal point arrived. She woke up to the fact that change was needed. "One morning, I forgot that my daughter was in the car. My mind was so consumed with work, that I drove straight to the office rather than drop her off at childcare. This experience in the car was my tipping point."

The Polarity Strategy helped her balance opposites. "Two conflicting values were causing great tension. My head said, 'Stay at the law firm'; and my heart said, 'Leave to be with your child.' . . . It is easy to make a quick decision when the head and heart are in agreement, but it is difficult to make a decision when the head and heart are not aligned."

As she began to use the Allowing Strategy, she realized, "After 10 years in the legal profession, I had lost my passion. I wanted to connect with my soul more. I decided to create balance by quitting the big firm, being a mother, and working part-time as a lawyer. The decision was driven by economics, too—my husband made enough money [so] that I didn't need to work. And I started doing volunteer work to help disadvantaged children."

By unknowingly using the Attraction Strategy, her next passionate purpose found her. After she volunteered with several nonprofits seeking a way to contribute, community leaders encouraged Shoemaker to use her interests, background, and time in an elected office. She won a heated local election to serve as president of the school board. "I was at the right place at the right time. I ran a great campaign."

Shoemaker advises that we find the courage to commit and then pursue persistently, "Don't be afraid to take chances. We all have to learn how to fail, learn from it, and do a better job next time. The trick with failure is to not take it personally. Too many people are paralyzed and cannot make a decision. Instead make a decision, go for it, and make midcourse corrections."

Linda Shoemaker didn't start out with the intention of changing the world; the bigger purpose grew as she aligned with her passion. "My main purpose in life is to make the world a better place," says this visionary philanthropist, education advocate, and community change agent. "You do not only need to be in a high-level, powerful position. A checker at the grocery store can have the right attitude and make the world a better place." With a meaningful purpose in mind, the resources came to pursue it. Work delivered great financial rewards, "It's like we won the lottery." Shoemaker and her husband started a private family foundation that focuses on providing a better life for disadvantaged children. Its annual grants to existing organizations, public policy initiatives, and existing public and private entities total over $500,000. But Shoemaker did not stop there—she founded a public policy think tank and supports other community nonprofit organizations.

Linda Shoemaker effectively applied the Pursuit of Passionate Purpose formula to find real rewards. Here's her advice for someone taking on a passionate purpose. "Be optimistic. Have the right, positive attitude. It won't be easy or a straight line. Realize that there will be changes and corrections as you go. There will be people who will say you can't do it. Yes, you may fail. Persevere and ride through the storms. Be open to learning along the way—see the process as a positive learning experience.

"You can have passion for whatever you do. Passion does not need to be grandiose. Too many people let opportunities pass because they're not ready or don't have all their ducks in line. I recommend being action oriented. Seize the opportunities."

PERSONAL DEVELOPMENT

Our life is the path of learning, to wake up before we die.
NATALIE GOLDBERG, *Long Quiet Highway*[1]

The Pursuit of Passionate Purpose approach works for personal development whether people are aware they are following it or not. For me and for others, it has delivered real rewards. I used it for the Degree Plan, Book Plan, and more.

Helping Self

Dawn,[2] the retired teacher and Seeker grew to know herself better and recognized she had already made an important contribution through motherhood and her 30-year teaching career. Jim Collins (see Chapter 3) changed his situation from being a poor kid who pilfered food from grocery stores to being a best-selling author and respected business professor. Mark Plaatjes (see Chapter 9) evolved from one more kid in a large South African family to world marathon champion. Karen Bernardi (see Chapter 3) transformed herself from a single, alcoholic mom living in a tent to a top-producing realtor. Alan Ehrlich makes his living as an emergency room doctor, but he pursues his passion for music as lead guitarist in a bluegrass band.

Many others in my study, too many to share in this book, followed the same process. They got to know who they were and what they valued, took action to nurture themselves, found and committed to a passionate purpose, pursued it unremittingly, and assessed progress along the way as a means to accept and make required midcourse adjustments.

Most of them have certain success strategies in common. They made significant progress toward their intention and increased their satisfaction with life as a result. Yet, most of them do not feel that they have arrived— they continue pursuing passionate purpose because they understand that the pursuit itself is the means to produce even more meaning and rewards. In each situation, regardless of good and bad influences, each person went through critical stages of deciding, committing, and pursuing. In so doing, they determined, for themselves and others, how to turn a good life into a great life.

Helping Others

Use this same formula to help others in their personal development. Whatever role you play—manager, coach, teacher, parent, or colleague—you can help others make a meaningful difference in the world and find personal growth. This chapter provides suggestions on how to do this.

My high-school German teacher, Fraulein Tali (see Chapter 8), changed my life's course when she commented, "I see you as an engineer." Meg Hansson, entrepreneur (see Chapter 3), Margot Zaher, life coach (see Chapter 5), and many others found the support they needed from outside themselves. Today, they provide encouragement to other people.

IMPLICATIONS FOR ORGANIZATIONS

Matthew Fox,[3] in *The Reinvention of Work,* warns us, "If there is no bliss in our work, no passion or ecstasy, we have not yet found our work."

Organizations can also use the Pursuit of Passionate Purpose approach to positively impact the bottom line or reach other goals. It is useful in directing strategic planning, marketing, finance, and organization development aspects of a firm, as well as for staff development, small group facilitation, and project management. Apply this formula to launch a new business, transform an established one, manage a project, resolve service issues, turn innovation into income, or generate solutions for critical problems. The success strategies can be applied in a large or small, for-profit or nonprofit organization, educational institution, or government agency.

Lynda Simmons (see Chapter 2) used such a process to build the largest nonprofit housing developer in the United States. Don Vanlandingham (see Chapter 11) did likewise to build a $500 million, for-profit technology company. Tom Chappell (see Chapter 5) and others applied this approach to building entrepreneurial ventures that blossomed into multimillion-dollar firms.

It delivered for my Career Plan, Business Plan, and other professional pursuits. I used it to help Radish and my consulting clients thrive, as well as to guide nonprofit organizations toward aggressive goals.

Highlights of Findings

More research is needed and is underway on the organizational aspects of passionate purpose. While there are unanswered questions relevant to business applications, we have learned a great deal:

- People are the most critical element in an organization's success. The work of the organization is a function of the work of the individuals and teams. Each person is following, knowingly or unknowingly, the four-stage process and determining—What do I value and find exciting, what do I want, how do I get it, and how are things going?
- Organizations that accomplish extraordinary results know how to unleash and match people's fervor with important organizational purposes. The manager's job is to place people in positions that allow them to work their passions, individually and in teams, in line with meaningful work purposes.
- An organization follows a comparable four-stage process:
  1. Know the organization (determining the values and core competencies—the passion of the organization).
  2. Find passionate purpose (discerning the needs in the marketplace to serve with the passion).
  3. Pursue purpose (establishing and implementing a plan for achieving the mission).
  4. Assess and adjust along the way (asking how things are going and what's next).

Managers may find the following approaches helpful:

- Allow opportunities for personal exploration so that people get to know themselves better. Consider company-paid education and training, job rotations, and varying project assignments.
- Use the feedback loop to build employees' self-confidence.
- Strengthen a sense of meaningfulness by giving people choices where possible.
- Provide validation of competency and progress through informal and formal assessments.
- Make a supportive environment and people available. Encourage a collaborative culture and provide staff access to a coach.

Work Applications

Here are examples of using this approach in strategic planning, marketing, and organization development.

Strategic Planning

Every organization, large and small, benefits from a strategic plan. The plan clarifies thinking, guides the pursuit, and provides various players with the means to align their passions with a worthwhile end—the overall purpose. Consider one of my nonprofit clients, which uses the Pursuit of Passionate Purpose approach to inspire members and direct the annual planning process. The Boulder Rotary, with over 300 members, held its annual planning session with about 50 of the club's leaders. The president laid the foundation by explaining the international and local strategic focus (*Know the Person and Organization*). My role as facilitator and speaker was to inspire members to make a meaningful difference by pursuing their own passionate purpose through Rotary and to offer best practices for the planning effort (*Find Passionate Purpose*). To encourage coordination, we formed teams for each avenue of service. Each team drafted a miniplan with annual goals, tactics to achieve the goals, budget requests, and expected resulting impacts (*Pursue Purpose*). Later, service team members had the opportunity to match their own passions with the club's purpose by committing to take on certain responsibilities. All the teams submitted their plans a few weeks later, and we combined them into an overall club strategic plan. Process is tracked quarterly with status reports that are shared with all teams (*Assess Progress*).

Marketing

A business cannot survive without satisfied customers who generate revenue. That is why I work with many clients to help them nurture customer relationships as a passionate purpose. The market-driven approach may include listening to the customers through focus groups, managing products and services to ensure they meet market needs, establishing user groups, or communicating effectively with the marketplace. As a result, customer needs are understood and used to guide organizational purpose. Additionally, information is gathered on employees' passions. The key is to align employees' passions with the organizational purpose of customer delight and then to pursue this objective relentlessly. The Pursuit of Passionate Purpose approach has delivered great results in this area.

Organization Development

One of my Fortune 100 clients, a multibillion-dollar player in the information systems arena with well-defined corporate values, committed to transforming their global finance organization. Once the central transition team determined areas for improvement, multiple strategies, and an action plan to make appropriate changes, the next challenge was to get local and worldwide financial officers committed to the plan. Employees in many different countries had unique gifts and interests. How could their passions be unleashed and aligned to pursue the overall corporate purpose?

Corporate finance used the Pursuit of Passionate Purpose approach to reaffirm values, embrace the purpose of organization transformation, and pursue it by drafting an overall plan. In continuing to *Pursue Purpose,* corporate finance partnered with the local CFOs to carry out the next level of implementation. Each country organization and its team members used the four-stage process, with the help of planning coaches, to determine what was of value, what parts of the overall purpose and business strategy were most pertinent to them, and how to execute relevant changes. The Pursuit of Passionate Purpose framework applied to many tiers: corporate, each country, and players within each territory.

RELATIONSHIPS

The important thing is not to think much but to love much; do, then, whatever most arouses you to love.

ST. TERESA OF AVILA[4]

Whether you are nurturing love, looking for your life's partner, striving to have a healthy baby, balancing work with family demands, seeking harmonious relationships, or pursuing a multitude of other personal goals, the Pursuit of Passionate Purpose approach is useful. I successfully used it for the Man Plan, Baby Plan, Family Plan, and Friendship Plan.

Deb,[5] computer scientist, pursued with all her might the intention of having a biological child. She became clear on what she valued, clarified and committed to the purpose, pursued the purpose by working with the best doctor in the world using aggressive interventions, and fulfilled her dream with a baby boy.

The second time around, it wasn't as easy. After three failed rounds of in vitro fertilization, she was faced with a difficult decision. Should she try again? She and her family were paying a huge price in monetary costs as well as in emotional suffering. In broadening the intention, they adopted their daughter from China. Deb advises, "The key is finding passion. You can make things happen if you want it enough. Be open to the possibilities."

André Pettigrew, resolved the tension between work and family by leaving his entrepreneurial venture and passionately pursuing public administration work. He was better able to balance his life with time for his family and his work (see Chapter 7).

Harry Nachman, 85, retired professional engineer, realized as a young man that "only love is real" after reading a Thornton Wilder[6] book. "There is a land of the living and a land of the dead and the bridge is love, the only survival, the only meaning." Love then became the source of all meaning in his life and nurturing loving relationships became his real purpose. He met Jean when he was 30, they married a few months later, and he has been passionately pursuing this love ever since. But his love does not end with his family; he loves friends, community, and causes such as marching during the civil rights movement.

SERVICE

A single hand's turn given heartily to the world's great work helps one amazingly with one's own small tasks.

LOUISE M. ALCOTT, *An Old-Fashioned Girl*[7]

Service is a passionate purpose in and of itself. Thank goodness that millions of people and organizations make a significant difference by advocating for causes without monetary profit. Yes, the Pursuit of Passionate Purpose formula also applies to the Service Plan.

Help for Others—Fred Ramirez Briggs's Story

After working long and hard to grow his telecommunications company into one of the largest Hispanic firms in Colorado, Fred Ramirez Briggs found an attractive exit strategy and sold out. Finally relaxing on a well-earned scuba-diving vacation, he received the call any parent would dread. His 20-year-old son was found dead. No amount of professional success substitutes for tragedy in the family.

No one knew what happened. Ryan had struggled with bipolar disorders for all his life. It may be that his medication triggered his deadly heart attack.

It was too late to help Ryan, but Fred chose to help others as a result of this heartbreak. Music had been one of Ryan's loves and a source of balance. So Briggs established the Ryan Briggs Memorial Foundation to provide funds for music therapy and other treatment to those suffering with Ryan's condition.

Service Leads to Significance

Likewise Morris Frank,[8] as a result of being blinded, brought guide dogs to the United States and cofounded The Seeing Eye. Yet the passionate pursuit of service doesn't have to be initiated by calamity. Linda Shoemaker is now able to be of great service as a result of hard work and good fortune. Eleanor Crow, has spent her work life, and now her retirement, fighting for civil rights for the underprivileged. Oak Thorne is helping save the planet by educating children on the value of the outdoors.

Service can be one of several passions that you pursue at the same time. Millions of people across the world volunteer and provide service in addition to their regular jobs.

Those who serve use the same four-stage process—they find what is meaningful to them and strengthen parts of themselves into the person they want to be, find a worthwhile purpose, pursue it relentlessly with their head, heart, and hands, and assess along the way.

HELP OTHERS USE THE SUCCESS FORMULA

There is no limit to applications for the Pursuit of Passionate Purpose approach. As Paulo Coelho,[9] states in *The Alchemist,* "When you want something, all the universe conspires in helping you achieve it." Purposes range from local applications such as singing in the church choir to international efforts working for world peace. You can help others learn the formula in their own personal development, work, relationships, and service pursuits. Tell them about the two-four-six rule and help them understand that there are *two steps* in the formula for a rewarding personal and professional life:

1. Follow the process.
2. Apply success strategies.

Follow the Proven *Four-Stage* Process

Here are ideas of how to help others during the process:

1. *Know and Nurture the Person.* Ask your friend, "What do you really value? What is important to you?" Notice and acknowledge your friend's gifts and traits, "I like your energy. Wow, you are so curious. You really are good at that." Provide ideas on how to strengthen these and other traits. Open the doors for your friend's personal exploration and growth, "Have you read this book?"
2. *Find Passionate Purpose.* When you notice your friend is passionate and fully engaged, ask, "How do you feel when doing this?" Affirm the connection between the activity and response, "Oh, let's remember that this makes you feel good. Remember to do this more." Help your friend see that exciting opportunities are everywhere. Have your friend make choices on what to pursue and take responsibility for priorities and time commitment. When helping others, be sure they are pursuing their dream, not yours. Counsel your friend to write down a clear, yet inspiring, statement of what is wanted.
3. *Pursue Purpose.* Recommend that your friend develop a plan for "how to get it" that is reasonable, focused, and broken into manageable parts. Provide suggestions on how to tap needed resources. Make the pursuit fun and playful.
4. *Assess Progress.* Acknowledge progress so that movement toward the goal is appreciated. Encourage your friend to define success as integrity of effort, not only attainment of the goal. Teach your friend to recognize and celebrate every success. Be a scorekeeper and cheerleader.

Apply *Six* Success Strategies

Encourage others to use these strategies:

1. Help your friend become aware of how certain activities, such as a schedule, physical activities, and meditation, assimilate disparate parts of self—head, heart, and hands—into an integrated person through the *Polarity Strategy.* When an ongoing tension or difficulty is present

between options, question whether there is dependence between the poles. Ask, "How can you encourage and embrace both alternatives?"

2. Help your friend paint a picture and engage the *Attraction Strategy*. "Close your eyes and see yourself happily attaining what you want. Feel, taste, smell, and hear all parts of the experience."

3. Encourage perseverance and the use of the *Persistence Strategy*. Urge your friend to divide and conquer a big goal by working it piece by piece. Help your friend set up a positive feedback loop: Commit to a small goal, work toward it, and celebrate progress. Genuinely praise efforts. Give compliments. Be a coach. Reinforce a sense of competency.

4. Help your friend accept a change in direction, when necessary. Eventually it may be the right time to let go of a pursuit. Follow the *Allowing Strategy* and surrender to the process.

5. Encourage use of the *Connections Strategy*. Assist your friend in making connections to the right people and establishing a support system. Help develop awareness of internal connections by asking, "Do you hear your inner voice? What does it say?"

6. Notice what energizes and what discourages your friend—help your friend learn how to use the *Pack Strategy*. Give feedback. Provide encouragement in recognizing and attending to the energizers. Suggest ways to reduce the impact of those discouraging factors.

My Path—The Purpose of It All

Radish survived without me. I survived without Radish. I intentionally worked to overcome my anger and hurt. I started to heal and let go of the desire for revenge. It took awhile for me to feel whole again, but my regenerative nature and other Pursuer traits did not let me down.

Slowly, I moved from the in-between into the *Know and Nurture the Person* stage. I read books, visited friends and family, and volunteered. I traveled to Egypt to find my destiny, but didn't find it on the Nile, in the tombs, at the pyramids, or on the summit of Mount Sinai. Destiny does not come from outside, although external factors are helpful. It comes from within. The lesson for me was: The answer lies within you—listen to your inner voice, your heart in harmony with your head and hands.

Before I flew to Paris for the next leg of the Egypt trip, I heard my inner voice saying, "Go home, go home." I didn't know why, but I knew that I had to return. I made the right decision by following my heart and arrived in time to grieve Uncle Wally's death with my family. There is an order, connectedness, and unity in the Universe that brings you where you need to be if you are open to possibilities.

What critical factors are part of the success formula for pursuing any passionate purpose? When I look back at my entrepreneurial pursuit through the Radish experience, I see a four-stage process:

1. A set of values that the founders established and lived by. In knowing "who we were," we laid the foundation of the firm.
2. A clear vision of what we wanted to achieve and intense passion aligned with that meaningful purpose of building a successful company with head and heart.
3. Determination and resilience directed toward getting what we wanted, while finding lots of enjoyment in the process.
4. Evaluation of how it was going, recognition and appreciation of success, and adjustments along the way.

The six success strategies were also at work:

1. Polarity recognition—trying to find a way to embrace both the head and heart purposes.
2. Attraction of the envisioned outcome through tremendous effort—thinking, feeling, and doing.
3. Persistence in working toward the bigger purpose part by part.
4. Allowing, ultimately letting go and surrendering to the process.
5. Connections to many proper people.
6. Energizers that outweighed the many hindrances—the trials, obstacles, and enemies—along the way.

That formula brought Radish to a place it never would have been without it—we made an impact and produced significant results. And in letting go of Radish, and eventually the desire for retribution, I brought myself to a transformed place with new possibilities. I allowed my heart to balance the drive of my head. By moving on from one era of my life purpose, I made room for another pursuit and even more significant rewards.

I learned to more broadly define success as integrity of effort, not only as attainment of the dream. I was a winner in the end, although it did not feel like it initially, because I knew I had lived out my days at Radish with integrity—remaining true to my highest convictions and maintaining effort.

Many rewards came from the pursuit itself—relationships with great people, learning and personal growth, recognition, and financial payback. The long-term rewards for me personally were a more meaningful life with a balanced whole self, worthwhile work today with helping dreamers and organizations fulfill their destiny, and ultimately through the birth of our daughter Annie, the rediscovery of true love—the core purpose of life for me.

As Viktor Frankl[10] asserts in *Man's Search for Meaning,* no one can take away your choice of how to behave. In the end, I was still in charge of myself and maintained my preferences on how to live my life. In letting go of Radish, I reaffirmed influence over my own choice. Ultimately, the only thing you have authority over is you. In the end, that power brings progress on pursuits of passionate purpose.

Success is self-determined. You can turn a good life into a great life. Yes, there are many influencers, both positive and negative. Yes, many people and spiritual forces help along the way. Yes, a process and strategies help move you to where you want to go. But in the end, life is exactly what you choose to make of it.

Now the choice is yours: to pursue or not to pursue the real rewards of life.

Life is short.
Follow your heart, in harmony with your head and hands.
Live your passion. Enjoy the process.
Begin now!

This is not the end. The story is not finished. Just as the Pursuit of Passionate Purpose approach is an ongoing spiral through the seasons of our lives, the process continues through each of you who follows your dreams to turn a good life into a great life, with real rewards.

Here's wishing you well in pursuing passionate purpose!

Epilogue

As the story goes, Radish lived happily ever after. About a year and a half after I left, the firm was sold for over $40 million to a public company that embedded VoiceView into its product line. All the Radish stakeholders received an easy exit strategy and a positive return for their investment. The head purpose was realized.

Many of the employees chose to work together in other ventures, some saying that their Radish participation was their best work experience yet. Much of the heart purpose was achieved and lives on.

As for me, the pendulum dynamically moves, with a little more ease now, between my head and heart to create a balanced life. After the in-between, I plunged into the Baby Plan. As its own challenging pursuit of passionate purpose, it eventually delivered a 7 lb., 9 oz. baby girl. While continuing to attend to the Family Plan, I then embraced the Service Plan and, among many volunteer projects, built a small nonprofit organization into an endowed foundation that helps low-income women attain economic self-sufficiency through education. This helped me reaffirm my worth and appreciate the Pursuit of Passionate Purpose approach as the formula for a rewarding personal and business life. Now, through my present Business Plan, a consulting, speaking, and research firm, I am a "catalyst for extraordinary results" helping individuals and organizations succeed by aligning passion with worthwhile purpose.

Appendix A

The "Pursuit of Passionate Purpose" Formula at a Glance

Based on the two-four-six rule, this is the *two-step* formula for a rewarding life:

1. Follow an iterative and ongoing *four-stage* process.
2. Apply *six* success strategies, which lubricate movement through the process.

Here are the tactics to effectively implement this formula.

FOLLOW THE PROVEN *FOUR-STAGE* PROCESS

1. *Know and Nurture the Person.* Get to know who you are and nurture your whole self.
2. *Find Passionate Purpose.* Foster passion, align it with a worthwhile purpose, and commit fully to the purpose.
3. *Pursue Purpose.* Develop and focus on implementing a plan by persistently involving people in partnership, resources, and communication.
4. *Assess Progress.* Evaluate progress, recognize success, appreciate, and determine what's next.

APPLY SIX SUCCESS STRATEGIES

1. *Polarity Strategy:* Instead of seeing a polarity as a problem to solve, honor opposites in life and allow dynamic movement between interdependent poles.
2. *Attraction Strategy:* Hold a broad intention and remain open to the opportunities that are everywhere, while thinking, feeling passionately, and taking action to get what you want.
3. *Persistence Strategy:* Mindfully persevere with focused determination using a *divide-and-conquer* approach.
4. *Allowing Strategy:* Be clear on *what* you want and allow *how* you get it to unfold.
5. *Connections Strategy:* Bring the proper people and web of life along and lessen the impact of improper ones.
6. *Pack Strategy:* Pack energizers and remove hindrances for the journey.

Appendix B
Tested Meditation Techniques

The Core Practice, developed by Shinzen Young[1] (www.shinzen.org), is a unique interactive, algorithmic approach to mindfulness meditation that consists of four basic steps:

1. Pay attention and accept **B**ody sensations.
2. Pay attention and accept mental **I**mages.
3. Pay attention and accept internal **T**alk.
4. Freely float attention among Body sensations, mental Images, and internal Talk—the **BIT**—and accept whatever you experience.

CORE PRACTICE BASIC MEDITATION SESSION

Sit comfortably, preferably in a quiet place without too many distractions. If possible, sit with upright posture aligning your head over your heart. Close your eyes, if possible, to help concentration. If not, just look into the distance with a softened, nonfocused gaze.

Determine the length of the session. Typically, it will range from 5 to 20 minutes for the entire cycle with approximately equal time given to each contact step.

Settle in by taking a few deep relaxing breaths and slowly letting them out:

Step 1. Establish and maintain simple *contact with your body sensations.* As a physical sensation arises in your body, carefully

(continued)

put your mental awareness on this sensation. Try not to interfere with the sensation, but allow it to change and "dance its dance." In this way, become mindful and accepting of what is. If something other than body sensations distracts you, gently bring your focus back. If there are no body sensations, pay attention to your breathing. After an appropriate amount of time, depending on your comfort and experience meditating, you may continue with the next contact step or move to the final transition.

Step 2. Next establish and maintain simple *contact with the mental images* of your thinking process. For most people, mental images associated with memories, planning, and fantasies tend to appear in the front of or behind their eyes. This location in space is called the mental screen. Rest your attention at your mental screen and be aware of any or no, clear or subtle image activity. Accept whatever images may or may not appear or change; try not to interfere. If your attention wanders into body sensations, mental talk, external sounds, or what have you, gently return to your mental screen. If no mental images appear, focus on the sense of brightness or darkness behind your eyes. After an appropriate amount of time, depending on your comfort and experience meditating, you may continue with the next contact step or move to the final transition.

Step 3. Next establish and maintain simple *contact with the verbal component, or your internal talk,* of the thinking process. Usually people find the talk home base in their head somewhere. Rest your attention at talk home base and listen to the activity without getting lost in the content. Accept whatever talk—clear, subtle, or none—may or may not appear and change. If you get pulled away from talk home base, gently return to it. If no talk is present, focus on the quietness. After an appropriate amount of time, depending on your comfort and experience meditating, you may continue with the next contact step or move to the final transition.

Step 4. Let your attention *freely float among BIT.* Accept whatever you experience. This is truly an awesome undertaking as you attempt to monitor the entire mind-body gestalt as it arises second by second. When the time is right, move to the final transition.

Finally when the time is right, savor any pleasant aspects of the session such as concentration, peace, energy, clarity, and so on as you slowly transition to your next activity.

Repeat this process over and over again as you like. Visit www.shinzen.org for more instruction, information, and insights.

APPRECIATION MEDITATION

This Appreciation Meditation is a variation on ancient loving kindness meditations.[2]

APPRECIATION MEDITATION SESSION

Sit comfortably, preferably in a quiet place without too many distractions. If possible, sit with upright posture aligning your head over your heart. Close your eyes, if possible. If not, just look into the distance with a softened, nonfocused gaze. Take in a deep breath and exhale slowly, letting out all the tensions and preoccupations of the day. Relax.

Start with yourself, because without appreciating yourself, it is close to impossible to be grateful to others. Hold a picture of yourself in your mind.

See yourself physically expressing gratitude to yourself in whatever way is right for you. Imagine your "hands," or physical being, giving a handshake, hug, smile, standing ovation, or whatever works best.

Then using your "head," recite the following affirmation inwardly: "I appreciate all you have and will continue to do in pursuing this passionate purpose. You are making a meaningful difference. You are making progress. You are competent. Thank you for being you." Modify the affirmation until it is right for you.

(continued)

Then with your "heart," send feelings of love, appreciation, and gratitude. Feel yourself being showered with appreciation. A smile covers your face, a warm glow sweeps over your body, and waves of good feelings permeate throughout and radiate everywhere.

Now gradually expand the focus of this meditation to others for whom you are appreciative. Hold a picture of one fellow being after another, or a group together. See yourself physically expressing thanks to the person(s). Recite the affirmation. Send feelings of gratitude and shower the person with appreciation. Feel a loving connection.

If appropriate, expand the focus to encompass spiritual forces in the Universe.

When the time is right, slowly bring your awareness to this situation and space.

BALANCE POLARITIES MEDITATION

Shinzen Young, mindfulness meditation teacher whose story is shared in Chapter 4, has another, more advanced approach to handling personal polarities. "If you want to resolve two opposites, find out what they have in common. Take joy and fear, for example. They are both body sensations, although they also trigger mental images. As such they are vibrating waves of pure energy. Waves can join into an integrated experience."

To better understand this, Young suggests that you consider something solid, such as ice cubes. They have difficulty merging. Instead, they bang and come apart. But they can easily unite, if you change them into water.

Let's explore another example for more advanced meditators. Perhaps you are faced with a decision—stay in your current job or leave? While meditating, you can experience each option as a constellation of body sensations, mental images, and internal talk. When you transform the stream of body sensations, images, and talk into waveforms, you don't suffer from a conflict between them. The streams merge into a unified waveform. You do not waste energy fighting yourself and probably make the best decisions. Realize that this approach may be new and requires practice.

LESSENING THE IMPACT MEDITATION

Normally, nonsupportive people affect you by stimulating uncomfortable body sensations, mental images, and internal talk. Using the Core Practice technique, observe your stream of BIT when these people are around and accept with equanimity. As much as possible, transform your BIT without concern for content into a waveform. The painful feelings that result from these people convert to neutral waves that will not hurt you. Through this conversion, the negative impact of nonsupportive people is purified out of your system.

PERSISTENCE MEDITATION

Start with the basic Core Practice session, but establish that the purpose is to strengthen focus and discipline. Determine an object of meditation and then focus on finer and finer pieces of that object. Establish a certain amount of time to sit that is considerably longer than your typical meditation session. Commit, also, to sit completely still without moving your body other than for breathing. As you sit completely still for a longer period, it may take more discipline on your part to maintain this practice. Reaffirm your clear purpose. Do not move. When your allotted time is up, and only then, slowly come back to broader awareness of your surroundings and room.

Notes

Acknowledgments
1. Sir Isaac Newton, *Letter to Robert Hooke* (February 5, 1675/1676).

Chapter 1: Pursuit Brings Real Rewards
1. Charles Dickens, *Tale of Two Cities* (Garden City, NY: Nelson Doubleday, 1920), book 1, chap. 1.
2. Richard Chang, *The Passion Plan: A Step-by-Step Guide to Discovering, Developing, and Living Your Passion* (San Francisco: Jossey-Bass, 2000), p. 19 defines the term "passions" as activities, ideas, or topics that elicit the emotion of passion. Passionate purpose is found when passion is aligned with purpose; it is one of these "passions." Pursuing passionate purpose means living your passions.
3. Viktor E. Frankl, *Man's Search for Meaning: An Introduction to Logotherapy,* 2nd ed. (New York: Pocket Books, 1963), p. 166.
4. Joseph Campbell, *The Hero of a Thousand Faces* (Princeton, NJ: Princeton University Press, 1989).
5. Kenneth W. Thomas, *Intrinsic Motivation at Work: Building Energy & Commitment* (San Francisco: Berrett-Koehler, 2000), p. 22.
6. These conclusions come from the analysis of data collected from participants in my research study.
7. See note 3. Frankl and others suggest that having a purpose is key to meaning in life.
8. Napoleon Hill, *Think and Grow Rich* (New York: Fawcett Columbine, 1937), p. 38.
9. Jim Collins, *Good to Great: Why Some Companies Make the Leap . . . and Others Don't* (New York: HarperCollins, 2001), p. 210.
10. See note 5, p. 44.
11. Mihaly Csikszentmihalyi, *Flow: The Psychology of Optimal Experience* (New York: HarperCollins, 1990).
12. Chris Hoffman, *The Hoop & The Tree: A Compass for Finding a Deeper Relationship with All Life* (San Francisco: Council Oak Books, 2000).

13. Mark Olsen and Samuel Avital, *The Conception Mandala: Creative Techniques for Inviting a Child into Your Life* (Rochester, VT: Destiny Books, 1992).
14. See note 4. He explains the hero's journey as the universal cycle of life in myths and in reality.
15. Daniel J. Levinson, *The Seasons of a Man's Life* (New York: Knopf, 1978) and *The Seasons of a Woman's Life* (New York: Knopf, 1996).
16. Cynthia Kneen, *Awake Mind, Open Heart: The Power of Courage and Dignity in Everyday Life, A Personal Journey through the Teachings of Buddhism and Shambhala* (New York: Marlowe & Company, 2003), p. 10.

Chapter 2: Profiles of People on Their Path

1. Mindfulness meditation is also known as Vipassana meditation or Insight meditation. The Core Practice is the basis for Shinzen Young's unique interactive, algorithmic approach to mindfulness meditation. Available through World Wide Web: www.shinzen.org.
2. David Crockett's motto in the War of 1812 as per John Bartlett, *Bartlett's Familiar Quotations* (Boston: Little, Brown and Company, 1882, revised 1980), citation 455:1.
3. Inputs from interviewees were qualitatively analyzed to determine energizers, or positive forces, and hindrances, or negative forces. Hindrances related to internal personal constraints such as doubt, lack of confidence, fears, not knowing your passion, or other factors related to low self-esteem were mentioned most frequently by the largest number of people.
4. Author interview with Dawn, retired elementary teacher, who asked not to be identified by her real name.
5. Bob is not this student's real name.
6. William Bridges, *Transitions: Making Sense of Life's Changes* (Reading, MA: Addison-Wesley, 1980). According to Bridges, there are three phases to transitions: ending, neutral zone, and beginning.
7. Author interview with Brian, who asked to not be identified with his real name.
8. Sue is not her real name.

Chapter 3: Know and Nurture the Person

1. Know thyself is the inscription at the Delphic Oracle, from *Plutarch, Morals*. These sayings throughout antiquity were variously attributed to the figures known as the Seven Sages [c. 650 to c. 550 B.C.]. The list is commonly given as Thales, Solon, Periander, Cleobulus, Chilon, Bias, Pittacus.
2. Based on quantitative analysis of data from research participants. Kenneth W. Thomas, *Intrinsic Motivation at Work: Building Energy & Commitment* (San Francisco: Berrett-Koehler, 2000), provides a good summary that there

is a human need for purpose; and Viktor E. Frankl, *Man's Search for Meaning: An Introduction to Logotherapy,* 2nd ed. (New York: Pocket Books, 1963), concludes that purpose gives meaning to life, and your ability to choose how to respond to a situation, even difficult ones such as being in a concentration camp, is something that no one can take away from you.

3. Abraham Maslow, *Toward a Psychology of Being* (New York: D. Van Nostrand, 1961).

4. Additional other elements that people mentioned as sources of meaning included: Everything, music, movement, athletics, and enjoyment. These can, in the broadest sense, be linked with growth.

5. Larry is not the real name. When appropriate in this book, names have been changed to protect people's identity.

6. Richard J. Leider, *The Power of Purpose* (New York: Ballantine Books, 1985), p. 52.

7. Erik H. Erikson, *Childhood and Society* [35th Anniversary Edition] (New York: W.W. Norton and Company, 1985). Integrity is explored on p. 268.

8. According to the Rotary International web site, www.rotary.org, the 4-Way Test, "which was created in 1932 by Rotarian Herbert J. Taylor, is one of the world's most widely printed and quoted statements of business ethics. The 4-way Test has been translated into more than a hundred languages and published in thousands of ways."

9. Anonymous quote used by many people without a clear source.

10. The list emerged from the data of this study, and then their role was substantiated via a study of secondary research.

11. See note 7. Trust and confidence are addressed on p. 247.

12. Johann Wolfgang Von Goethe, *Faust [1808–1832].* Mephistopheles and the Student.

13. Judith Briles, *The Confidence Factor* (Denver, CO: Mile High Press, 2001), has good suggestions. Many of the recommendations are consistent with my study's findings on how to build confidence.

14. Mark Sanborn, president of the National Speakers Association, quoted Albert Einstein in his 2003/2004 "Voices of Experiences" president's message.

15. David Hawkins, MD, PhD, *Power vs. Force: The Hidden Determinants of Human Behavior* (Sedona, AZ: Veritas, 1998).

16. Dr. Norman Vincent Peale, *The Power of Positive Thinking* (Philadelphia: Running Press, 2002).

17. See note 7. Industry is discussed on p. 259.

18. See note 7. Regenerativity is discussed on p. 266.

19. Jim Collins, *Good to Great: Why Some Companies Make the Leap . . . and Others Don't* (New York: HarperCollins, 2001), p. 3.

20. Janet Hagberg and Richard Leider, *The Inventurers: Excursions in Life and Career Renewal,* 2nd ed. (Reading, MA: Addison-Wesley, 1982). Inventure is a term meaning adventure internally.

21. Madame Chiang Kai-shek, *I Confess My Faith* (New York: Methodist Church, Board of Missions and Church Extension, Joint Division of Education and Cultivation, Editorial Department, 1943).

22. St. Teresa of Avila (1577), *Interior Castle,* E. Allison Peers, translator, Reissue ed. (New York: Image, 1972), is a great literary work on experiential mysticism in Christianity. At the center of her teaching is prayer. Thomas Keating, *Open Mind, Open Heart: The Contemplative Dimension of the Gospel,* Reissue ed. (New York: Continuum International Publishing Group, 1994), has made Centering Prayer accessible to modern times and people. Visit www.contemplativeoutreach.org for more information.

23. Mindfulness meditation is also known as Vipassana meditation or Insight meditation. This definition of meditation practice comes from Shinzen Young as explained in "Purpose and Method of Vipassana Meditation." Available through the World Wide Web: www.shinzen.org.

24. This quote from Shinzen Young is taken from his lectures and web site, and is available through the World Wide Web: www.shinzen.org.

25. Andrew Weil, MD, *Self Healing* newsletter (September 2003): 8.

26. The Core Practice is the basis for Shinzen Young's unique "interactive algorithmic" approach to mindfulness meditation. More information is available at www.shinzen.org.

27. Anna Quindlen, "Doing Nothing is Something," *Newsweek* (May 13, 2002): 76.

Chapter 4: Find Passionate Purpose

1. Geog Wilhelm Friedrich Hegel, "Introduction," *Philosophy of History* (1832).

2. Martin Luther King Jr., *I have a Dream: Writings and Speeches that Changed the World* (HarperSanFrancisco, 1992), Speech at Civil Rights March on Washington, August 28, 1963.

3. Mihaly Csikszentmihalyi, *Flow: The Psychology of Optimal Experience* (New York: HarperCollins, 1990).

4. Richard Bach, *Jonathan Livingston Seagull: A Story* (New York: MacMillan, 1970).

5. Kenneth W. Thomas, *Intrinsic Motivation at Work: Building Energy & Commitment* (San Francisco: Berrett-Koehler, 2000), reports that a sense of meaningfulness, choice, competency, and progress provides essential rewards.

6. Jim Collins, *Good to Great: Why Some Companies Make the Leap . . . and Others Don't* (New York: HarperCollins, 2001).

7. In *Gallup Management Journal*'s fourth national survey of U.S. workers, only 35 percent of workers aged 18 to 24 are engaged, or deeply involved in their work. Engagement was slightly less for other age groups: 29 percent aged 25 to 34, 30 percent aged 35 to 49, and 29 percent aged 50 and older are engaged.

8. George Bernard Shaw, *Back to Methusulah* (1921), pt. I, act I. The more popular version of this saying is tributed to Robert Kennedy, "Some men see things and say, 'why?' I dream things that never were and say 'why not?' ."
9. Paulo Coelho, *The Alchemist: A Fable about Following Your Dream* (New York: HarperCollins, 1993).
10. Oprah Winfrey as referenced in *The Quotable Woman* (Philadelphia: Running Press, 1991), p. 159.
11. James Allen, *As a Man Thinketh* (New York: Grosset & Dunlap, 1907), p. 42.
12. Lewis Carroll, *Alice's Adventures in Wonderland* (New York: Dell, 1991) and *Through the Looking Glass: And What Alice Found There* (Market Drayton, England: Tern Press, 2001).
13. Author interview with Martha Arnett, retired university secretary. She was referring to raising four daughters, working full-time, and caring for her polio-crippled husband.
14. Antoine De Saint-Exupery, *The Little Prince* (New York: Harcourt Brace Jovanovich, 1943).
15. Shinzen Young, mindfulness meditation teacher, explains that emotions are experienced as body sensations. Visit www.shinzen.org for more information.
16. Mary Daly, *Minnesota Women's Press* (1993).
17. See note 5.

Chapter 5: Pursue Purpose

1. Esprit Entrepreneur 2003 forum, Boulder Development Commission (October 15, 2003).
2. Ralph Iron (1883) also known as Olive Schreiner, *The Story of an African Farm: A Novel* (New York: Crown, 1987).
3. Shinzen Young. "Benefits of Mindfulness Meditation," (1998–2002). Available through the World Wide Web: www.shinzen.org.
4. Paulo Coelho, *The Alchemist: A Fable about Following Your Dream* (New York: HarperCollins, 1993).
5. Maria Goeppert Mayer, in Barbara Shiels, *Winners: Women and the Nobel Prize* (Minneapolis, MN: Dillon Press, 1985).
6. The *Wall Street Journal* and many other publications covered this story about the ScreenPhone in 1991.
7. Tom Chappell, *The Soul of a Business: Managing for Profit and the Common Good* (New York: Bantam Books, 1993).
8. Tom Chappell, *Managing Upside Down: The Seven Intentions of Values-Centered Leadership* (New York: William Morrow, 1999).
9. Matthew Fox, *The Reinvention of Work: A New Vision of Livelihood for Our Time* (New York: HarperCollins, 1994), p. 96.

10. David Kiersey and Marilyn Bates, *Please Understand Me: Character & Temperament Types* (Del Mar, CA: Prometheus Nemesis Book Company, 1984). The basics of the Myers-Briggs Type Indicator are explained.

11. Joseph Campbell, *The Hero with a Thousand Faces* (Princeton, NJ: Princeton University Press, 1949).

12. O. Fred Donaldson, PhD, "Chrysanthemum Swords: Towards an Understanding of Play as a Universal Martial Art," *Somantics* (Spring/Summer 1984); and "Going Out to Play: A Personal Oath of Peace," *Peace Journal*, vol. 1 (Winter 1988–1989).

13. "Can Saying Cheese Make More Dough?" *US Banker* (November 2003).

14. Jennifer Louden, *The Couple's Comfort Book: A Creative Guide for Renewing Passion, Pleasure, & Commitment* (New York: HarperCollins, 1994), p. 133, reports on the work of Dr. William Fry of Stanford University on laughter.

15. Viktor E. Frankl, *Man's Search for Meaning: An Introduction to Logotherapy* 2nd ed. (New York: Pocket Books, 1963), pp. 68–69.

16. Katharine Graham, in Jane Howard, "The Power That Didn't Corrupt," *Ms.* (1974).

Chapter 6: Assess Progress

1. Kurt Lewin's Social Change Theory is the underlying basis for this Force Field Analysis. Kurt Lewin, *Field Theory in Social Science* (New York: Harper & Brothers, 1951).

2. Kenneth W. Thomas, *Intrinsic Motivation at Work: Building Energy & Commitment* (San Francisco: Berrett-Koehler, 2000).

3. James Allen, *As a Man Thinketh* (New York: Grosset & Dunlap, 1907), p. 42.

4. Jim Collins, *Good to Great: Why Some Companies Make the Leap . . . and Others Don't* (New York: HarperCollins, 2001), p. xii.

5. Rachel Snyder, *365 Words of Well-Being for Women* (Chicago, IL: Contemporary Books, 1997), p. 37.

6. Erika Stutzman, "Making Workers Happy," *Daily Camera* (December 6, 2003): 1E.

7. Bob Nelson and Dean R. Spitzer, *The 1001 Rewards & Recognition Fieldbook: The Complete Guide* (New York: Workman Publishing, 2003).

8. I personally developed this Appreciation Meditation for pursuits of passionate purpose. I was influenced by Shinzen Young based on information from his retreats, web site, and article on loving kindness and Jack Kornfield, *A Path with Heart: A Guide through the Perils and Promises of Spiritual Life* (New York: Bantam Books, 1993).

9. The serenity prayer may date back to A.D. 500, but it is usually credited to Reinhold Niebuhr, a twentieth-century theologian.

10. Anna Eleanor Roosevelt, *This Is My Story* (New York: Harper & Brothers, 1937).
11. See note 1.

Chapter 7: Polarity Strategy

1. Antoine De Saint-Exupery, *The Little Prince* (New York: Harcourt Brace Jovanovich, 1943), p. 70.
2. Gia-fu Feng and Jane English, *Tao Te Ching* (New York: Alfred A. Knopf, 1972).
3. John Heider, *The Tao of Leadership: Leadership Strategies for a New Age* (New York: Bantam Books, 1986), p. 3.
4. Rahima Baldwin Dancy, *You Are Your Child's First Teacher* (Berkeley, CA: Celestial Arts, 1989).
5. Barry Johnson, *Polarity Management™ Identifying and Managing Unsolvable Problems* (Amherst, MA: Human Resource Development Press, 1992), p. 21.
6. Sometimes the head energy, as defined here, is known as the Yang and the heart energy is known as the Yin. The Yin/Yang concept is explored more by Harriet Beinfield and Efrem Korngold, *Between Heaven and Earth* (New York: Ballantine Books, 1981), pp. 49–59.
7. David Keirsey and Marilyn Bates. *Please Understand Me: Character & Temperament Types* (Del Mar, CA: Prometheus Nemesis Book Company, 1984). A good overview of the Myers-Briggs Type Indicator is given.
8. See note 5, p. xii.
9. See note 5, p. 23.
10. See note 6.
11. Polarity Map® and Polarity Management™ are trademarks of Barry Johnson of Polarity Management Associates. See www.PolarityManagement.com.
12. Intensive Polarity Management™ workshop run by Barry Johnson and Sally Sparhawk through Associated Consultants International, September 5–6, 2003.
13. See note 5. Realize this approach has tremendous depth and wide application from a life-time of research; only a simple overview is presented in this chapter. On-line Polarity Management™ training sessions are available at www.PolarityManagement.com.
14. Comparable to my personal Yin/Yang story shown in Figure 7.1, this situation may represent the Yin/Yang of the organization.
15. Exercises offered by Dr. Peter Lyons, chiropractor and kinesiologist.

Chapter 8: Attraction Strategy

1. Lynn Grabhorn, *Excuse Me, Your Life is Waiting: The Astonishing Power of Feelings* (Charlottesville, VA: Hampton Roads, 2000), p. 5.

2. David Hawkins, MD, PhD, *Power vs. Force: The Hidden Determinants of Human Behavior* (Sedona, AZ: Veritas, 1998), p. 105.

3. The Hicks Family at P.O. Box 690070, San Antonio, TX 78269; and Lynn Grabhorn, *Excuse Me, Your Life Is Waiting: The Astonishing Power of Feelings* (Charlottesville, VA: Hampton Roads, 2000), have some very insightful information about this concept.

4. Margot Zaher, *The Incredible Power of Intention,* electronic newsletter (June 5, 2000).

5. Napoleon Hill, *Think and Grow Rich* (New York: Fawcett Columbine, 1937), p. 53.

6. Sarah Ban Breathnach, *Simple Abundance: A Daybook of Comfort and Joy* (New York: Warner Books, 1995), p. 4. This is a statement that a confessor, a lovely nun, made to the author.

7. Simone Weil, *Gravity and Grace* (New York: Putnam, 1952).

8. Deepak Chopra, *The Seven Spiritual Laws of Success: A Practical Guide to the Fulfillment of Your Dreams* (San Rafael, CA: Amber-Allen, 1994).

9. Author interview with technology entrepreneur, who requests that his name not be disclosed. Mike is not his real name.

10. See note 5.

11. James Allen, *As a Man Thinketh* (New York: Grosset & Dunlap, 1907), p. 60.

12. Albert Einstein, scientist, has been quoted as speaking about imagination.

13. Maxwell Maltz, *Psycho-Cybernetics* (North Hollywood, CA: Wilshire Book Company, 1960); and Maxwell Maltz, *Live and Be Free Thru Psycho-Cybernetics* (New York: Warner Books, 1975).

14. See note 5, p. 89.

15. See note 13, *Psycho-Cybernetics,* pp. 28–29.

16. See note 5, pp. 49–50.

17. Florence Scovel Shinn, *The Game of Life and How to Play It* (Marina Del Ray, CA: DeVorss, 1925), p. 87.

18. Louise L. Hay sold millions of copies of her classic books *Heal Your Body* (Carlsbad, CA: Hay House, 1976); and *You Can Heal Your Life* (Carlsbad, CA: Hay House, 1984).

19. James L. Adams, *Conceptual Block Busting: A Guide to Better Ideas* (New York: W.W. Norton and Company, 1974). Adams offers creative approaches to overcoming perceptual, emotional, cultural and environmental, and intellectual and expressive blocks.

20. See note 12, *Live and Be Free thru Psycho-Cybernetics,* p. 97.

Chapter 9: Persistence Strategy

1. Napoleon Hill, *Think and Grow Rich* (New York: Fawcett Columbine, 1937), p. 152.

2. Natalie Goldberg, author of *Writing Down the Bones,* shares this wisdom from her Zen meditation teacher, Katagiri Roshi, in her writing courses.
3. As per *Bartlett's Familiar Quotations* (Boston: Little, Brown and Company, 1882, revised 1980), citation 133:21. This is an ancient political maxim cited by Machiavelli. Shinzen Young uses this approach in his mindfulness meditation teachings, summarized in Appendix B.
4. Natalie Goldberg author of *Writing Down the Bones,* shares this wisdom from philosopher Dogan in her writing courses.
5. Kenneth W. Thomas, *Intrinsic Motivation at Work: Building Energy & Commitment* (San Francisco: Berrett-Koehler, 2000).
6. Mike is not his real name.
7. Pavlov's behaviorial model is based on the premise that stimuli bring forth certain responses. Ivan Petrovich Pavlov, "The Scientific Investigation of the Psychical Faculties or Processes in the Higher Animals: The Huxley Lecture on Recent Advances in Science and Their Bearing on Medicine and Surgery," *British Medical Journal,* vol. 2, no. 2388 (October 6, 1906).
8. The doom loop is discussed in Chapter 8 of Jim Collins, *Good to Great: Why Some Companies Make the Leap . . . and Others Don't* (New York: HarperBusiness, 2001), pp. 164–187.
9. See note 1, p. 152.

Chapter 10: Allowing Strategy

1. John Heider, *The Tao of Leadership: Leadership Strategies for a New Age, Lao Tzu's Tao Te Ching Adapted for a New Age* (New York: Bantam Books, 1985), p. 43.
2. The Hicks Family (P.O. Box 690070, San Antonio, TX 78269) has some worthwhile teachings on this concept.
3. Jon Kabat-Zinn, *Wherever You Go There You Are* (New York: Hyperion, 1994), p. 53.
4. "*Fortune* Checks Out 25 Cool Companies for Products, Ideas, and Investments," *Fortune* (July 11, 1994).
5. Dozens and dozens of publications, newspapers, and periodicals covered this news.
6. "Radish Hits the Road," *PC Week* (April 4, 1994).
7. Author interview with Deb, computer scientist, who asks that her real name not be disclosed.
8. Florence Scovel Shinn, *The Game of Life and How to Play It* (Marina Del Ray, CA: DeVorss Company, 1925), pp. 9–10.
9. John Heider, *The Tao of Leadership: Leadership Strategies for a New Age, Lao Tzu's Tao Te Ching Adapted for a New Age* (New York: Bantam Books, 1985), p. 155.

10. Shinzen Young, mindfulness meditation teacher, shares this insight on reducing suffering in life during his lectures and on his web site www.shinzen.org.
11. This fable of the Cling-Ons was told to me years ago. The source is unknown.
12. These affirmations have been created, modified and used over the years. They have been influenced by many sources, some known and others unknown at this point. An inspirational source for affirmations is by Louise L. Hay, *Heal Your Body* (Carlsbad, CA: Hay House, 1982); and another is by Louise L. Hay, *You Can Heal Your Life* (Carlsbad, CA: Hay House, 1984).

Chapter 11: Connections Strategy

1. Jim Collins, *Good to Great: Why Some Companies Make the Leap . . . and Others Don't* (New York: HarperCollins, 2001).
2. Scripture passage John 16:24.
3. The Seeing Eye, a nonprofit organization based in Morristown, New Jersey, continues its important work to help blind people.
4. It is interesting to note that the religious or philosophical preferences of the study's sample represent the major religions and beliefs in the United States, including Christian, Nonreligious/secular, Jewish, Muslim, Buddhist, Agnostic, Atheist, Hindu, Unitarian Universalist, Humanist, and others.
5. Fred I. Steele, *Physical Setting and Organization Development* (Reading, MA: Addison-Wesley, 1973).

Chapter 12: Pack Strategy

1. The people who participated in this research study noted the positive forces encouraging them in their various pursuits of passionate purpose. Using qualitative research techniques, inputs from all participants were analyzed and consolidated into the energizers most frequently mentioned. These are reported here.
2. Dan Millman, *Way of the Peaceful Warrior: A Book that Changes Lives* 2nd ed. (Tiboron, CA: H.J. Kramer, Distributed by Publisher's Group West, 1984), p. 104.
3. Kenneth W. Thomas, *Intrinsic Motivation: Building Energy & Commitment* (San Francisco: Berrett-Koehler, 2000).
4. The people who participated in this research study noted the negative forces discouraging them in their various pursuits of passionate purpose. Using qualitative research techniques, inputs from all participants were analyzed and consolidated into the hindrances most frequently mentioned. These are reported here.
5. Jack Kornfield, *A Path with Heart: A Guide through the Perils and Promises of Spiritual Life* (New York: Bantam Books, 1993). This names the demons as: grasping and wanting, anger, fear, boredom, judgment, sleepiness, restlessness, and doubt.

6. Author interview with Dawn, retired elementary teacher, who asked not to be identified by her real name.
7. Joseph Campbell, *The Hero of a Thousand Faces* (Princeton, NJ: Princeton University Press, 1989).
8. Natalie Goldberg, *Writing down the Bones: Freeing the Writer Within* (Boston: Shambala, 1986). This concept is communicated in her workshops and books as her philosophy of life.
9. Author interview with Deb, computer scientist and mother, who asked not to be identified by her real name.
10. Bob, a student, is not his real name.

Chapter 13: Put Passionate Purpose to Work

1. Natalie Goldberg, *Long Quiet Highway: Waking up in America* (New York: Bantam Books, 1993), p. xiii.
2. Author interview with Dawn, which is not her real name, retired teacher.
3. Matthew Fox, *The Reinvention of Work: A New Vision of Livelihood of Our Time* (New York: HarperCollins, 1994), p. 94.
4. St. Teresa of Avila (1577), *Interior Castle,* E. Allison Peers, translator, Reissue ed. (New York: Image, 1972).
5. Author interview with Deb, mother and computer scientist, who asks that her real name not be used.
6. Thornton Wilder, *The Bridge over the San Luis Rey* (New York: Albert & Charles Boni, 1928), pp. 234–235.
7. Louise May Alcott (1870), *An Old-Fashioned Girl* (Cleveland; New York: World Pubublishing Company, 1947).
8. Public presentation by Bill Mooney, storyteller, who impersonates Morris Frank on behalf of The Seeing Eye organization.
9. Paulo Coelho, *The Alchemist: A Fable about Following Your Dreams* (New York: HarperCollins, 1993), p. 23.
10. Viktor E. Frankl, *Man's Search for Meaning: An Introduction to Logotherapy* 2nd ed. (New York: Pocket Books, 1963).

Appendix B: Tested Meditation Techniques

1. Shinzen Young, *A Complete Guide to the Core Practice* (2001), available from www.shinzen.org.
2. I personally developed this appreciation meditation for pursuits of passionate purpose. I was influenced by Shinzen Young's article on loving kindness available at his web site: www.shinzen.org; and Jack Kornfield, *A Path With Heart: A Guide through the Perils and Promises of Spiritual Life* (New York: Bantam Books, 1993), p. 19, and many guided meditations at retreats.

About the Author

Theresa M. Szczurek, PhD, helps organizations and individuals succeed by aligning their passions with purpose. Offering success strategies she used in taking her company, Radish Communications Systems, to over $40 million in six years, Szczurek works with emerging and established organizations worldwide in marketing, strategic planning, economic development, and organization development to reenergize workforces and produce extraordinary results. An award-winning business leader and speaker featured in *Fortune, PC Week,* and many other publications, her audiences have included AT&T, Polish Chamber of Commerce, Brown University, and many others. Her presentations include: Pursuit of Passionate Purpose, From $0 to $40 Million, Innovation into Income, Become a Champion of Change, Practical Persistence, and Build Customer Delight and the Money Will Follow.

Previously, Szczurek worked as an engineer for Bell Laboratories and then moved into worldwide marketing for AT&T. She has earned an MS in Operations Research from Stanford University and an MBA and PhD in Business Administration from the University of Colorado. Her first book was *Champions of Technological Change: How Organizations Successfully Implement New Technology* (Garland, 1994).

As a community leader, she works relentlessly for the advancement of the underprivileged. She has been honored as Rotarian of the Year, Business and Professional Women's Visionary Award recipient, and Colorado Technology Incubator's Model of Excellence.

Szczurek can be reached through her consulting, research, and speaking firm, Technology and Management Solutions (www.TMSworld.com or www.pursuitofpassionatepurpose.com). She lives with her husband, Richard A. Davis, and daughter, Annie, in Boulder, Colorado, where she enjoys hiking, biking, and being a Girl Scout leader.

Index